MONEY

There is gold and a multitude of rubies
But more precious are the lips of knowledge.

MONEY

Fourth and Revised Edition

LAWRENCE S. RITTER

&

WILLIAM L. SILBER

Basic Books, Inc., Publishers

NEW YORK

Library of Congress Cataloging in Publication Data
Ritter, Lawrence S
    Money.
    Selected Readings p. 335
    Includes index.
        1. Money. 2. Money—United States. 3. Monetary
policy—United States. I. Silber, William L., joint
author. II. Title.
    HG540.R57 1981   332.4   80–68171
    ISBN: 0–465–04718–1 (cloth)
    ISBN: 0–465–04720–3 (paper)

CONTENTS

PART II

THE POWER OF THE PURSE

PART III

FEDERAL RESERVE POLICY MAKING

PART IV

FISCAL POLICY AND DEBT MANAGEMENT

PART VI

MONEY AND NATIONAL PRIORITIES

PART VII

INTERNATIONAL FINANCE

EPILOGUE

PART I

In the Beginning

1

A BOOK FOR THE CURIOUS

In 1931, Babe Ruth received a salary of $80,000 from the New York Yankees. His after-tax take-home pay was $68,-500. Today, some baseball players are making $800,000 a year and taking home about half that or $400,000. Are they really that much better off?

Actually, they are somewhat *worse* off! Consumer prices in 1981 are six times higher than in 1931. At 1981 prices, $400,000 can only buy what $67,000 could buy fifty years ago. Babe Ruth's $68,500 was worth *more* in terms of purchasing power than $400,000 today!

All of which is not meant to prove that Babe Ruth was a better baseball player than the modern stars (which he was), but that inflation distorts economic relationships. Athletes making hundreds of thousands of dollars will make do, inflation or no inflation, but for most people rising prices are a more painful matter. As your income goes up, you may think you are earning more and moving up the ladder, but if prices are rising faster it is a mirage. You may be earning more dollars, but each dollar is worth less and less, so that after all is said and done you are no better (and maybe worse) off than you were before.

What does all this have to do with money? It is widely believed that increases in the price level are synonymous with increases in the money supply. The reason for this book is to explore precisely and thoroughly the influence of money on

the economy. How it affects the price level, what it does to
the volume of employment, whether it enhances or inhibits
economic growth, and what role it plays in the attainment
of national priorities. In short, this is a book about money
and monetary policy.

Other questions also spring to mind. Is money responsible
for the ups and downs of stock prices? Why is the housing
industry apparently so susceptible to changes in monetary
policy? Is gold an essential part of our monetary system or
a vestigial remnant of bygone days? Why do we now have
floating exchange rates?

These questions have been highlighted in recent years by
the rebirth of monetary policy as an instrument of national
economic policy, and also by widely publicized debates between the Monetarists and the Keynesians. The Monetarists are the standard-bearers of monetary policy and the
Keynesians the champions of fiscal policy. In recent years,
for example, great controversy arose between them as to
whether inflation could best be stopped by exclusive reliance on monetary policy or by increased taxes, a tool of
fiscal policy.

We will explore the intricacies of money and monetary
policy in the following way. Part I lays the foundations for
understanding problems of the sort we have mentioned
above. In particular, Chapters 2 and 3 deal with the essen-
tials of money and its relationship to the overall economy,
and Chapter 4 with the crucial debate between the Monetarists and the Keynesians. How does this theoretical confrontation lead to alternative policy recommendations for solving
real-world problems?

Against this background, Part II examines, in detail, the
impact of monetary policy on the economy. How does it
work? What effect does it have on the price level? What are

some of the implications of high interest rates? Part III, in the same vein, explores the execution of monetary policy, including the mechanics of who pushes which levers at what times. How can an outsider tell which levers are being pushed? Is there a better way to go about the whole business?

Having explored the execution and the effects of monetary policy, we return in Part IV to the controversy between the Monetarists and the Keynesians, this time concentrating on the potentialities of fiscal policy. Is the policy split in the real world as deep as the ideological chasm that appears to separate these two groups?

Part V takes an in-depth look at some puzzling issues that swirl in the wake of both monetary and fiscal policy. Can knowledge of the intricacies of monetary policy help in forecasting the stock market? What is meant by financial intermediation and disintermediation?

Parts VI and VII explore two areas that have attracted widespread attention recently: national priorities and international finance (exchange rates, balance of payments deficits, gold, devaluation, and all that). It is said that only two men in the whole world really understand what international finance is all about—and they disagree. Finally, we end up with our crystal ball and try to fathom what money and the financial system might look like in the Brave New World of the twenty-first century.

This is not a long book. Perhaps it is even too short to do full justice to the ground it covers. Nevertheless, after you finish it, we hope you will be more informed about money and its role in economic life, and more capable of satisfying your curiosity about what is happening today and what is likely to happen tomorrow in the sphinx-like world of monetary policy.

2

ALL THAT GLITTERS

"The lack of money is the root of all evil," said George Bernard Shaw. While that might be somewhat of an exaggeration, there have been numerous periods in history when it appeared to be more true than false. There have also been rather lengthy episodes when the opposite seemed true: when economic disruption apparently stemmed not from too little money, but from too *much* of it.

From this line of thought, the question naturally arises: What is the "right" amount of money? Not too little, not too much, but just right. And how can we go about getting it?

Questions of this sort used to be considered heresy, back in the days when the economy was viewed as a marvel of perpetual motion, sparked by divine inspiration in the form of gold (which gave money intrinsic value) and human intelligence (which told us to stay out of the way and let things work out by themselves). Flanked by the twin eternal verities —the gold standard and the balanced budget—*laissez faire* reigned supreme. Let nature take its course, and everything will turn out for the best in this best of all possible worlds.

Today we are no longer so sure. Aggregate spending on the nation's output of new goods and services—the economy's gross national product (GNP)—is no longer seen as inevitably producing full employment, stable prices, a high rate of economic growth, balance in international payments, and all the other things we expect our economy to yield. We have experienced too many instances of GNP falling short of the mark, or overshooting it, to retain blind faith in any built-in self-correcting thermostat. So today we deliberately try to influence the course of economic events. We tinker, meddle, turn switches, push buttons, pull levers, and try to make things better.

But are they really any better? The answer is far from clear. Nevertheless, for most people the issue now is not *whether* the government should intervene, but how, when, and to what extent. The ends are not particularly new—high employment, price stability, economic growth, and balance of payments equilibrium—but the means are. The means most frequently used today to influence the economy's direction are *monetary policy* (the subject of this book) and *fiscal policy.* How well do they work? Are they appropriate to achieve their purposes? Can they be improved?

Very few people still equate paper money with rampant inflation, unbalanced budgets with creeping socialism, and Keynes with Marx. But the emotional content of the argument has not disappeared. It has merely moved next door— to the debate between the Monetarists and the Keynesians, between monetary policy versus fiscal policy, and to controversy over the execution of monetary policy.

As a first approximation, monetary policy involves regulating the money supply and conditions in financial markets in order to achieve the goals of national economic policy. Fiscal policy involves changing government spending and tax rates for similar purposes. We will return to fiscal policy later in the book. First, however, let us set the framework for our main concern—money and monetary policy.

The Supply of Money

How large a money supply should we have in the United States? What *is* money, anyway? And how much of it do we actually have?

Money is just what you think it is—what you spend when you want to buy something. The Indians used beads, Eskimos used fishhooks, and we use *currency* (coins and dollar bills) and, most of all, *demand deposits* (checking accounts) in banks.

Money is used (1) as a means of payment—a medium of exchange—but it has other functions as well. It is also used (2) as a store of value, when people hold on to it, and (3) as a standard of value (a unit of account) when people compare prices and thereby assess relative values. But most prominently money is what you can spend, a generally acceptable medium of exchange that you can use to buy things or settle debts.

How much money do we actually have?

It amounted to $400 billion at the end of 1979, roughly $110 billion in the form of currency outside banks and $290 billion in demand deposits at banks. However, the answer is not quite as simple as that, because there is more than one definition of what constitutes "money." This definition of money—currency outside banks plus demand deposits—is the most popular one, but it is not the only one.

Currency and checking accounts are spendable at face value virtually anywhere, at any time, so they are the most "liquid" assets a person can have. A liquid asset is something you can turn into the generally acceptable medium of exchange quickly without taking a loss—as compared with "frozen" assets, for example, which can be sold or liquidated on short notice only at a substantially lower price. Currency and checking accounts are the most liquid assets you can have (because they *are* the medium of exchange), but they are not the only liquid assets around. Savings deposits and government bonds are rather liquid, although you can't spend them. To spend them, you first have to exchange them for money. At the other extreme, real estate and vintage automobiles typically rank fairly low on the liquidity scale: If you have to sell quickly, you're likely to take a beating on the deal.

Thus liquidity is a continuum, ranging from currency and demand deposits at the top of the scale to a variety of frozen assets at the bottom. As a result, what we call "money" is not a fixed and immutable thing, like what we call water (H_2O), but to a great extent is a matter of judgment. There are several different definitions of money, each of which drops one notch lower on the liquidity scale in drawing the line between "money" and "all other assets."

Every week, for example, the *Wall Street Journal* and the *New York Times* report money supply data based on several different definitions of money. In fact, each definition has its own unique label, just like Campbell's soup or Heinz pickles (except there are only four varieties, not fifty-seven).

The narrowest definition of money (labeled M1A) consists of currency outside banks ($110 billion at the end of 1979) and demand deposits at commercial banks only ($275 billion). On this basis, the money supply was $385 billion at the end of 1979.

Until recently, commercial banks were the only financial institutions permitted to issue checking accounts, and they are still responsible for the overwhelming proportion of them. However, the financial system is constantly changing and evolving. One recent innovation occurred a few years ago, in the 1970s, when thrift institutions—mutual savings banks, savings and loan associations, and credit unions— started issuing demand deposits for the first time, and financial institutions also began to offer automatic transfer services from some savings deposits to demand deposits. These checkable deposits amounted to $15 billion at the end of 1979; if they are included in the money supply, and they should be, it becomes $400 billion instead of $385 billion. This is the money supply definition we used previously— currency plus deposits on which checks may be written at all sorts of banks (known as M1B).

M2 drops a rung lower on the liquidity scale to include such assets as passbook savings deposits and small-size time deposits at commercial banks and thrift institutions, as well as shares in money market mutual funds. Time deposits are different from passbook savings deposits in that they have a scheduled maturity—such as six months or two years—and if you want to withdraw your funds earlier you suffer a substantial penalty by having to forfeit part of the accumulated interest. Money market mutual funds pool the funds of many small savers and invest in high-yielding short-term assets; most of them permit their shareholders to withdraw funds on demand. All these summed to $1,100 billion at the end of 1979; added to the previous $400 billion yields a money supply figure of $1,500 billion (M2).

M3 consists of M2 plus large-size ($100,000 and over) time deposits at all depositary institutions. These amounted to $200 billion at the end of 1979, to make a grand total of $1,700 billion as the money supply (M3).

So what is the money supply in the United States? Is it $385 billion (M1A) or $1,700 billion (M3), or something in between? Each definition of money has its adherents, but by and large most economists prefer the common-sense definition of money—M1B—because it includes everything that is generally acceptable as a means of payment but no more. Once you go beyond currency and checking accounts, it is hard to find a logical place to stop, since many things (bonds, stocks, waterbeds) contain liquidity in varying degree. Throughout this book, therefore, we will for the most part stick to the common-sense definition of money (M1B)— currency plus all demand deposits.

Now that we know what money is, a crucial question still remains: *how much of it should there be?*

In theory, the answer is simple enough; presumably the supply of money affects the rate of spending, and therefore we should have enough money so that we buy, at current prices, all the goods and services the economy is able to produce. If we spend less, we will have idle capacity and idle people. If we spend more, we will wind up with higher prices but no more real goods or services. We need a money supply, in other words, that is large enough to generate just the right amount of spending to give us a GNP that represents full employment at stable prices. More money than that would mean more spending and inflation, and less money would mean less spending and recession or depression.

In practice, unfortunately, the answer is not quite so simple. Precisely how much money will give us that much spending? The answer is not clear, because any given amount of money can conceivably be spent more or less rapidly, thereby generating a rather wide range of potential spending. In brief, the velocity of money, its rate of turnover, is as important as the supply. It is so important, in fact, that we will devote all of the next chapter to velocity and its implications.

Where, in all of this, does gold fit in? Regardless of what you might have heard, the amount of gold does *not* deter-

mine the money supply. Indeed, it has very little influence on
it. In 1968, the last remaining link between the money supply
and gold was severed, when a law requiring 25 percent gold
backing behind most of our currency was repealed. If that is
all news to you, it is a good indication of just how unimportant the connection between gold and money has always
been, at least in our lifetime.

Both demand deposits and currency can be increased (or
decreased) without any relation whatsoever to gold. Does
that disturb you? Does it lead you to distrust the value of
your money? Then send it to us. We'll be delighted to pay
you ninety cents on the dollar, which should be a bargain if
you believe all you read about a dollar being worth only sixty
cents, or fifty cents, or whatever the latest figure might be.

If gold is not the watchdog, what is? What supervision is
there over the creation (and destruction) of money? In other
words, who controls and formulates monetary policy? Before
we get into the details, let's back off for a moment and ask:
why all the fuss over money? What might the economy look
like without it?

The Importance of Money: Man Beats Barter

What good is money in the first place? In other words, why
was money invented (by Sir John Money in 3016 B.C.)?

For one thing, without money individuals in the economy
would have to devote more time to buying what they want
and selling what they don't. In other words, people would
have less time to work and play. A barter economy is one
without a medium of exchange or a unit of account (the

measuring rod function of money). Let's see what it might be like in a barter economy.

Say you are a carpenter and agree to build a bookcase for your neighbor, who happens to raise chickens and pays you with seventeen pounds of feathers and a dozen eggs. You decide to make one pillow for yourself, so you now have sixteen pounds of feathers to exchange for the rest of the week's groceries, and hopefully something left over to pay the plumber for fixing the outhouse roof which leaks. All you must do is find a grocer whose wife just gave birth and therefore needs a few extra pillows (hopefully she had trip- lets), and you still have to look around for a plumber with similar needs.

What's more, you have to remember that a loaf of bread exchanges for six ounces of feathers (it also exchanges for eleven books of matches or three boxes of crayons or one Yankee Yearbook, but never mind because you don't have any of these things to spare). And of course all the other items on the grocer's shelf have similar price tags—the tags are bigger than the items.

Along comes money and simplifies matters. Workers are paid in something called money, which they can then use to pay their bills and make their purchases (medium of ex- change). We no longer need price tags giving rates of ex- change between an item and everything else that might con- ceivably be exchanged for it. Instead, prices of goods and services are expressed in terms of money, a common denomi- nator (unit of account).

The most important thing about the medium of exchange is that each and every person be confident that it can be passed on to someone else—that it be generally acceptable in trade. Paradoxically, a person will accept the medium of exchange only when certain that it can be passed on to someone else. One key characteristic is that the *uncertainty* over its value in trade must be very *low*. People will be more willing to accept the medium of exchange if they are certain what it is worth in terms of things they really want. The uncertainty of barter transactions makes people wary of exchange: if I want to sell my house and buy a car and you want to do just the reverse, we might be able to strike a deal except for the fact that you've got shifty eyes and are likely to rip me off by passing me a lemon. Hence no deal: I'm uncertain about the value of the thing I accept in exchange. The medium of exchange, which is handled often in many transactions, becomes familiar to us all and can be checked carefully for fraud, thereby reducing uncertainty in trading.

Closely related to the low-uncertainty-high-exchangeability syndrome is the ability to hold on to the medium of exchange without its deteriorating in value. It must be a good store of value. Otherwise, as soon as I accept the medium of exchange, I'll try to get rid of it, lest it be worth fewer and fewer goods and services tomorrow or the day after. If price inflation gets out of hand and I have little confidence that the medium of exchange will hold its value, I'll be reluctant to accept it in exchange; in other words, it won't be the medium of exchange for very long. This means we begin to slip back into barter, spending more time exchanging goods and less time producing, consuming and enjoying them.

The medium of exchange also usually serves as a unit of account. In other words, the prices of all other goods are expressed in terms of, say, dollars. Without such a unit of account, you'd have to remember the exchange ratios of soap for bread, knives for shirts, and bookcases for haircuts (and haircuts for soap). The unit of account reduces the information you have to carry around in your brain—freeing that limited space for creative speculation.

So money is a good thing. It frees people from spending too much time running around bartering goods and services, and allows them to undertake other endeavors—production, relaxation, contemplation, and temptation.

It is important to emphasize that people hold the medium of exchange—money—not because it has any intrinsic value but because it can be exchanged for things to eat, drink, wear, and play with. The *value* of a unit of money is determined, therefore, by the prices of each and every thing—more accurately, the average level of all prices. If prices go up, a unit of money (a dollar) is worth less because it will buy less; if prices go down—use your imagination—a dollar is worth more because it will buy more. So when we noted that the dollar was worth only 50 cents it meant simply that the dollar could now buy what 50 cents could have bought a few years ago (because prices have doubled).

What all this suggests is that the value of the dollar has nothing to do with gold or any other precious metal. And this reminds us to get back to the question of who determines how many dollars are floating around. As we might expect, this has something to do with the level of prices, inflation, and the "value of a dollar."

The Central Bank and Money Creation

The monetary authority in most countries is called the central bank. A central bank does not deal directly with the public; it is rather a bank for banks, and it is responsible for the execution of national monetary policy. In the United States the central bank is the Federal Reserve, created by

Congress in 1913. It consists of twelve district Federal Reserve Banks, scattered throughout the country, and a Board of Governors in Washington. This hydra-headed monster, which some view as benign but others consider an ever-lurking peril, possesses ultimate authority over the money supply.

As noted previously, the money supply consists of currency and checking accounts. *Currency* is manufactured by money factories—the Bureau of Engraving and Printing and the Mint—and then shipped under rather heavy guard to the Treasury and the Federal Reserve for further distribution. For the most part it enters circulation when people and business firms cash checks at their local banks. Thus it is the public that ultimately decides what proportion of the money supply will be in the form of currency, with the Federal Reserve Banks wholesaling the necessary coins and paper to local banks. The Federal Reserve is not particularly concerned with the fraction of the money supply that is in one form or another, but rather with the *total* of demand deposits plus currency.

Most of the money supply (three-quarters of it) is in the form of *demand deposits,* and most of the demand deposits (95 percent of them) are in commercial banks. Demand deposits in commercial banks come into being when commercial banks extend credit—that is, when they make loans or buy securities. Demand deposits vanish, as silently as they came, when banks contract credit—when bank loans are repaid or banks sell securities. It is precisely here, through its ability to control the behavior of commercial banks, that the Federal Reserve wields its primary authority over the money supply and thereby implements monetary policy. This process of money creation by the banks under the influence of the Federal Reserve is sufficiently important and complex to deserve further explanation.

When a bank makes a loan to a consumer or business firm, it typically creates a checking account for the borrower's use. For example, when you borrow $1,000 from your friendly neighborhood bank, the bank will take your IOU and give you a checking account in return. From the commercial bank's point of view, it has an additional $1,000 of assets (namely, your IOU); this is matched by an additional $1,000 of liabilities (namely, your checking account). You could, of course, ask for $1,000 in $10 bills right then and there, stuff them in your pocket, and depart. But more likely you would be equally satisfied with the demand deposit, because by writing checks on it you can make payments just as well as with currency. The creation of this $1,000 in demand deposits means the money supply has increased by $1,000.

Similarly, when a bank buys a corporate or government bond, it pays for it by opening a checking account for the seller. Assume you are holding a $1,000 corporate or government bond in your investment portfolio, and you need cash. You might sell the bond to your local bank, which would then add $1,000 to your checking account. Once again, from the point of view of the bank, its assets (bonds) and liabilities (demand deposits) have gone up by $1,000. Just as by a bank loan, money has been created; the supply of money in the economy has increased by $1,000.

Conversely, when you repay a bank loan by giving the bank a check, the bank gives you back your IOU and at the same time lowers your demand deposit balance. If a bank sells a bond to an individual, the same reduction in demand deposits occurs. The supply of money declines. To repeat: banks create money (demand deposits) when they lend or

buy securities, and destroy money when their loans are repaid or they sell securities.

Can they do this without limit? Is there any control over
their ability to create and destroy money? No they can't and
yes there is, and that is where the Federal Reserve comes into
the picture.

A commercial bank cannot always expand its demand
deposit liabilities by making loans or buying securities. Commercial banks that are members of the Federal Reserve System, and they include those that do most of the banking
business, must hold reserves against their demand deposit
liabilities—the current requirement is reserves of about 15
percent against demand deposits. *These reserves must be held
in the form of vault cash or as a deposit in their regional
Federal Reserve Bank.* Therefore, only if a commercial bank
has "excess" reserves, reserves over and above its requirements, can it create new demand deposits by making loans
and buying securities.

Once a bank is "loaned up," with no more excess reserves,
its ability to create money ceases. And if it has deficient
reserves, not enough to support its existing deposits, the bank
must somehow get additional reserves. Otherwise, it has no
choice but to call in loans or sell securities in order to bring
its deposits back in line with its reserves. If a bank has
demand deposits of $10,000 but only $1,400 in reserves, it
would be $100 short of meeting its required reserves. One
way to set itself right with the Federal Reserve would be to
call in $667 worth of loans. This would reduce its demand
deposits to $9,333, at which level its $1,400 of reserves sat-
isfies the legal 15 percent requirement.

It is through the fulcrum of these reserves that the Federal
Reserve influences commercial bank lending and investing
and thereby the money supply. The Federal Reserve manipu-

lates the reserves of the banking system and the amount of demand deposits that they can support in several different ways.

In the first place, within prescribed limits established by Congress, the Federal Reserve can specify the reserve requirement percentage. Lowering the percentage, say from 15 to 10 percent, will instantly and automatically increase banks' excess reserves, enabling banks to make more loans (or buy securities) and to expand demand deposits. If reserve requirements were lowered from 15 to 10 percent, the bank with the $100 reserve deficiency would suddenly find itself with $400 in excess reserves. Raising the percentage, say to 20 percent, will just as quickly reduce excess reserves or create deficiencies, pressuring banks to call in loans (or sell securities), thereby reducing demand deposits.

Second, through facilities available for "discounting," member banks can temporarily borrow reserves from their regional Federal Reserve Bank at a price (the discount rate). For example, the problem bank, with demand deposits of $10,000 but only $1,400 in reserves, could avoid the embarrassment of having to call in loans if it were willing to borrow the needed $100 in reserves from its regional Federal Reserve Bank. The ability to borrow these reserves means that the money supply can remain unchanged. A bank could also take the initiative and borrow additional reserves to make *new* loans and thereby *increase* the money supply. The Federal Reserve influences the willingness of banks to borrow reserves by manipulating the rate it charges on such loans. A lower discount rate will tend to make borrowing reserves more attractive to the commercial banks, and a higher rate will tend to make it less attractive.

Third, and most important of all as a means of day-to-day policy making, the Federal Reserve can buy or sell government securities (open market operations), thereby enlarging or diminishing bank reserves. About $400 billion worth of marketable government securities are held as investments by the public—by individuals, corporations, financial institutions, and so on. These government securities came into being when the United States Treasury had to borrow to finance past budget deficits. Some are long-term bonds, running twenty or thirty years until maturity, and others are shorter term, all the way down to government securities that are issued for only a few months, called Treasury bills. The existence of this pool of widely held marketable securities, with many potential buyers and sellers, offers an ideal vehicle through which the Federal Reserve can affect bank reserves.

When the Federal Reserve *buys* government securities in the open market, much as you would buy a stock or a bond on one of the stock exchanges, it pays for them with a check drawn on itself. When the seller deposits that check in a commercial bank, and the bank presents the check to the Federal Reserve for payment, the bank's deposits at the Federal Reserve Bank—its reserves—increase. With more reserves, the bank can make loans and increase its demand deposits.

Take the following concrete example. When the Federal Reserve buys $1,000 in government securities from an insurance company (or from any individual, for that matter), it pays the insurance company with a $1,000 check drawn on itself. When the insurance company deposits the check in its commercial bank, a demand deposit of $1,000 is created for it, and the bank now has the Federal Reserve's check as an asset. This bank, in turn, presents the check for payment at its local Federal Reserve Bank and receives in exchange reserves equal to $1,000, the amount of the check. So far, the money supply has gone up by $1,000, and the bank has additional reserves. On the basis of these additional reserves, the banking system can now create *more* demand deposits by making new loans.

But what the central bank giveth, the central bank can taketh away. If the Federal Reserve *sells* government securities out of its portfolio, it *receives* a check for them, drawn on some commercial bank; the Federal Reserve collects by reducing that bank's deposit at the Federal Reserve Bank, thus diminishing the bank's reserves. Result: both the money supply and bank reserves fall.

Note that the Federal Reserve could achieve the same ends —that is, change the money supply and bank reserves—by buying or selling any asset, such as record albums or any type of bond or stock. The reason for limiting its open market operations to the purchase and sale of government securities is quite obvious: who would determine whether the Federal Reserve should buy Bob Dylan or Barry Manilow? General Motors stock or IBM? The Federal Reserve is smart enough, at least in this respect, to keep its hands out of the public hair.

To summarize: these techniques—setting reserve requirements, varying the discount rate, and open market operations—put the reserves of the commercial banking system (and their demand deposit potential) pretty tightly under the control of the Federal Reserve, thereby giving it sufficient leverage with which to control the money supply.

But does it really matter? What difference does it make whether the money supply increases or decreases?

Does Money Matter?

We have come full circle, back to the question that started us off: how much money should we have in the United States? What effects does monetary policy have on the economy?

Monetary policy consists of varying the amount of money in the economy, presumably increasing it (or, more realistically, increasing the rate at which it is growing) during a recession, to stimulate spending; and decreasing it (or increasing it at a less than normal rate) during a boom, to inhibit spending.

But whether just changing the money supply really can influence people's *spending* in any consistent way is not that obvious. Many appear to believe that monetary policy affects people's wealth and in that fashion influences their spending. Clearly, if people have more money and less of nothing else, they are wealthier and will probably spend more. But *pure* monetary policy—that is, monetary policy alone, without any accompanying fiscal policy (such as a budget deficit)— usually does not alter people's wealth *directly*.

An expansion in the money supply via pure monetary policy does not increase wealth directly, because the public gives up an asset or incurs a liability as part of the very process through which currency or demand deposits rise; the reverse occurs when demand deposits decline. For example, if the money supply is increased by Federal Reserve open market purchases of securities, the increased demand deposit acquired by the public is offset by the reduction in its holdings of government securities (they were purchased by the Federal Reserve). In any subsequent expansion of demand deposits by bank lending or security purchases, the public acquires an asset (demand deposits) but either creates a liability against itself in the form of a bank loan or sells to the bank an asset of equal value, such as a government bond. What a change in the money supply *can* do directly is alter people's *liquidity.* Money, after all, is the most liquid of all assets. A liquid asset, as mentioned before, is something that can be turned into cash—that is, sold or "liquidated"— quickly, with no loss in dollar value. Money already *is* cash. You can't get more liquid than that!

Since monetary policy alters the liquidity of the public's portfolio of total assets—including, in that balance sheet, holdings of real as well as financial assets—it should thereby lead to portfolio readjustments that involve spending decisions. An increase in the money supply implies that the public is more liquid than formerly; a decrease in the money supply implies that the public is less liquid than before. If the public had formerly been satisfied with its holdings of money relative to the rest of its assets, a change in that money supply will presumably lead to readjustments throughout the rest of its portfolio.

In other words, these changes in liquidity should lead to more (or less) spending on either real assets (cars and television sets) or financial assets (stocks and bonds). If spending on real assets expands, demand for goods and services increases, and GNP is directly affected. If spending on financial assets goes up, the increased demand for stocks and bonds drives up securities prices. Higher securities prices mean lower interest rates. The fall in interest rates may induce more spending on housing and on plant and equipment (investment spending), thereby influencing GNP through that route.

At this point, it is worth noting that while monetary policy does not alter wealth directly, it does have an indirect wealth effect through its impact on interest rates and securities prices. Lower interest rates mean higher securities prices, and higher interest rates mean lower securities prices.* Capital losses are familiar to us all, and perhaps capital gains as well—even if only on paper. Such changes in the values of stocks and bonds in an individual's portfolio may very well alter his or her spending on real goods (a new home) or even on real bads (pornography). This indirect wealth effect provides another link between monetary policy and GNP.

Underlying the effectiveness of monetary policy, however, is still its initial impact on the liquidity of the public. But whether a change in the supply of liquidity actually does influence spending depends on what is happening to the demand for liquidity. If the supply of money is increased but the demand expands even more, the additional money will be held and not spent. "Easy" or "tight" money is not really a matter of increases or decreases in the money supply in an absolute sense, but rather increases or decreases relative to the demand for money. Indeed, changes in monetary policy are most often couched in terms of increases or decreases in the rate of growth of money, rather than in terms of absolute changes. In the past decade, we have had few periods in

---

*To avoid falling into the well-known Galbraithian footnote phobia ("No footnotes are sillier than footnotes"—John Kenneth Galbraith, *The Great Crash* [Boston: Houghton Mifflin, 1961], p. xxiii), we hereby offer our one and only:

Since it comes up again and again, it is worth devoting a moment to the *inverse* relationship between the *price* of an income-earning asset and its effective *rate of interest* (or yield). For example, a long-term bond that carries a fixed interest payment of $10 a year, and costs $100, yields an annual interest rate of 10 percent. However, if the price of the bond were to rise to $200, the effective rate of interest would drop to $^{10}/_{200}$ or 5 percent. And if the price of the security were to fall to $50, the yield would rise to $^{10}/_{50}$ or 20 percent. Conclusion: a rise (or fall) in the price of a bond is reflected, in terms of sheer arithmetic, in an automatic change in the opposite direction in the effective rate of interest. To say the price of bonds rose or the rate of interest fell are but two different ways of saying the same thing.

which the money supply actually decreased, yet we have had many periods of tight money because the *rate* of growth was so small that the demand for money rose faster than the supply.

If people always respond in a consistent manner to an increase in their liquidity (the proportion of money in their portfolio), the Federal Reserve will be able to gauge the impact on spending and GNP of a change in the money supply. But if people's spending reactions vary unpredictably when there is a change in the money supply, the central bank will never know whether it should alter the money supply a little or a lot (or even at all!) to bring about a specified change in spending.

The relationship between changes in the money supply and consequent changes in spending returns us once again to the speed with which money is spent, its rate of turnover or velocity, the subject of the following chapter. In subsequent chapters, we shall delve deeper into the influence of money and monetary policy on the economy—including interest rate effects, wealth effects, and maybe even a few special effects.

3

MONEY IN ACTION

When the Federal Reserve increases the money supply by $1 billion, how does it know how much of an effect this will have on people's spending and thereby on GNP? Say we are in a recession, with GNP $20 billion below prosperity levels. Can the Federal Reserve induce a $20 billion expansion in spending by increasing the money supply by $2 billion? Or will it take a $10 billion—or a $15 billion—increase in the money supply to do the job? As we noted at the end of the previous chapter, if people always respond in a consistent manner to an increase in their liquidity (the proportion of money in their portfolio), the Federal Reserve will be able to gauge the impact on GNP of a change in the money supply. But if people's spending reactions vary unpredictably when there is a change in the money supply, the central bank will never know whether it should alter the money supply a little or a lot to bring about a specified change in spending.

Clearly, this is the key puzzle the Federal Reserve must solve if it is to operate effectively. After all, the central bank is not in business to change the money supply just for the sake of changing the money supply. Money is only a means to an end, and the end is the total volume of spending (GNP); when the chips are down, GNP will determine whether the overall economy is performing well or poorly.

How stable is the public's propensity to spend on goods and services out of increased liquidity? Does the public react to a change in the money supply predictably enough to allow the central bank to calculate the effect of its actions on GNP? Or is the reaction so unpredictable that the Federal Reserve can do no more than probe and pray?

The Missing Link

When the money supply increases, the recipients of this additional liquidity probably spend some of it on goods and services, increasing GNP. The funds thereby move from the original recipients to the sellers of the goods and services. Now *they* have more money than before, and if they behave the same way as the others, they too are likely to spend some of it. GNP thus rises further—and at the same time the money moves on to a still different set of owners who, in turn, may also spend part of it, thereby increasing GNP again.

Over a period of time, say a year, a multiple increase in spending and GNP could thus flow from an initial increase in the stock of money. Whether this expansion in GNP is large or small, relative to the change in the money supply that set it going initially, depends on two things: first, on how much of the new money is respent on real goods and services at each stage; and second, on how quickly the respending takes place. If a large fraction of the increased money is respent by each recipient soon after he receives it, GNP will expand a great deal relative to the increase in the stock of money. On the other hand, if a small fraction (or none) of the increased money is respent, or if it is held a long time at each stage, or if many financial transactions intervene, the expansion in GNP during the year will be quite small relative to the enlarged money supply.

This relationship between the increase in GNP over a period of time and the change in the money supply that brought it about is important enough to have a name: the velocity of money. Technically speaking, it is found, after the process has ended, by dividing the increase in GNP by the increase in the money supply that started it all.

We similarly can compute the velocity of the *total* amount of money in the country by dividing total GNP (not just the increase in it) by the total money supply. This gives us the average number of times each dollar turns over to buy goods and services during the year. In 1979, for example, with a GNP of $2,370 billion and a money supply of $400 billion, the velocity of money was 2,370 divided by 400, or 5.9 per annum. Each dollar, on the average, was spent about 6 times in purchasing goods and services during 1979.

With this missing link—velocity—now in place, we can reformulate the problem of the Federal Reserve more succinctly. The Federal Reserve controls the supply of money. Its main job is to regulate the flow of spending. The flow of spending, however, depends not only on the supply of money but also on that supply's rate of turnover, or velocity, and this the Federal Reserve does *not* have under its thumb. Since any given supply of money might be spent faster or slower—that is, velocity might rise or fall—a rather wide range of potential spending could conceivably flow from any given stock of money.

The *ideal* situation for the central bank is a stable velocity, or at least one that is changing slowly and predictably over time. If velocity is stable or predictable, or close to it, the Federal Reserve can induce almost any volume of spending it wants simply by adjusting the money supply to the known velocity. For example, the velocity of the total money supply is now about 6. If an *addition* to the money supply also turns over 6 times a year in the purchase of goods and services, then the Federal Reserve knows for sure that if it increases the money supply by a billion dollars the end result will be an increase in GNP of $6 billion. In that case, the Federal Reserve has it made; monetary policy alone would be both necessary *and sufficient* to control aggregate spending.

At the other extreme, the *worst* situation from the point of view of the monetary authorities is if velocity fluctuates randomly or perversely. If velocity moves randomly up and down without rhyme or reason, it would be impossible to gauge the impact on GNP that might result from a change in the money supply. If movements in velocity are perverse, that would mean that every time the Federal Reserve increased the money supply by 10 percent, velocity would respond by falling 10 percent. Monetary policy would be impotent. Changes in the money supply would merely be offset by an opposite change in velocity, leaving spending (and therefore GNP) unaltered. The public would not be responding to changes in liquidity and would be deciding by itself how much it would spend, irrespective of the actions of the Federal Reserve. Under such circumstances, monetary policy would be close to useless as a tool of national economic policy.

Living with Velocity

The facts are that velocity is neither perfectly stable nor fully predictable. Unfortunately for the Federal Reserve, it does not operate in a world designed for its own convenience. With a money supply of about $400 billion today, a miscalculation of only 0.1 in velocity means a $40 billion swing in GNP. But all is not necessarily lost. While velocity is not fixed, neither do its movements appear to be random or perverse. If the Federal Reserve could discover the underlying determinants of fluctuations in velocity, it might still be able to coexist with such a moving target.

With that in mind, examining the past may provide a clue to developments in the future. The velocity of the money supply (M1B) reached an annual peak of slightly over 4 times per year in 1918. It fell slightly during most of the 1920s and then regained that peak of 4 in 1929. Thereafter, during the Depression and World War II, velocity fell almost continuously to an all-time low of 2 in 1946. In that year GNP was about $210 billion and the money supply $105 billion; each dollar, on the average, was being spent only twice.

Since then, however, velocity has risen considerably. It rose to 2.5 by 1950; to 3 by 1955; 3.5 in 1960; reached 4 (the previous peak) in 1964; continued on upward, beyond its previous peak, to 4.5 in 1968; hit 5 in 1973; and now, still climbing, it is approaching a turnover rate of about 6 times per annum. The increase since World War II has been steady and even, with only slight dips now and then, usually in recessions, to interrupt an otherwise unbroken upward climb.

But, of course, facts alone do not speak for themselves. Understanding requires interpretation. Why has velocity behaved this way, especially in the past 35 years? After World War II it was generally expected that velocity would accelerate somewhat. Unexpected, however, has been the magnitude of the increase and its duration.

Perhaps the main reason for the extent of the postwar rise in velocity has been the increasing attractiveness of financial assets *other than money*—bonds, stocks, savings and loan shares, money market mutual funds, and savings accounts in commercial banks—as prudent and desirable outlets in which to invest excess cash. These assets are often highly liquid, almost as liquid as money, and yet they pay relatively high rates of interest. Attractive yields on financial assets other than money have led more and more people to wonder why they should ever hold any idle cash aside from what they need for day-to-day transactions purposes. And traditional concepts about how much cash on hand is really necessary for doing business have also come under reexamination. If cash for day-to-day transactions purposes can be pared down, then some of it can be loaned out to earn more interest. The money that is put to work moves to borrowers who can use it for current purchases. As a result, a larger volume of current spending flows from the same stock of money.

Corporate treasurers, in particular, have found that it pays dividends to scrutinize their cash holdings intensively. Could they manage to get along with somewhat less in the till than they had previously thought of as "normal," and invest a portion in high-yielding Certificates of Deposit at commercial banks or in U.S. Treasury bills (short-term government securities)? Increasingly, the answer has been yes, and imaginative new techniques of cash management have been developed to facilitate the process (also some not so imaginative old techniques, such as becoming "slow payers" when bills come due).

This trend has not escaped the attention of consumers. They have learned to economize on money by substituting lines of credit at retail stores and financial institutions in place of cash reserves; in addition, the growing use of credit cards has drastically reduced household needs for day-to-day transactions money. What was formerly held in the form of demand deposits or currency, for emergency use or for current payments, now shifts to higher interest-bearing savings deposits.

In summary, it is clear that velocity has not been stable; however, neither has it fluctuated randomly or perversely. There is a discernible pattern in the movements of velocity during the postwar period—a persistent long-run rise with minor short-run dips during recessions. Even though we may not be able to pinpoint all the specific determinants, we can still see broad cause-and-effect relationships.

Higher interest rates clearly lead to an increase in velocity by inducing business firms and households to economize on money. They hold less, lend out the excess, and others (the borrowers) can then spend it. Once learned, techniques of cash management are not easily forgotten, so that even in recessions, when interest rates fall, velocity does not drop back very far.

Furthermore, the long-run upward trend in velocity over the past quarter century suggests that fundamental structural relationships between the money supply and the spending habits of the community are apparently in the process of transition. New payment methods are developing (credit cards are a prime example), as financial innovation occurs side by side with technological innovation in industry. Such financial innovation, however, rarely takes root overnight. Established payment habits are likely to change only gradually.

Thus, although velocity is not fixed, neither is it likely to change drastically in the short run. The Federal Reserve may be able to live with it, even though it is a moving target. By gaining further insight into what makes velocity move, the central bank might be able to establish a range of probabilities as to where velocity is likely to be tomorrow and the day after, and act on that basis. In other words, a morning line on velocity (not unlike the one your local bookie puts out on the races at Hialeah)—provided the odds are unemotionally calculated and continuously reassessed in the light of emerging evidence—might still enable the Federal Reserve to come out a winner.

4

THE MONETARISTS VERSUS THE
KEYNESIANS

Each baby girl and tiny man
That's born into a family nest
Is either a little Keynesian
Or else a little Monetarest.

At an economics conference in the late 1960s, Robert Solow, a prominent Keynesian from MIT, commented as follows on a paper presented by Milton Friedman: "Another difference between Milton and myself is that everything reminds Milton of the money supply; well, everything reminds me of sex, but I try to keep it out of my papers."

Monetarists do, in fact, make so much of the money supply that they are rather easy to caricature. It appears frequently in their professional papers circulated among economists; it figures prominently in their policy recommendations to the government; and some have even shown how it can make money in the stock market. But so far, at least, no evidence has been presented on its qualifications as an aphrodisiac. Don't, however, rule out the possibility.

The President of the United States will use very different approaches in economic policy making depending on whether his orientation is Keynesian or Monetarist. As a Keynesian, he and the Chairman of his Council of Economic

Advisers would spend considerable time pressing the Congress for countercyclical tax and expenditure legislation. If he were a Monetarist, he would expend more effort trying to convince everyone that things will get better by themselves; but if something simply must be done, then he would turn to the Federal Reserve. The Eisenhower administration had essentially a Monetarist course, while the orientation of economic policy under Kennedy and Johnson was primarily Keynesian. The Nixon, Ford, and Carter administrations have used a little bit of everything.

What are the underlying differences between these two schools? And how do their theoretical disputes affect their policy recommendations?

The Monetarist View

The Monetarists used to be called Quantity Theorists. Their lineage can be traced at least as far back as Jean Bodin in the sixteenth century, through John Locke, David Hume, and then through the nineteenth century classical economists, David Ricardo and John Stuart Mill, up to Irving Fisher in the 1920s and 1930s, and now Milton Friedman in the 1970s and 1980s. Historically, they used to be concerned primarily with the relationship between the quantity of money and prices, viewing the money supply as the main determinant of the price level. The modern Quantity Theorists—or Monetarists—no longer believe changes in the money supply affect only the price level. As they see it, the role of money can be much broader than that; in the *short run* it is the crucial determinant of economic activity.

According to the Monetarists, there is a direct and reliable link between the money supply and GNP. That link is the predictability of monetary velocity. Because of it, a change in the money supply will change aggregate spending and GNP by a predictable amount.

The chain of transmission from the money supply to GNP can be visualized as working roughly in the following fashion. Assume that the Federal Reserve increases the money supply through open-market purchases of government securities. This increases the liquidity of the public; they are now holding cash in place of government securities. However, people do not want simply to hold this additional money. According to the Monetarists, people want money mainly as a medium of exchange for day-to-day transactions purposes, or to hold for a short while before making purchases. Based on the current volume of transactions—represented by the current GNP—they already had just about the amount of money they needed. So, finding themselves with some extra money, they proceed to spend it on real assets, on real goods and services, thereby driving up GNP.

If the money supply is increased during a recession, then the increased spending will primarily raise employment and real output; on the other hand, if the economy is already close to full employment, then the increase in GNP will consist mainly of higher prices.

How high will GNP go? The answer, according to a simple version of Monetarism, is that spending on real goods and services will continue to climb until GNP has risen to the point where the relationship between it and the money supply becomes the same as it had been before the money supply was increased by the Federal Reserve. That relationship, of course, is exactly what we mean by monetary velocity (GNP/M). When GNP has reached the point where it once again stands in its previous ratio to the money supply, the public will finally be satisfied to hold the increased stock of money as a medium of exchange and spending will level off.

The same thing could be said in still another way. The increase in the money supply makes the public's portfolio of assets more liquid than it had been. This increased liquidity leads to the purchase of additional (less liquid) real assets until the portfolio's liquidity is restored to its former state.

A decrease in the money supply works in similar fashion, except in the opposite direction. When the Federal Reserve reduces the money supply through open market sales of government securities, the public finds itself short of cash relative to the volume of business being done. Spending on goods and services contracts, driving GNP lower until the previous relationship between GNP and the (now smaller)

"Frank, how ever did you find this guru?"

Drawing by D. Fradon; © 1968 *The New Yorker Magazine, Inc.*

money supply is restored. Faced with a shortage of liquidity, the public cuts back its spending until GNP drops to the point where the original ratio of GNP to the money supply is reestablished and velocity falls back to "normal." GNP will then stabilize in line with the smaller money supply.

This particular view of the money-GNP relationship is quite inflexible. Most Monetarists would insist only that velocity be predictable, not necessarily a fixed and unchanging number—in other words, as money supply goes up, GNP rises by a predictable amount because the demand for money is related in a reliable way to GNP. Money demand might even depend on interest rates, but that relationship is predictable and stable as well. In either case, it is clear where the Monetarists got their name. The *ideal* situation for the central bank is a stable velocity, or at least one that is changing slowly and predictably over a period of time, and this is precisely *the* main assumption of the Monetarists. If velocity is stable (or predictable, as reasonable Monetarists argue), the Federal Reserve can induce almost any volume of spending it wants simply by adjusting the money supply to the known velocity.

In the Monetarist World, there is no need to even pay any attention to fiscal policy (the Keynesians' pet). Changes in the money supply can do the whole job, and stabilization policy should concentrate on that and that alone. No wonder Monetarists blame the Federal Reserve whenever *anything* goes wrong! Of course, there's still the question of whether we really need an active stabilization policy—a subject we'll discuss below.

The Keynesian View of Money

The gospel according to Saint John—the late John Maynard Keynes, that is—is that the channels through which the money supply affects GNP are rather different. They are less direct and also less reliable, primarily because velocity is not viewed as very stable in either the short or the long run.

The chain of transmission from the money supply to GNP can be visualized as follows. Assume once more that the Federal Reserve increases the money supply by open market purchases of government securities. Again, this increases the liquidity of the public. However, people *may* want simply to hold this additional liquidity. The entire process might end right there, before it has hardly begun. The public gets additional money and hoards it. Period. The money supply has increased but GNP is unaffected. Velocity has fallen. In the Keynesian World, unlike the Monetarist World, the public holds cash not only for day-to-day transactions purposes but *also* as idle balances or as a pool of liquidity for possible speculation in the stock and bond markets.

Suppose the Monetarists have a point: that people do *not* want to hold the additional cash. Finding themselves with more money, they proceed to spend it. In the Monetarist World they would spend it primarily on *real* assets, on real goods and services, thereby directly driving up GNP. In the Keynesian World, however, they would spend it not on real assets but on *financial* assets, such as stocks and bonds. The prices of securities rise and interest rates fall. The increased money supply may also increase the availability of credit as well as lower its cost. But GNP still has not been affected.

This drop in interest rates and increased availability of credit *may*, then, induce some business firms or consumers to borrow and purchase real goods and services. *Finally,* GNP has been affected.

A decrease in the money supply works in similar fashion. The Federal Reserve reduces the money supply so that the public finds itself short of cash. The public may just hold less cash and that's the end of it. GNP will not be affected. Or, in an effort to get more cash, the public may try to sell some *financial* assets (or buy less than it had been buying), driving securities prices down and interest rates up. The higher rates, and accompanying decreased availability of credit, *may* lead to less borrowing and less spending, finally reducing GNP.

To summarize the Keynesian view: a change in the money supply can only affect aggregate spending and GNP if it *first* changes interest rates and/or the availability of credit, and *then* only if business or consumer spending is sensitive to those changes. In this way of looking at things, there's many a possible slip 'twixt the cup and the lip.

Is the Private Sector Inherently Stable?

A prominent issue currently dividing Monetarists and Keynesians is whether the private sector of the economy is inherently stable. Monetarists tend to believe that GNP will be relatively unaffected by autonomous shifts in investment spending. Keynesians argue that unless there is an active attempt at stabilization, the level of economic activity and unemployment will fluctuate considerably when buffeted by entrepreneurial animal spirits. While these beliefs have often taken on a religious fervor, they are grounded in the rather prosaic mechanisms of economic theory.

Monetarists, reflecting their classical ancestry, argue that any exogenous decrease in investment spending would be countered automatically by either increased consumption or other investment spending. The mechanism could be attributed, somewhat mysteriously, to the fixed money stock, hence a relatively fixed level of total spending based on the quantity theory. Or, to a reduction in interest rates that would follow a drop in exogenous investment. The fall in interest rates would, in turn, stimulate other categories of investment spending, reduce saving (thereby increasing consumption), and make up for the initial drop in investment.

As long as that mechanism worked, there would be no need to intervene by pushing policy buttons, either monetary or fiscal. The level of GNP would not be buffeted by exogenous shocks.

Keynesians are less impressed with the automatic offsets to gyrations in investment spending. First, the mysterious quantity theory linkage between money and GNP is simply not part of the picture. Moreover, interest rates do not necessarily respond to a drop in investment. And even if interest rates did decline, there's no guarantee that they will induce very much investment. You can forget about any help from consumption—if anything, it makes matters worse by declining with falling GNP. Thus, according to Keynesians, it is essential for the government to step in and stabilize GNP.

Fluctuations in the price level are another source of stability, according to Monetarists. If, for example, consumption and investment don't rise fast enough to offset an initial decline in investment spending, the resulting unemployment will drive down prices. A fixed money stock with lower prices means a larger real supply of money (that is, in terms of its purchasing power over goods and services). This could stimulate spending directly via the quantity theory. Alternatively, the larger real supply of money would lower interest rates, and investment spending would increase still further. The Keynesian response to such price effects is twofold: first, prices rarely decline; and second, the spending effects are too slow to rely upon to restore full employment.

The Monetarist-Keynesian confrontation on the need for an active stabilization policy rests on empirical assessments of the speed and power of the natural stabilizers in the economy—fluctuating interest rates and prices. It would seem a rather straightforward task to measure such real-world characteristics and thereby ascertain who is correct. But, as we'll see in the next chapter, that is simply not the case.

The Interest Rate: Where Does It Go and Why?

Returning to the monetary mechanism, it is obvious that, to Keynesians, one of the keys to the effectiveness of monetary policy is what happens to interest rates on financial instruments. Unless the increased liquidity produced by an expanding money supply lowers interest rates (and unless the decreased liquidity produced by contracting the money supply raises interest rates), monetary policy is probably impotent.

Even the wealth effect of monetary policy, mentioned near the end of Chapter 2, which has been invoked by latter-day Keynesians, operates through interest rates: Lower interest rates imply higher securities prices, and higher interest rates imply lower securities prices. Such changes in wealth may or may not have a significant impact on spending. But if an expansionary monetary policy is to carry with it a wealth effect, it must lower interest rates; if contractionary monetary policy is to have a wealth effect, it must raise rates.

Monetarists, however, do not view interest rates as a major link in the transmission belt between a change in the money supply and the ultimate impact on spending. Indeed, in one version of Monetarism, if interest rates do not change at all it probably indicates a very *powerful* monetary policy, since presumably the entire change in liquidity is spent *directly* on goods and services and none at all in financial markets.

The controversy between Monetarists and Keynesians over interest rates is even more complex. Milton Friedman has argued that an *expansionary* monetary policy *raises* interest rates and a *contractionary* monetary policy *lowers* interest rates; just the reverse of standard Keynesian analysis. How does Milton do it? Here's the point: An increase in the money supply *may initially* lower interest rates, if the increased liquidity is spent on financial assets. But that is only the beginning. Once GNP responds to the increased money supply (as it must in the Monetarist world) the transactions demand for money will increase, thereby driving interest rates upward. But this is hardly new. Mainstream Keynesians certainly wouldn't disagree. The Monetarists argue, however, that the "income effect" of the increased money supply will overwhelm the initial "liquidity effect" so that interest rates snap back past original levels.

If pressed on this last point, Keynesians might even acquiesce as well: after a while rates *could* rise past the original equilibrium—it all depends on the speed and strength of the response in GNP to monetary expansion. They would focus their attention on the interim period—before GNP expands. And this interim period is sufficiently long to justify the statement: Expansionary monetary policy *means* lower interest rates while contractionary policy *means* higher rates.

But there's more. Until now we've ignored inflation. And while the Monetarist-Keynesian debate on inflation will be explored in Chapter 6, it plays a key role in the response of interest rates to monetary policy. In particular, if expectations of inflation are generated by an expansionary monetary policy, then this will cause a *further* increase in the level of interest rates. The reason is as follows: A credit instrument promises to repay the principal of the loan after a certain time period plus an interest payment as a reward to the lender. The interest and principal are fixed in dollar terms. For example, a $1,000 one-year note which promises $50 in interest yields five percent. This is the nominal yield. If the rate of increase in prices during the year is 2 percent, then it takes $1,020 at the end of the year to buy what $1,000 would have purchased a year earlier. Thus, in *real* terms the lender is receiving an interest return of only about 3 percent. It is simply a fact of life, therefore, that the nominal rate of interest minus the rate of inflation equals the real rate of interest. But financial experts aren't dumb. If lenders expect prices to rise by 2 percent during the next twelve months and want to receive 5 percent in real terms, they will demand 7 percent from borrowers. As long as borrowers expect the same rate of inflation, they will go along with the higher nominal rate of interest. After all, if they were ready to pay 5 percent with no inflation, they should be equally eager to borrow money at 7 percent with 2 percent inflation—they will be paying off the loan in "cheaper" dollars.

What might lead *both* borrowers and lenders to expect inflation and then arrive at a higher nominal rate of interest? You guessed it—an expansionary monetary policy! When such inflationary expectations are tacked on to the income effect, Monetarists contend that it is virtually certain that these two will dominate the initial liquidity impact and expansionary monetary policy will lead to higher interest rates. An analogous argument can be made for contractionary monetary policy lowering interest rates.

Notice, by the way, that the Quantity Theory foundations of Monetarism are clearly visible in these arguments. Increases in money lead to inflation via the quantity theory. The interest rate is determined by savers and investors. They "pierce the veil" of money and refuse to let inflation interfere with their agreed-upon *real* rate of interest. Thus an "inflation premium" is added to the real rate and increases in money supply raise the nominal or stated rate of interest.

The story just told of interest rates rising due to the inflationary expectations generated by expansionary monetary policy has taken on an added dimension called rational expectations. In particular, inflationary expectations that incorporate the predictions of economic models, such as the quantity theory of money, as well as the predictable behavior of policy-makers, are called rational expectations. They are rational in the sense that all potentially relevant information is brought to bear on the formulation of expectations. Nothing is left out.

The consequences of such apparently innocuous logic are simply amazing. In particular, if policy-makers are expected to increase the money supply in an effort to lower interest rates, there will, in fact, be no effect at all on real interest rates since such anticipated money stock movements will have been already incorporated in portfolio decisions. For example, the liquidity effect of the anticipated increase in money stock will have already raised bond demand to take advantage of anticipated capital gains; thus no further bond price increases occur when the money stock actually increases. All that's left is the quantity theory effect which says that increases in money stock raise prices. Thus, the anticipated rate of inflation generated by expansionary monetary policy pushes up nominal interest rates. There simply aren't any intermediate steps. Rational expectations provide a closer link between money and prices and between money growth and inflation and severs the usual Keynesian connection between money and interest rates.

While the rational expectations story sounds convincing, we must remember that the simple quantity theory operates only at or near full employment. At lower levels of economic activity, there is considerable slippage between money and prices. Even near what we designate as full employment there are wage and price rigidities because of contractual arrangements that interfere with any proportional relationship between money and prices.

Can we really be this far in a book on money and not be sure which way interest rates respond to monetary ease or stringency? Yes and no—unequivocally.

Monetarists and Keynesians generally agree that *initially* an expansionary policy lowers interest rates (and a contractionary policy raises them). But for how long? If the impact on real spending is strong, or if expectations of price changes are generated, the initial interest rate change will be reversed and rates may very well snap back past what they had been originally. Thus interest rates could be either lower or higher at some point after an expansionary monetary policy, depending on the speed and strength of the response in GNP and on what happens to expectations regarding inflation. (Similarly, interest rates could be either higher or lower at some point after tight money begins, depending on the same factors.)

The question of the strength of monetary policy in affecting GNP will be explored in detail in the following chapter.

It should be obvious, however, that the Monetarist view implies a very direct and certain impact of money supply on economic activity. Money is only a temporary abode of purchasing power. Any increase in the money supply will soon be spent on goods and services. Thus Monetarists tend to believe that an expansionary monetary policy will be followed, rather shortly, by *higher* interest rates (and that a contractionary monetary policy will be followed by lower interest rates).

To Keynesians, the link between monetary policy and GNP is more tenuous. Changes in the money supply may or may not affect spending significantly. It depends partly on how much money the public wants to hold idle, and on the reaction of spending to changes in interest rates and credit availability. Most Keynesians—but by no means all—tend to believe that an expansionary monetary policy will be followed by *lower* interest rates for quite a while (and that a contractionary policy will be followed by higher rates for a considerable interval).

As an aside, we may note at this point that the Keynesians' skepticism regarding the efficacy of monetary policy is paralleled by their opposite stance on fiscal policy. Fiscal policy, you recall, is concerned with the manipulation of government expenditure and tax rates in order to influence economic activity. Keynesians believe that a change in government spending alters GNP directly; a change in tax rates alters consumer spending, also changing GNP. However, the Monetarists take issue with these alleged truths of Keynesian economics. We shall return to the details of fiscal policy and the arguments over its effectiveness in Chapter 12.

Is It Money or Credit?

A subsidiary but important debate between the Monetarists and the Keynesians is whether the Federal Reserve, in conducting monetary policy, should look only at the money supply or at overall credit conditions as well.

The Keynesian analysis is a *credit,* as opposed to a strictly *monetary,* chain of causation. In a sense, money per se is seen as not too important until it finds its way into the hands of a potential spender. To a Monetarist, anyone holding money is a likely spender. But to a Keynesian, a loan transaction may be necessary to move money from its current owner, who may be holding it idle, to a borrower who wants to spend it. Thus the Keynesians take a credit view, concerned with financial assets, credit availability, the direction of interest rates, the reaction of lenders and borrowers to rate changes, and the role of financial markets as conduits for funds.

To a Monetarist, all this is excess baggage, more harmful than helpful. It is money that counts, money per se, and its effects on GNP are not roundabout but direct. To look at anything else is only a distraction.

As an illustration of a case where the two views diverge, assume that funds move from an individual to a business firm in a loan transaction (say the purchase of a newly issued corporate bond). The money supply remains the same; the corporation now has more but the individual has less. To a Monetarist, there will be no net change in spending since there has been no change in the money supply; the business firm, with more money, will increase its spending, but this will be offset by the lender, with less money, decreasing his. A Keynesian, on the other hand, would say that the result is more likely to be a net increase in spending; the lender is probably parting with what were idle balances, which in the till of the borrowing corporation will now be activated. The money supply is unchanged, but its velocity will increase. The Federal Reserve adheres essentially to a credit, rather than a strictly monetary, approach. Indeed, it frequently shies away from the term *monetary policy* in favor of the broader *monetary and credit policy.* Open market operations, reserve requirement changes, and discount rate movements affect credit conditions at least as much as they affect the money supply. Credit conditions include, among other things, interest rates on a wide variety of securities, the volume of activity in the various financial markets, bank reserve positions, credit extensions by commercial banks, and the flow of funds into and out of other financial institutions. The Federal Reserve considers all such credit conditions as well as the money supply when it decides what action it should or should not take.

A Compromise?

Monetarists claim that monetary policy should be conducted only for the purpose of controlling the money supply. Keynesians argue that interest rates and credit availability are at least as significant, maybe even more so. Monetarists contend that changes in the money supply are the major reason for fluctuations in GNP. Keynesians maintain that credit conditions are more important than the money supply, and, in any event, that fiscal policy is more important than either.

Ultimately, these differences can be settled only by empirical tests. As is often true in economic research, however, the factual evidence necessary to resolve the issues has been ambiguous at best and misleading at worst. There are credible (and incredible) empirical studies by eminent economists that come to diametrically opposite conclusions.

In its usual posture of deep humility, the Federal Reserve has refused to declare either interest rates or the money supply as the supreme channel through which monetary policy influences real economic activity. As the Federal Reserve sees it, concentrating solely on money market conditions and interest rates can lead to uncontrolled and even perverse movements in the money supply. Similarly, by focusing only on the money supply and related aggregates, interest rates are seen as subject to wider fluctuations than otherwise.

In a world of uncertainty, the Federal Reserve can never be perfectly sure of the source of the decline in economic activity that it seeks to prevent, or the cause of the inflationary pressures it seeks to thwart. Under such circumstances, it feels obliged to focus on *both* monetary aggregates *and* interest rates in the formulation and execution of monetary policy. These points are sufficiently important to warrant further elaboration by way of some examples.

Assume that a decline in economic activity is on the horizon, precipitated by a reduction in business investment spending. The correct course to follow would be expansionary monetary policy: lower interest rates, increase the rate of growth in the monetary aggregates to pump liquidity into the economy, and thereby thwart the impending contraction with both barrels. If the Fed looked at interest rates as its only guideline, it would observe a fall in rates simply because business firms have decided to spend less and borrow less and because there is a diminished need for cash with a decline in economic activity. The Fed might simply do nothing, since interest rates are already falling—in which case the money supply would not increase at all.

Or, if the decline in economic activity is sufficiently great and interest rates fall by more than anticipated, policy-makers may be induced to cut back on the money supply, thereby lessening the decline in rates but *lowering* the monetary aggregates. By requiring, under such circumstances, faster growth in the aggregates as a target of monetary policy, the Fed guards against such a perverse outcome.

Suppose, on the other hand, that the decline in economic activity is precipitated by an increased demand for liquidity by households—they want to hold a greater percentage of their portfolio in the form of cash. This would lead to less spending and lending by households, hence higher interest rates, and on both counts lower economic activity. The correct course to pursue is, once again, expansionary monetary policy to increase bank reserves and the money supply at a faster rate in order to provide for the increased demand for liquidity and to lower interest rates to encourage spending. If the Fed learned its lesson from the previous example and therefore concentrates only on the aggregates, it will expand the money supply. But if households' demand for liquidity is increasing at a faster rate, their spending will still decline, they will lend less, interest rates will continue to rise, and the contraction in economic activity will not be prevented. By requiring, under such circumstances, lower interest rates as a target of monetary policy, the Fed guards against such errors.

As long as there is uncertainty over the cause of fluctuations in economic activity, *both* interest rates and monetary aggregates must be used as targets of monetary policy. Monetarists place more emphasis on money supply and related aggregates, since they view velocity and the public's demand for liquidity as relatively stable and predictable. Keynesians rely more on interest rate targets, because they are less convinced of a stable demand for liquidity and a predictable velocity. The Federal Reserve—also known as the Great Compromiser—uses both.

PART II

The Power of the Purse

5

HOW EFFECTIVE IS MONETARY POLICY?

If monetary policy is to alter GNP, it cannot do it by mystic incantations. It has to do it by changing the consumer spending of households, the investment spending of business firms, or the expenditures of governments, either federal or state and local.

What categories of spending does monetary policy affect? To what extent? With what time lags? Complementing the theoretical discussion in the previous chapter and the velocity analysis of Chapter 3, the purpose of this chapter is to present the state of knowledge in this area as precisely—that is, in terms of numbers—as possible.

Time Lags in Monetary Policy

By their own admission, Federal Reserve officials are not omniscient. If the economy starts to slip into a recession, it takes time before the experts realize what is happening so they can take steps to correct it. Similarly, if inflation begins to accelerate, it takes a while before the evidence verifies the fact.

Prompt recognition of what the economy is doing is not as easy as it sounds. For one thing, the available data are often inadequate and frequently mixed: new car orders will rise while retail department store sales are falling; farm prices may be dropping while employment in urban areas is rising. Furthermore, the economy rarely proceeds on a perfectly smooth course, either up or down. Every upsweep is interrupted from time to time by erratic dips; every decline into recession is punctuated irregularly by false signs of progress, which then evaporate. Is a change only a brief and temporary interruption of an already existing trend, or is it the start of a new trend in the opposite direction? No one is ever perfectly sure. This problem of getting an accurate "fix" on what is happening in the economy, or what is likely to happen in the near future, is called the *recognition lag* in monetary policy. In 1968–69, for example, the Federal Reserve did not recognize that inflation was as serious a problem as it turned out to be until rising prices had gathered too much momentum to be halted. In 1975, the shoe was on the other foot: preoccupation with massive inflation continued even as the economy slipped into the worst recession since the 1930s.

As soon as the recognition lag ends, the *impact lag* begins, spanning the time from when the central bank starts using one of its tools, say open market operations, until an effect is evident on the ultimate objective—aggregate spending in the economy. It may take weeks before interest rates change significantly after a monetary action has begun. Changes in credit availability and money supply also take time. And a further delay is probable before actual spending decisions are affected. Once monetary policy does start to influence spending, however, it will most likely continue to have an impact on GNP for quite a while.

Regarding the recognition lag, rough evidence suggests that the Federal Reserve generally starts to ease about half a year or more after a boom has already run its course, whereas it starts to tighten only about three months after the trough in a business cycle. This evidence is less than definitive, and it is likely that under some circumstances the monetary authorities will sense what is going on and take action more promptly than under other circumstances. Nevertheless, the inference that the central bank is typically more concerned with preventing inflation than with avoiding recession probably contains a grain of truth.

The impact lag is most conveniently discussed, along with the strength of monetary policy, in terms of the results that formal econometric models of the economy have produced. An econometric model is a mathematical-statistical representation that describes how the economy behaves. Such a model gives empirical content to theoretical propositions about how individuals and business firms, lenders and borrowers, savers and spenders, react to economic stimuli. After such relationships are formalized in a mathematical expression, data on past experience in the real world are used to estimate the precise behavioral pattern of each sector. A model, therefore, is based on real-world observations jelled into a formal pattern by the grace of statistical techniques. Thrown into a computer, the model simulates the economy in action and grinds out predictions based on the formal interactions the model embodies.

Our knowledge of how best to construct such a model is still fairly rudimentary. The same data can produce different results depending on the theoretical propositions used to construct the model. As one cynic put it, "If one tortures the data long enough, it will confess."

A Keynesian model, for instance, would incorporate different behavioral assumptions than a Monetarist model and hence grind out an alternative set of predictions. Furthermore, the data we have available to feed in are not all that we would like. In any case, past relationships are not always reliable guides to future behavior; if they were, the favorite would always win the football game and marriages would never end in divorce.

Nevertheless, despite all their shortcomings, such models, if carefully and objectively constructed, are probably superior to casual off-the-cuff observations followed by inadequately supported generalizations. They are superior, that is, provided they are always taken with a healthy dose of skepticism.

The Federal Reserve Board, together with economists at the Massachusetts Institute of Technology and the University of Pennsylvania, has developed an econometric model of the behavior of economic aggregates in the United States. Many other economists have done similar work at other universities and financial institutions. But our discussion will be based primarily on the Federal Reserve–MIT–Penn (FMP) model, called the Federal Reserve model for short, which was prepared specifically to evaluate the impact of stabilization policies on economic activity. The results of Monetarist models, such as the one constructed at the Federal Reserve Bank of St. Louis, will be contrasted with the Fed model.

The Impact of Monetary Policy on GNP

The latest edition of the Federal Reserve model—and there have been numerous editions—includes virtually every conceivable linkage (maybe) between monetary policy and real economic activity. Interest rate effects, wealth effects, and credit availability are all explicitly articulated in mathematical splendor. As a first approximation to measuring the impact of monetary policy, let us look at what the model says about the effect of changes in the money supply on spending (i.e., on GNP). An increase in the money supply of $1 billion produces an increase of $1.5 billion in GNP after six months. At the end of one year GNP rises by $2.5 billion, and at the end of two years it is nearly $6 billion above its initial level. After three years, economic activity is still rising, producing an increase of more than $10 billion in GNP above its original level.

These results imply a rather long lag before the full effects of an increase in the money supply are felt on spending. If the Federal Reserve undertakes an expansionary monetary policy now, it will have to contend with the effects of such policies well into the future. This can create serious problems for monetary policy, as we shall see later.

Monetarists, especially those of the St. Louis variety, are unhappy with the Fed model. They don't like the detailed description of the transmission mechanism between money and economic activity, suspecting that the architects of the model may have unwittingly left out some of the *direct* links between money and spending. Exactly what these links are is not for us to know—but money works in mysterious ways, so we must have faith. The Federal Reserve Bank of St. Louis pits the midwestern virtue of simplicity against the sophisticated system produced by the Boston-Philadelphia-Washington Establishment.

The simple St. Louis model relating GNP directly to money produces a much faster and initially larger impact of money on economic activity. According to the St. Louis model, an increase of $1 billion in the money supply raises GNP by over $3 billion after six months and by over $5 billion after one year, roughly double the impact derived from the Federal Reserve model over the same time intervals. After one year, however, the St. Louis model finds no additional impact of money on GNP.

Federal Reserve economists counter that the little black box connecting money and GNP in the St. Louis model does not lend itself to scientific evaluation. It is impossible to tell how much of the change in GNP is really due to changes in money supply and how much is due to other things that are changing at the same time. In short, the St. Louis model is too simple to be trusted by Easterners.

Some economists have argued that the effectiveness of monetary policy is asymmetrical—that is, monetary policy is more effective in stopping inflation than in getting us out of recession. They reason that the high interest rates and curtailed availability of credit that characterize tight money cannot help but force restrictions on spending, while the low interest rates and ample credit availability that are typical of easy money will not necessarily induce people to borrow and spend. You can lead a horse to water, as the saying goes, but you can't make him drink.

The Federal Reserve model provides some support for an asymmetrical response to tight versus easy money. In particular, a *decrease* of $1 billion in the money supply lowers GNP by $4 billion after one year and by $8 billion after two years. Thus the impact of tight money is more than one-third larger than the impact of easy money. The St. Louis model, however, makes no distinction between periods of easy or tight money. According to the Monetarists, money is money and if you want it and don't have it, it is equally as disturbing as when you have it and don't want it. (Yes, the sentence is written correctly; we checked it three times and so did the proofreaders.)

Returning to the question of time lags, it should be noted that it takes time for an open market operation by the Federal Reserve to have an impact on the money supply. Reserves provided through open market purchases, for example, must work their way through the banking system as banks make loans and buy securities. If we take as the starting point for monetary policy an injection of about $300 million worth of reserves via an open market purchase, this raises the money supply by about $1 billion after six to nine months. GNP, meanwhile, increases by a little less than $1 billion after six months, by about $2 billion after one year, as compared with our previous figure of $2.5 billion. If we measure the lag in monetary policy from the point in time when the Federal Reserve injects reserves through open market operations, the total lag becomes somewhat longer than was suggested in the first two paragraphs of this section.

The Effect of Monetary Policy on Interest Rates

The impact of monetary policy on interest rates is also generated by our econometric models. Here again Monetarist models differ somewhat from the Keynesian variety. *All* models show that interest rates decline and remain below their original levels for at least six months to a year after an expansionary monetary policy, and that they are above their original levels for a similar period after a contractionary monetary policy. The Fed model, for example, shows that a $1 billion increase in reserves via open market purchases by the Federal Reserve lowers the corporate bond rate by one-fourth of 1 percentage point initially; after some slight readjustment upward during the next twelve months, it levels off and remains below its original level for a considerable length of time.

The more sensitive three-month Treasury bill rate reacts with greater gyrations to an open market purchase. Immediately following a $1 billion purchase of government securities by the Federal Reserve, the bill rate declines by more than 1 percentage point. But after a year the bill rate is only one-half of 1 percentage point below its original level, and it eventually comes to rest about one-third of 1 percentage point below its starting point. Under certain conditions, the Fed model does suggest that interest rates could rise above their original levels in response to an expansionary monetary policy: namely, when inflationary price expectations are especially strong. Even here, however, the decline in rates lasts at least through the second year of expansion. In contrast, there are some Monetarist models that show the Treasury bill rate snapping back to its original level and going above within six to twelve months after an expansionary monetary policy.

Thus far we have discussed the overall impact of monetary policy on GNP, but we have not explored the particular categories of spending involved. Monetary policy does not have an equal impact on all types of expenditure. Which kinds of spending does it affect most, and which kinds of spending appear to be relatively immune?

Investment Spending

One would expect interest rates and investment spending to move in opposite directions: an increase in interest rates, for example, should lower investment spending. If the cost of borrowing rises, business firms should presumably be less willing to incur new debt in order to build new factories or buy new equipment. The historical record shows, however, that interest rates and business investment almost always move in the *same* direction. As in most cases where fact contradicts economic theory, one of them must give ground —and it is usually fact.

In the historical record, many things are happening simultaneously, so that separate strands of cause and effect are not sorted out. Investment spending is influenced by a number of factors besides interest rates—by sales expectations, changes in anticipated profitability, pressures from competitors who may be installing new equipment, the degree of capacity currently being utilized, the availability of internal funds (undistributed profits and depreciation reserves), expectations regarding labor costs, and expectations regarding inflation, to name only some. An increase in interest rates may inhibit investment, and yet investment may, in fact, rise if a number of these other elements shift sufficiently to offset the effect of a rise in interest costs.

The actual change in investment spending from one year to the next reflects the net impact of *all* the variables influencing it, not just interest rates alone. We would expect, however, that if interest rates had not risen, investment would probably have expanded even further.

Econometric methods permit us to isolate specific factors, allowing us to experiment in the "laboratory" of statistical

techniques, as it were. The effects of interest rates on investment, for example, can be examined holding all other influences constant. The results show that a rise in interest rates
does reduce investment spending. In the Federal Reserve's
model, for example, an increase of one percentage point (say,
from 10 to 11 percent) in the corporate bond rate lowers
business spending on new plant and equipment by about half
a billion dollars after one year, by about $2.5 billion after two
years, and by $4 billion after three years.

In this instance, the time lag is clearly quite substantial. In
most cases, investment decisions are not made in the morning and executed in the afternoon. Decisions regarding the
installation of new machinery and the construction of new
plants are usually made many months in advance of their
actual execution. Thus an increase in rates does not promptly
affect investment spending. What it does affect is *decisions*
currently being made about plans that will not actually be
implemented until months or years in the future.

The Federal Reserve model does reveal, however, that
there is one category of investment spending that is extremely sensitive to a change in interest rates. That category
is residential construction, which, although it is not business
investment, is still generally considered a form of investment
because of the long time horizon involved, with returns accruing for many years into the future. An increase of one
percentage point in the interest rate lowers housing expenditures by $2 billion within nine months and by $3 billion after
a year. In addition to this interest rate effect, residential
construction is also affected by monetary policy through
credit rationing by financial institutions engaged in mortgage
lending. Some of the implications of this strong relationship
between monetary policy and home-building are explored
further in Chapter 18.

Small business perhaps deserves special mention in any discussion of the impact of monetary policy on investment expenditures. Spokesmen for small business have always contended that during periods of tight money commercial banks discriminate against them in their allocation of scarce loanable funds.

The evidence on this is not altogether clear, but it is likely that small firms are indeed at a disadvantage relative to large borrowers during periods when banks are short of funds. Furthermore, large firms have access to the corporate bond market, the commercial paper market, and other alternative sources of funds, while small firms do not.

On the other hand, the extension of trade credit (delayed payment for supplies) from large to small firms tends to offset some of these disadvantages. In effect, through their supplier-customer relationships, large firms pass their access to funds on to smaller firms in the form of trade credit. To some extent this alleviates the problem, although it is not likely that it eliminates it.

State and Local Government Spending and Consumer Spending

Construction expenditures by state and local governments also appear sensitive to the actions of the monetary authorities. Municipal bond flotations are often reduced, postponed, or completely canceled during periods of high and rising interest rates. Many municipal governments have self-imposed interest rate ceilings that eliminate them from the market when rates go up. In other instances, when interest costs become too heavy, local voters become reluctant to approve bond issues for school construction and other projects, since the higher interest burden implies the immediate or eventual imposition of higher property or sales taxes.

The Federal Reserve model indicates that a 1 percentage point rise in the interest rate cuts state and local government spending by almost $2 billion after six months. Subsequently, however, the impact declines as municipalities rethink their problems and, typically, proceed sooner or later with much of their planned expenditures.

Consumer spending, according to the Fed model, is influenced by monetary policy directly through the wealth effect of monetary actions on the values of stocks and bonds in household portfolios, and indirectly through the impact on the level of income. About one-third of the impact of monetary policy on GNP after one year occurs through changes in consumer spending, with another third coming from residential construction and the remainder divided between plant and equipment spending by businesses and spending by state and local governments. The effects on consumer spending continue to build up during the second and third years following a monetary action, while the impact on housing tends to stabilize as credit rationing by financial institutions becomes less important. After the first year, the thrust of monetary policy is reinforced by the delayed effects on business plant and equipment spending.

Lags Again

The evidence presented by both Monetarists and Keynesians suggests that monetary policy does have a significant impact on economic activity, with much of the impact distributed over two calendar years. There are powerful short-run effects but, at least as far as the Federal Reserve model is concerned, even more powerful long-run effects.

When the initial *recognition lag* is combined with the *impact lag*, however, the usefulness of monetary policy as a stabilization device becomes less obvious. Suppose a boom tops out in January but the Federal Reserve does not realize it is over until July, at which time monetary policy starts to ease. Its pre-July tightness may still be having depressing effects through the first half of the *following year*, but by then we might well be in the middle of a recession and in need of exactly the opposite medicine. The Federal Reserve, of course, will be providing that opposite medicine, but its expansionary effects may be so long delayed that they might not take hold until we are in another boom, thus once again making matters worse. Monetary policy will be a destabilizer rather than a stabilizer!

We shall return to the crucial topic of time lags in Chapter 11, where we discuss the optimum execution of monetary policy.

6

IS MONEY THE INFLATION CULPRIT?

Arthur F. Burns, former Chairman of the Board of Governors of the Federal Reserve System, once told a visitor, "One of the greatest evils of inflation is that it leaves the President with no easy choices." When asked whether he thought the voters appreciate a real effort to stop inflation, he responded, "I like to think you are rewarded at the polls. But even if the reward isn't at the polls, I come from a culture where there is a belief in a reward in the hereafter."

Those of you who have been valiantly searching for the Eleventh Commandment can now rest easy; "Thou shalt fight inflation" has just been added to the Scriptures!

To most of us, inflation is not something we pray for or against in houses of worship, but something we encounter in supermarkets, department stores, and, of course, doctors' offices. Needless to say, prices today are quite different even from what they were only twenty-five years ago. Workers and businessmen whose incomes have risen along with the rising prices of the past quarter century can still visit their favorite stores and hospitals, although they probably can't stay as long as they used to in either place. But inflation is a more painful matter for many others, especially for the elderly and for retired or disabled people whose incomes are more or less fixed for the rest of their lives. At a sustained annual increase of 6 percent, prices will double every twelve years; at an increase of 8 percent, they will double every nine years; and if prices go up at the rate of 10 percent annually, they will double every seven years.

Under such circumstances, it is obvious that retirement incomes of a fixed dollar amount gradually melt away. A retirement income that is initially adequate slowly becomes marginal and, as the years continue to unfold, approaches the level of sheer subsistence. About the only thing many older people can hope for is that they reach the hereafter before inflation does.

Who is responsible for inflation? Is money the culprit? Can we bring an inflationary spiral to a halt if we clamp down on the money supply? Can wage-price controls help?

Too Much Money Chasing Too Few Goods

The classic explanation of inflation is that "too much money is chasing too few goods." The diagnosis implies the remedy; stop creating so much money and inflation will disappear.

Such a diagnosis has indeed been accurate, painfully so, during those hard-to-believe episodes in history when runaway hyperinflation skyrocketed prices out of sight and plunged the value of money to practically zero. Example: prices quadrupled in revolutionary America between 1775 and 1780, when the Continental Congress opened the printing presses and flooded the country with currency. The phrase "not worth a continental" remains to this day. Germany after World War I was even more extreme; prices in 1923 were 34 billion times what they had been in 1921. In Hungary after World War II it took 1.4 nonillion pengoes in

1946 to buy what one pengo could purchase a few years earlier (one nonillion equals 1,000,000,000,000,000,000,000,-000,000,000).

Pathological breakdowns of this sort are impossible unless they are fueled by continuous injections of new money in ever-increasing volume. In such cases, money is undoubtedly the inflation culprit, and the only way to stop the avalanche from gathering momentum is to slam a quick brake on the money creation machine.

Creeping Inflation

However, hyperinflation is not what we have been experiencing in this country in recent years. During World War II, consumer prices rose by about 30 percent. In the immediate postwar years (1945–49), after wage and price controls were removed, they climbed another 30 percent. None of this was unexpected or particularly unusual. Prices typically rise in wartime and immediately thereafter.

The unusual thing about prices and World War II is not that they rose so much during and immediately after it, but that they have never declined since. Quite the contrary—prices have continued onward and upward to this day, virtually without interruption, producing the longest period of continuous inflation in American history. In all prior wars, prices had gone up during and immediately after hostilities, but then had fallen back somewhat. Not this time. In all prior peacetimes, price increases had been interrupted from time to time by occasional corrective periods of stable or declining prices. No longer.

From 1950 through 1980, the cost of living increased in every year but one (1955). The annual rate of inflation over the entire thirty-year period averages out at close to 4 percent per year. Prices are now more than triple what they were in the late 1950s. They are more than double what they were in 1970.

This is not hyperinflation. It is not like America in 1775, Germany in 1923, or Hungary in 1946. This is a different sort of animal—nibbling away doggedly, insistently, without pause, at the purchasing power of the dollar. Prices do not skyrocket, they only creep—some years 6 percent, some years 10 percent—but always in the same direction, always up, up, up.

This type of inflation is something new. Is money the culprit here, too? Can creeping inflation, like hyperinflation, be stopped simply by slamming the brakes on the money supply? To work our way around these questions, it will be helpful to examine the recent inflation process a bit more closely.

Demand Pull

We understand fairly clearly—as well as anything is understood in economics, anyway—why the price level rises when aggregate demand exceeds the limits of the economy's full capacity output. This is the orthodox inflation setting, exemplified in starkest form in wartime when we simply cannot produce enough goods and services to satisfy all would-be purchasers at existing prices. The excessive spending (in relation to the available supply of goods and services) bids prices up, thereby eliminating some potential buyers and, in effect, rationing the available short supply among those able and willing to pay more.

War thus generates the classic form of demand-pull inflation, with competition among buyers for the available goods and services driving prices higher. People are put to work producing war goods—which are bought by the government —but the incomes they receive, unless siphoned off by higher taxes, are as available as ever for the purchase of private consumer goods and services. At the same time, the output of civilian goods is curtailed as war production takes precedence.

Part of the reason for our inability to eliminate the inching up of prices is simply that we have never really brought World War II to a complete end. An entire generation has grown up that has never fully known peace. Intermittently, in the past quarter century, the financial, manpower, and matériel resources of the nation have been mobilized in an effort to produce both guns *and* butter. Budget deficits, shortages, and accelerated consumer and business buying plans have periodically converged, with the swollen aggregate demand outpacing the economy's productive capacity.

Cost Push

But that cannot be the whole story. There have been periods of relative tranquillity, primarily in the late 1950s and early 1960s, and since the Vietnam War ended, when international tensions eased and slack developed in the economy. But even then prices continued upward. For example, aggregate demand from government, business, and consumers was in no sense excessive during the years 1974 and 1975. If anything, demand was sluggish. Unemployment averaged about 7 percent of the civilian labor force during that two-year period, and occasionally exceeded 9 percent. Nevertheless, consumer prices rose 11 percent in 1974 and 9 percent in 1975.

Why should prices rise when spending is slow and we are far below full employment of our labor force and full capacity utilization of our industrial plant? In past years, before World War II, these were the very times when prices *fell* and the impact of prior inflation was to some extent ameliorated. Some new ingredients have evidently entered the picture since the 1930s and drastically altered the economy's response mechanism.

One such ingredient is the economic strength of labor unions. The American Federation of Labor was founded in 1886, but the real power of trade unions to influence money-wages came with the passage of the Wagner Act and related legislation half a century later. On the basis of government encouragement of unionism as a declared principle of public policy, the expansion of the economy from the depression of the 1930s into the war boom of the 1940s carried with it an enormous growth in union membership. The ranks of organized labor jumped from 3 million members in 1933 to 9 million in 1940 and to 15 million in 1946. Today, union rolls list almost 25 million members. The Taft-Hartley Act of 1947 corrected some union abuses, but it put hardly a dent in their new-found power to extract wage increases in excess of productivity growth, thereby generating round after round of higher production costs.

The second new ingredient—closely related to the economic power of organized labor, although not so recent an arrival—is the substantial market power of big business. Be-

cause of the nature of modern technology, which often results in lower unit production costs as the scale of operations
expands, a few large firms dominate many major manufacturing industries. Their size enables these industrial giants to
exert a degree of control over their prices that would be
impossible in a thoroughgoing competitive environment,
thereby permitting them, to some extent, to pass on cost
increases to their customers.

The third new ingredient is the Employment Act of 1946,
under which the government assumed responsibility for
maintaining high employment through the use of its monetary, fiscal, and related powers. According to the Employment Act, "it is the continuing policy and responsibility of
the federal government to use all practicable means . . . to
promote maximum employment, production, and purchasing power." Without the support of the Employment Act,
neither Big Labor nor Big Business, individually or in concert, could sustain a wage-price spiral for very long. In the
absence of the Employment Act, labor would have to take
more seriously the possibility that it might be jacking up
money-wages too far—that excessive wage demands might
force businessmen to cut back on their hiring. Businessmen
would similarly have to guard against pricing their products
out of the market. But such restraints are relaxed by the
presence of a full employment guarantee underwritten by Big
Government, standing ready to "insure prosperity" with injections of purchasing power should employment or sales
decline too far.

Finally, in the past few years these three ingredients driving up prices have been joined by a fourth element: *imported*
inflation. When the international oil cartel raised oil prices
400 percent late in 1973, we suddenly realized that our domestic price level has become extremely sensitive to actions

quite beyond our control. Political extortion in the form of the 1973 Arab oil embargo had devastating economic impact. The prices that we have to pay for certain key imports from abroad—like oil and some other raw materials—have a pervasive influence on our own cost of living. When a well-organized international cartel, like the Organization of Petroleum Exporting Countries (OPEC), sets artificially high prices for its products and successfully limits its output to keep those prices up, the consequences include higher consumer prices in the United States (and elsewhere) regardless of the state of our domestic economy.

All of this has created an environment of inflationary expectations. And such expectations feed on themselves by forcing labor and business to enter contractual arrangements that pass on higher wages and prices in a never-ending spiral. The old-fashioned pattern of demand-pull inflation—excess aggregate spending, greater than the economy's productive capacity, pulling prices up—has not disappeared. Witness the Korean War period, the 1956–57 episode, and Vietnam. But demand-pull (or buyers') inflation has been joined in the postwar period by a new form of inflation: cost-push (or sellers') inflation. Even when aggregate spending subsides, as from 1958 through 1964 and again in 1969–70 and 1974–75, prices still rise. The distinguishing feature of cost-push or sellers' inflation is a rising price level while the economy is still below a full employment (full capacity) rate of production.

Indeed, even when full employment is far distant on the horizon, Big Labor and Big Business start to turn the screws. Backed by substantial market (and political) power of their own, underwritten by a high employment guarantee that provides some immunity from the consequences of their actions, strong unions and large corporations begin throwing their weight around and marking wages and prices up even when aggregate demand is weak and anemic. As we move closer to full employment, they gradually become more aggressive until, in the immediate neighborhood of full employment, the pressure for higher wages and prices becomes literally explosive. At this point, for all practical purposes, cost-push and demand-pull become virtually indistinguishable as they interact and reinforce one another.

Actually, it is somewhat artificial to separate the two kinds of inflation to begin with; wage increases in excess of productivity growth mean higher costs for the businessman, thereby putting upward cost pressure on prices. Those same higher wages also mean larger incomes for wage-earners, thereby generating a step-up in consumer spending that yanks prices up from the demand side. The stage is then set for a new round of wage negotiations based on the increase in the cost of living, as the process feeds on itself and continues ad infinitum. Or is it ad nauseam?

Money and Creeping Inflation

Unlike hyperinflation, money is not so obviously the culprit when it comes to the real problem of our times, creeping inflation. The "fit" between the money supply and the cost of living exists, but it is rather loose and a bit baggy.

Take, for example, the four decades from 1930 to 1970:

1. From the end of 1930 to the end of 1940, the money supply increased by 70 percent, but prices, instead of rising, fell 15 percent.
2. From 1940 to 1950, the money supply increased by 175 percent, but prices rose by only 80 percent, less than half as much.

"*I've called the family together to announce that, because of inflation, I'm going to have to let two of you go.*"

Drawing by Joseph Farris; © 1974 *The New Yorker Magazine, Inc.*

3. From the end of 1950 to the end of 1960 provides the best fit; the money supply grew by about 25 percent and the consumer price index rose by about 20 percent.

4. However, from 1960 through 1970 the relationship sags again; the money supply increased by 40 percent, but prices by just 20 percent.

Upon further examination, even the close relationship during the 1950s turns out to be less impressive. During the first half of the decade the money supply increased twice as fast as prices, while during the second half prices increased twice as rapidly as the money supply. At the end of the 1960s, the money supply was about 4½ times larger than it had been in 1940, but prices were "only" about 2½ times higher.

This is not meant to imply that money has nothing to do with creeping inflation. Quite the contrary, it has a great deal to do with it, if only because, sooner or later, people will not be able to continue buying the same amount of goods and services at higher and higher prices unless the money supply increases. If the money supply today were no larger than it was in 1940 ($40 billion), or even than it was in 1950 ($115 billion), prices would have stopped rising long ago—and so would real economic activity.

Over the long run, an increase in the money supply is a *necessary* condition for the continuation of inflation, creeping or otherwise.

But it is not a *sufficient* condition. Increases in the money supply will not raise prices if velocity falls (as in the 1930s). Even if velocity remains constant, an increase in the money supply will not raise prices if production expands. When we are in a depression, for example, the spending stimulated by an increase in the money supply is likely to raise output and employment rather than prices. Furthermore, in the short run at least, and sometimes the short run is a matter of several years, increased spending and inflation can be brought about by increases in velocity without any increase in the money supply.

Nevertheless, it bears repeating that inflation can only persist for any length of time by grace of the central bank. If the inflation is primarily demand-pull, a cutback—or mere stability—in the money supply will sooner or later put an end to further increases in spending and thereby eliminate, or at least substantially moderate, the upward drift of prices. If the inflation is primarily cost-push, a cutback or stability in the money supply will sooner or later make it difficult, if not impossible, for business firms to sell their products at higher and higher prices—and thereby make it equally impossible for them to continue granting wage increases in excess of productivity growth, no matter how strong labor may be.

Let us end this section with a summary statement of the role of money in the inflation process. Does more money *always* lead to inflation? No, but it can under certain circumstances, and if the increase is large enough it probably will. Case 1: If the central bank expands the money supply while we are in a recession, the increased spending it induces is likely to lead to more employment and a larger output of goods and services rather than to higher prices. Case 2: As we approach full employment and capacity output, increases in the money supply become more and more likely to generate rising prices. However, if this increase is only large enough to provide funds for the enlarged volume of transactions accompanying real economic growth, inflation still need not result. Case 3: Only when the money supply increases under conditions of high employment *and* exceeds the requirements of economic growth can it be held primarily responsible for kindling an inflationary spiral.

The time horizon and the extent of inflation are also relevant. In the short run, an increase in monetary velocity alone (generated by increased government or private spending), with a constant or even declining money supply, can finance a modest rate of inflation. The longer the time span, however, and the higher prices rise, the less likely that velocity can do the job by itself. Over the longer run, the money supply must expand for inflation to persist.

Conclusions: more money does not always lead to inflation (Cases 1 and 2), but sometimes it does (Case 3). In the short run, inflation can make some headway without any change in the money supply, but rising prices cannot proceed too far too long without the sanction of the central bank.

Does More Inflation Cause Higher Interest Rates?

Unlike many of the questions we have discussed, there is relatively little controversy over the proposition that an increase in the rate of inflation leads to higher interest rates. This is true whether we go from no inflation at all to a rate of inflation of 5 percent, or whether the rate of inflation jumps from 5 percent to 10 percent. Irving Fisher, of Quantity Theory fame, was the first to recognize that inflation, or more precisely, expectations of inflation, would lead to higher interest rates on bonds. In particular, Fisher argued that the nominal or monetary interest rate on a bond was equal to a "real" rate plus the expected rate of inflation. A higher expected rate of inflation would lead to a higher nominal yield.

Recall our discussion in Chapter 4, where the Monetarist-Keynesian debate over the response of interest rates to monetary policy was analyzed. Part of that discussion emphasized that a lender who is satisfied with a $1,000 one-year note which promises $50 in interest will demand a higher interest payment, say $70, if the price level is expected to increase by, say, 2 percent during the year. The reason: with 2 percent inflation, it takes $1,020 at the end of the year to buy what $1,000 would have bought a year earlier. Thus, when expected inflation rises from zero to 2 percent, the nominal yield on a bond must rise from (say) 5 percent to 7 percent to keep lenders happy.

Who cares if lenders aren't happy? Why not let them be unhappy, with the interest rate remaining at 5 percent? Under such conditions they might very well refuse to lend their funds because they would only receive 5 percent in nominal terms, which is reduced to 3 percent in real terms by inflation. If lenders refused to part with their funds, borrowers would be unable to borrow. And that would make *them* unhappy as well. So borrowers, realizing that they'll be repaying their loan with cheaper dollars, and to get their hands on funds with which they expect to make even more money, agree to raise the nominal interest rate on their promissory notes to lenders. That way everyone's happy, including Irving Fisher who said it all along: the nominal rate of interest rises by the expected rate of inflation.

Can we really be this far in our book and finally arrive at an issue on which everyone agrees? Don't be ridiculous! The story just told, of lenders and borrowers joyously arriving at a 2 percent increase in the nominal rate on bonds when expected inflation jumps by 2 percent, takes time to work itself out. In the short run, lenders might be induced to accept a lower real rate of interest. Thus, instead of the nominal rate of interest rising by 2 percent, it might rise by less, in which case the real rate would fall when expected inflation jumps by 2 percent. Eventually, as lenders adjust their cash balances and borrowers alter their investment plans, the real rate returns to its long-run level and the nominal rate rises above the real rate by the expected rate of inflation.

How long is the long run? Ah, if we only knew the answer to that question, how simple life would be. We get closer to

Irving Fisher's result even in the short run—say within six months—as the delay in borrower and lender reactions gets shorter. Furthermore, when expectations of inflation respond quickly to economic forces, the Fisher result is likely to occur still more quickly. On the other hand, when delays are long and expectations of inflation respond slowly, then it takes longer for nominal rates to rise by the full amount of the expected inflation. As a general rule, it is a good bet that an increase in nominal rates of interest will closely follow a jump in inflationary expectations, but nominal interest rates are unlikely to respond immediately by the full amount suggested by Fisher.

The Trade-off between Price Stability and Employment

Since inflation is not something we want any more of, and since the monetary and fiscal tools to curb it are at hand, why don't we just use them and put a stop to these never-ending increases in the cost of living?

The reason we hesitate is because of an apparent conflict of national objectives. The cost of price stability—in terms of the unemployment necessary to get it—is too high. If we pursued monetary (and fiscal) policies with the determination necessary to put a total and complete brake on inflation, we would probably find ourselves with catastrophic rates of unemployment, at least in the short run. We do not want any more inflation, but we do not want any more depressions either. And so far we have been unable to find a solution to the problem of stopping rising prices without simultaneously bringing on at least a recession.

To put the problem succinctly, it seems that we cannot have both price stability and full employment at the same time. If we want stable prices, we have to sacrifice full employment. And if we want a high level of employment, we have to give up stable prices. Exactly what are the terms of this trade-off?

On the basis of our past experience, the accompanying illustration—known as a Phillips Curve, after its popularizer, Professor A. W. Phillips—gives a rough idea of the cost, in terms of unemployment, of various degrees of price stability. For example, point A (1 percent inflation, 5½ percent unemployment) represents the situation in 1963; point B (4 percent inflation, 3½ percent unemployment) represents 1968.

As the Phillips Curve indicates, obtaining absolute price stability during the 1960s would have required an estimated 8 percent unemployment rate. Furthermore (and this the chart does not indicate), for many years the black unemployment rate has been approximately twice the national average. An overall national unemployment rate of 8 percent, which is about what it would have taken to eliminate inflation completely during the 1960s, implies a black unemployment rate at the deep depression level of 16 percent. Even worse, the black teen-age unemployment rate has been averaging *six or seven* times the overall jobless rate for many years; an overall national unemployment rate of 8 percent means a black teen-age unemployment rate of about 50 percent.

The optimum choice among this array of less-than-happy alternatives is not amenable to a purely economic solution.

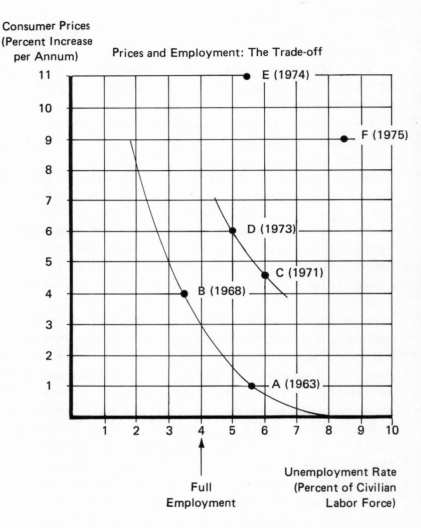

Consumer Prices
(Percent Increase
per Annum)   Prices and Employment: The Trade-off

If we move to the left on the curve and choose low unemployment, some people will be hurt by the resulting inflation. On
the other hand, if we move toward the right on the curve and
choose something close to stable prices, other people will be

hurt by the resulting unemployment. An economist, as an economist, has no basis on which to judge which is better. Resolution of this conflict of interests fundamentally involves personal value judgments and assessments of the social implications of the alternatives more than it involves economics.

But things are even more complicated. Historical relationships are subject to change. Since the 1960s, a bad situation has gotten even worse, as points C, D, E, and F on the diagram indicate. Today, a policy-maker who looks at the 1960s' Phillips Curve and chooses absolute price stability will get not 8 percent unemployment but evidently lots more to boot, judging from points E and F. Not to mention 1979, which is completely off the chart with slightly less than 6 percent unemployment and 13 percent inflation!

What happened? Where has the Phillips Curve of the 1960s gone?

To the right—along with other elder statesmen—is the simplest answer, and the one that appeals to most Keynesians. The trade-off between stable prices and full employment has simply gotten worse because of structural changes that have taken place in the economy. A changed composition of the labor force, an expansion in the demand for skilled labor but not for unskilled, more aggressive union behavior, increased market power in the hands of the large corporations, the oil situation, and other factors have all pushed the Phillips Curve to the right.

The Monetarist Challenge to the Phillips Curve

And yet there is a still more mind-boggling possibility—no Phillips Curve at all. The trade-off between stable prices and high employment is illusory. That towering iconoclast, Milton Friedman, has pounced on still another victim!

The Monetarist reasoning goes something like this: Government policies to increase employment generate rising prices; some additional employment can initially be bought with higher prices. But workers are not fools. They soon realize that rising prices are eroding the value of their pay raises. If they were satisfied with 3 percent pay raises when prices were stable, now they will want more to keep pace with inflation. If we assume 4 percent inflation has been generated, for example, workers will want 7 percent pay raises to get a 3 percent *real* wage increase. If employers believe they can pass on such a wage increase in the form of higher prices, they will grant it—thereby making the inflation worse. Then, as the day follows the night, unions will want even larger money-wage increases next year to wind up with another real wage hike. Thus expectations of further inflation snowball through round after round of ever-growing wage settlements promptly followed by corresponding price increases.

This has become known as the "accelerationist" hypothesis. It implies ever-increasing rates of inflation to maintain unemployment at its lower level. It also suggests that if and when unemployment rises, the inflationary expectations that caused the spiral will remain for a while, thereby leaving us with both high unemployment and high inflation.

On such grounds, Friedman argues that there is no true trade-off between employment and prices, because in the long run you can't fool all of the people very much of the time. You may be able to buy some additional employment with higher prices for a while, but as soon as workers catch on that their pay raises are more imaginary than real, either the inflation will accelerate or businessmen will begin to lay off workers. In either case, the Phillips Curve doesn't give the correct answer to the question of how high prices would rise if employment were increased by a given amount.

What should be done? Nothing—says Friedman. Let the economy find its own "natural" rate of unemployment. Don't try to lower unemployment by countercyclical monetary-fiscal policies, because they'll only produce inflation. It will only help for a short while, and the more you do it the worse things will get!

Is all this true? To some extent, yes. In the long run, the trade-off between employment and prices does get worse, as the chart indicates. But most of the evidence points to a rather long run—such as five years—before all the employment effects of increased inflation are wiped out. We can still use inflation to buy some employment—but less than we thought and for a shorter time period.

Wage-Price Controls and All That

There are other means that have been proposed to help resolve the inflation-unemployment quandary. These include manpower training programs, index-linked contracts throughout the economy, escalating annuities and social security payments, wage-price guidelines, and outright controls.

Manpower programs are aimed at shifting the dismal Phillips Curve to the left. There is substantial agreement that the fundamental cause of the present position of the Phillips Curve is the failure of labor markets to operate effectively. Less inflation would be associated with any given level of aggregate demand and employment if workers who are between jobs could be placed more quickly, if disadvantaged workers who make up the "hard core unemployed" could be retrained with skills that are in short supply, and if artificial barriers to entry were removed from certain trades and occupations. Manpower programs designed to rectify some or all of these structural maladjustments in the way our economy utilizes its labor force might very well permit us to coexist with an unfriendly Phillips Curve by pushing it to the left.

Since the basic problem with inflation is that it imposes costs—in the form of erosion of purchasing power—on certain segments of the public (widows living on pensions, and others whose income is more or less fixed in dollar terms), it is conceivable that one way to get around the problem of inflation is to compensate those who suffer most. This could be achieved by linking annuities and social security payments, and perhaps many other contracts as well, to some cost-of-living index. This has been billed as "living with inflation" by James Tobin of Yale and Leonard Ross of Columbia. Brazil has often been cited as a country that successfully used widespread indexation—that is, escalator or cost-of-living clauses—as a means of softening the impact of inflation. The main drawback of such arrangements is that they do not get at the heart of the problem, the root causes of inflation, and thus they may induce complacency about inflation and increase the likelihood of hyperinflation.

Which brings us to wage-price controls. There are many types of wage-price policies—the strong variety, best approximated by wartime controls with stiff legal sanctions and rationing; the intermediate kind, such as voluntary wage and price guidelines with vague and largely unspecified penalties; and the weak variety, consisting of appeals to labor and business to act with restraint and integrity. Well, as the poet said, "Integrity ain't all it's cracked up to be"—so much for the effectiveness of the weak form of wage-price controls. As for the strong form of controls—few would argue, save perhaps John Kenneth Galbraith, that the benefits flowing from a full-blown set of wage-price controls would even remotely justify the bureaucratic costs and inefficiencies typically incurred in their implementation.

Wage-price controls once again involve trying to shift the Phillips Curve to the left. This time, however, we merely try to suppress some of the inflation associated with a given level of employment. But the costs cannot really be escaped. Inflation is inequitable—to those living on relatively fixed incomes. But so are wage-price controls—to those who were slow in joining the inflationary wage-price spiral before the controls were imposed. Even more serious is the interference of wage-price controls with the price mechanism that is so vital in channeling resources to where they are most desired in a decentralized unplanned economy. Indeed, even centrally planned economies appear to be moving toward *greater* reliance on decentralized price-profit signals to direct resources to their best uses.

Many European countries that have experimented with rather permanent wage-price controls (called "incomes policies" across the Atlantic) have concluded that they don't really work. Methods of getting around controls are developed as time passes, making them both ineffective and more inequitable. As an interim measure, however, temporary wage-price controls may have a greater justification and a better track record. If conditions are ripe for a slowdown in inflation, but inflationary expectations have become a way of life, imposition of controls may have some shock value. By some standards, the three-month wage-price freeze of 1971 was a success, probably for this reason. Furthermore, when business and labor believe that controls are a temporary phenomenon, there is less incentive to incur the moral indignation of friends and neighbors by evasion.

Unfortunately, we cannot provide a happy ending to our story on inflation. The current state of the art does not have a solution to the confrontation of stable prices and full employment. Money is at the root of inflation in the long run but not the short run. The Phillips Curve is alive and well in the short run but not the long run. Wage-price controls work in the short run but not the long run. Living with inflation, as suggested by Tobin and Ross, may be a good idea —but for how long?

7

ARE HIGH INTEREST RATES

ALWAYS BAD?

It is time for a pop quiz. Compare yourself with the experts. Check all those you know, way down deep, are more true than false:

High interest rates
( ) result from collusion between Wall Street and Big Business.
( ) make the rich richer and the poor poorer.
( ) create economic disaster.
( ) raise prices and cause inflation.

We all think we know the answers. But do we? Have we ever really thought them through?

The Conspiratorial Interpretation of Interest Rates

There is a deep-seated suspicion in American society that conspiracy is everywhere afoot. Television programs are awful because "they" want them that way. Stocks go up or down because "insiders" are rigging the market. Rents are high because the landlords are ganging up on the rest of us.

The Yankees always won because that's how "they" wanted it; now "they" don't want it that way any more, so the Yankees win only some of the time. We've all seen too many Westerns. So why should interest rates be any different?

Insofar as interest rates are concerned—and regardless of the merits of these other matters—it is in fact extremely doubtful that any one person or group in the United States, aside from perhaps the Federal Reserve and the United States Treasury, has anywhere near enough power even to influence interest rates, much less set them.

That statement may be a slight exaggeration. But even if it is, it is still much closer to reality than the more popular conspiratorial theory of interest rate determination. The simple reason is that in this country there are too many lenders engaged in the business of lending, and therefore too many alternatives open to most would-be borrowers, to make it possible for any tightly knit clique of lenders (or borrowers, for that matter) to control the price of credit. They would love to. Who doubts that? But they are not *able* to. The wish, as ninety-three-year-old George Bernard Shaw commented when he considered marrying Brigitte Bardot, is not always father to the deed.

Suppose that the three largest banks in the United States —the Bank of America, Citibank of New York, and Chase Manhattan, with aggregate assets of more than $200 billion at the end of 1979 (of total commercial bank assets of $1,350 billion)—were to decide, in concert, to raise interest rates above prevailing levels during a time when there was *no overall upward pressure on rates.* Could they pull it off?

Not very likely. Quite aside from the antitrust laws, their business customers would simply shift to other banks, or decide to raise their funds in the commercial paper market, or float bonds in the nationwide corporate bond market, or utilize any one of a wide variety of other potential alternatives. Consumers could also shift to another bank, or to a savings and loan association, or to their local credit union. If the three would-be monopolists wanted to continue doing very much business, they would have little choice but to bring their rates back into line.

Even the Federal Reserve does not have enough power to set interest rates at whatever level it pleases, whenever it wishes. The central bank may control the supply of credit, but it does not control the demand for credit, and both are involved in the determination of its price.

The facts of life, in this case at least, are rather prosaic. There is considerable competition in the market for loanable funds: competition among lenders for potential creditworthy borrowers and competition among borrowers for the available supply of funds. Lenders charging more than prevailing rates will price themselves out of the market and lose business to their competitors. Borrowers trying to borrow at cheaper than prevailing rates will find themselves outbid for funds by others.

The Rich Get Richer and the Poor Get Poorer

Inequality in the distribution of income may possibly be getting worse. However, there is some hopeful evidence to the contrary in a few countries, including the United States, Great Britain, Scandinavia, and Castro's Cuba. But whatever the facts, the fault hardly lies with the interest rate, high or low.

The blame for continued bedrock poverty in the United

States might conceivably be attributed to capitalism, but if so—and the evidence is less than convincing—it has little to do with the interest rate. Socialist and communist economies have interest rates just as capitalist ones. Indeed, regardless of the type of economic system, wherever funds are scarce and have alternative immediate as well as future uses there will be interest rates, whatever they are called.

It deserves mention, by the way, that financial institutions *pay out* interest as well as take it in. Currently the largest category of bank costs is interest paid out to depositors, a larger cost item than even wages and salaries. Assuming that all bankers are rich and all depositors poor, an unlikely assumption if there ever was one, the flow of interest on savings deposits—which increases when interest rates rise—redistributes income from the rich to the poor. The financial position of small depositors and bondholders is often ignored when the income-redistribution effects of high interest rates are discussed.

The fact of the matter is that the causes of poverty in this country have little to do with interest rates. The primary reasons for most of our poverty are much less complicated than the intricacies of money, financial markets, or fluctuations in interest rates. The poor get poorer because to a large extent they are elderly or unskilled or black or Puerto Rican or Mexican-American or Indian. They get poorer because they are elderly and inflation erodes their savings, or because they are unskilled and unable to compete in the job market, or because the skills they do possess have been made obsolete by the onrush of technology.

For many, poverty is quite simply the bitter legacy of several centuries of sharp-edged bigotry; the fruit of persistent, widespread, and systematic prejudice against racial, religious, and nationality minorities in education, housing, and employment. They get poorer not because interest rates are high but because they get third-rate educations in inferior schools, because they are denied access to clean and decent housing, because they encounter a mountainous avalanche of employer discrimination in job advancement and union discrimination in admission and apprentice requirements, because they are tangled up in a topsy-turvy welfare system that penalizes initiative, discourages family ties, and fosters dependency and cynicism.

For the most part, high interest rates are a contrived scapegoat. The elimination of hard-core poverty does not lie in perpetually low interest rates. It lies in an overhaul of our educational system, in adequate job-training programs, in more sensible welfare and social security arrangements, and in the maintenance of a high-employment economy without inflation within which there is full and complete equality of opportunity for everyone. (Will everyone please rise for a singing of our national anthem!)

Do High Interest Rates Create Economic Disaster?

Tight money and the high interest rates it typically induces are designed to prevent inflation or at least slow it down. However, some object strenuously to its use as an anti-inflationary weapon on the grounds that it is a very dangerous instrument that cannot be used in moderation—that if effective at all, it is likely to be *too effective,* setting off a financial crisis.

Thus, Alvin Hansen, for years the foremost American Keynesian, wrote in 1949:

> The monetary weapon has the peculiar characteristic that it is scarcely at all effective unless the brakes are applied so vigorously as to precipitate a collapse. Those who glibly talk about controlling inflation by monetary policy have failed to consider that moderate monetary measures by themselves alone are relatively ineffective, while drastic measures may easily turn the economy into a tailspin.

A decade later, in 1959, in a report for the Joint Economic Committee of the Congress, practically the same thesis was reasserted by Warren Smith, who several years later was to become a member of President Johnson's Council of Economic Advisers: "It is perhaps just as well that monetary controls have not been very effective; if they had been, they might have been disastrous."

Ten years later, in 1969, the same views were put forth by others, particularly the labor unions, as soon as monetary policy began to tighten. And, as if such episodes were scheduled decennially, tight money during 1979 was again attacked by organized labor as courting potential disaster.

Assessments of monetary policy along these lines are paralyzing. If taken seriously, monetary policy would be employed so gingerly in fighting inflation that it could hardly be anything but useless. We have now had, in the postwar period, three decades of more-or-less active countercyclical monetary policy, sometimes devoted to offsetting recession and sometimes to counteracting inflation. And thus far, tight money, periodically imposed, has not precipitated either Hansen's tailspin or Smith's disaster.

Every economic policy involves some degree of risk. The Federal Reserve might indeed go too far. But on the basis of the record up to now, the potential depression risk involved in actively employing tight money to check inflation appears to be far less than the potential inflation risk of being afraid to ever use monetary policy at all.

In the years before World War II, mass unemployment was the dominant economic problem in this country. In the broad sweep of the postwar period, the major concern has not been depression, but inflation. We can't effectively fight the economic problems of the 1980s, if we continue to be hypnotized by the problems of the 1930s.

Do High Interest Rates Make Inflation Worse?

Although the announced purpose of tight money is to restrain inflation, complaints against its use have consistently come from critics who assert that the higher interest rates produced by tight money make inflation *worse* rather than better. Since interest is one of the costs of doing business, it is argued, higher interest rates, like higher wages, tend to *raise* rather than lower prices.

Long-time Congressman Wright Patman of Texas, who died in 1976 after forty-eight years in the House of Representatives, was a leading proponent of this point of view, along with spokesmen for organized labor. Surprisingly, there is possibly more truth in this position than most professional economists—who refuse to take it seriously and typically dismiss it out of hand—are willing to admit.

Higher interest rates *do* increase costs, and thereby push prices up from the supply side. They also *do* result in larger incomes for lenders, owners of savings deposits, and bond-holders, enabling them to increase their spending and thereby helping pull up prices from the demand side. Cost-push and demand-pull. On the surface, at least, higher interest rates are not so different from higher wage rates. If the latter are inflationary, why not the former?

The standard response to these arguments is that interest is so small an element of business costs, and of income, that higher rates don't matter that much. But such a response raises more questions than it answers. Indeed, it goes so far that it all but destroys the orthodox case for higher interest rates made by the proponents of monetary policy themselves —which is that higher rates lower investment spending, decrease aggregate demand, and thus reduce inflationary pressures. If interest is so minute an element of business costs, then how can higher rates be expected to significantly affect investment spending, as the proponents of monetary policy claim?

The fact is that interest is *not* a negligible item in business costs. In expenditures for long-lived plant or equipment, particularly, it may be a crucial component of costs. For example, if you buy a $50,000 house (it's very cheap, better check for termites) and get a mortgage for the full amount at 9 percent interest for thirty years, before all is over and done with you will be paying $93,000 in interest and the $50,000 house will wind up costing you $143,000. If the interest rate increases to 10 percent, your total interest payments will add up to $105,000 and the house will cost you $155,000, more than triple its list price.

Furthermore, interest is no trivial component of national income. In recent years it has been running at about 10 percent of personal after tax income.

The orthodox response, then, to the "higher interest rates raise prices" argument is wrong. If that were the only answer, the heretics would be far more correct than the traditionalists, even on the traditionalists' own grounds. The answer, if there is any, will have to be found elsewhere.

The answer to the "high interest rates raise prices" school of thought lies in a closer examination of the assumed similarity between the effects of higher wage rates and the effects of higher interest rates. In the previous chapter we pointed out that higher wage rates are inflationary. Wage increases in excess of productivity gains mean higher costs, thereby putting upward cost pressure on prices from the supply side. Higher wages also mean larger incomes for wage-earners, thereby generating an increase in consumer spending that pulls up prices from the demand side. Interest rates appear to do the same thing—and they do. Higher interest rates *do* raise costs and incomes, and *do* thereby generate cost-push and demand-pull inflationary pressures.

In the previous chapter we also pointed out, however, that wage increases, *alone,* could not fully explain either cost-push or demand-pull inflation. To maintain inflation for any sustained period of time, wage increases must be accompanied by continued injections of new money: permissive increases in the money supply are a necessary condition for the continuation of inflation. If the central bank does *not* increase the money supply, or actually reduces it, inflation will sooner or later peter out, regardless of the strength of unions or the monopoly power of business.

Similarly, high interest rates accompanied by monetary expansion are also inflationary. But rising interest rates attributable to tight money—monetary restriction—are not.

Rising interest rates that result from tight money should be equated *not* with higher wages plus an enlarged money supply, which is typically the equation that is implied, but with higher wage rates accompanied by a constant or lower money supply—as if every time wages increased by so many percent, the central bank automatically cut back the rate of growth in the money supply a similar percent. For this, in general terms, is what happens when interest rates rise during a period of *tight* money.

Such higher interest rates, like higher wages under similar circumstances, may raise the price level briefly, but if the central bank sticks to its guns it will not go up far or for long. With a constant or lower money supply, further increases in the price level eventually would be difficult to finance. At that point the higher interest rates will choke off some spending and total expenditures will stop rising. Then the inflation process will grind to a halt (regardless of the higher costs) as a result of tight monetary policy.

PART III

Federal Reserve

Policy Making

8

WHO'S IN CHARGE HERE?

Monetary policy is the responsibility of the Federal Reserve, but to whom is the Federal Reserve responsible?

The answer to that question is so complex that if we unravel it successfully (which is not too likely a prospect), we will either have unveiled one of the great socioeconomic creations in the annals of civilization, comparable to the invention of inside plumbing, or unmasked one of the most devious schemes ever contrived by the mind of man to camouflage the true locus of clandestine power.

According to some, the Federal Reserve is responsible to the Congress. But it is the President, not Congress, who appoints the seven members of the Board of Governors of the Federal Reserve System who occupy the stately building at 20th Street and Constitution Avenue, Washington, D.C. The President also selects from among those seven the Chairman of the Board of Governors, the principal spokesman for the central bank.

On that basis, one might surmise that the Federal Reserve is responsible to the executive branch of government, in the person of the President and his (or her) administration. However, since each member serves a fourteen-year term, the current President can appoint only two of the seven-member Board of Governors, unless there are deaths or resignations. Even the Chairman may be the appointee of the previous administration. Furthermore, it is Congress that created the

Federal Reserve (not in its own image) in 1913, and it is Congress, not the President, that has the authority to alter its working mandate at any time. In 1935, for example, Congress chose to throw two administration representatives off the Board of Governors—namely, the Secretary of the Treasury and the Comptroller of the Currency, both of whom had been ex officio members—simply because they were representatives of the executive branch.

Others, more cynical, have suggested that the Federal Reserve is mostly responsible to the private banking community, primarily the 5,600 commercial banks that are member banks of the Federal Reserve System. The member banks do in fact choose the presidents of each of the twelve regional Federal Reserve banks, including the president of the most aristocratic of all, the Federal Reserve Bank of New York. It may or may not be significant that the annual salary of the President of the Federal Reserve Bank of New York is $110,-000, while that of the Chairman of the Board of Governors in Washington is $57,500.

Who's in charge here? Who, indeed?

Formal Structure

The statutory organization of the Federal Reserve System is a case study in those currently popular concepts, decentralization and the blending of public and private authority. A deliberate attempt was made in the enabling congressional legislation (the 1913 Federal Reserve Act) to diffuse power over a broad base—geographically; between the private and public sectors; and even within the government—so that no one person, group, or sector, either inside or outside the government, could exert enough leverage to dominate the thrust of monetary policy.

As noted in the formal organizational diagram on p. 106, the Board of Governors of the Federal Reserve System consists of seven members, appointed by the President with the advice and consent of the Senate. To prevent presidential board-packing, each member is appointed for a term of fourteen years, with one term expiring at the end of January in each even-numbered year. Furthermore, no two board members may come from the same Federal Reserve District. The Chairman of the Board of Governors, chosen from among the seven by the President, serves a four-year term. However, his term is not concurrent with the presidential term, so an incoming President could find himself saddled with an already appointed Chairman for part of his first term in office. The Board is independent of the congressional appropriations process and partially exempt from audit by the government's watchdog, the General Accounting Office, since its operating funds come from the earnings of the twelve regional Federal Reserve Banks.

The regional Federal Reserve Banks, one in each Federal Reserve District, are geographically dispersed throughout the nation—the Federal Reserve Bank of New York, the Federal Reserve Bank of Kansas City, the Federal Reserve Bank of San Francisco, and so on. Each Federal Reserve Bank is privately owned by the member banks in its district, the very commercial banks it is charged with supervising and regulating. Each member commercial bank is required to buy stock in its district Federal Reserve Bank equal to 6 percent of its own capital and surplus. Of this 6 percent, 3 percent must be paid in and 3 percent is subject to call by the Board of Governors. However, the profits accruing to owner-

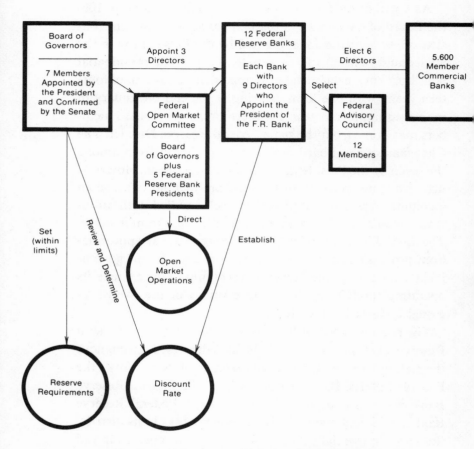

The Formal Structure and Policy Organization of the Federal Reserve System

ship are limited by law to a 6 percent annual dividend on paid-in capital stock. The member bank stockholders elect six of the nine directors of their district Federal Reserve Bank, and the remaining three are appointed from Washington by the Board of Governors. These nine directors, in turn, choose the president of their Federal Reserve Bank, subject to the approval of the Board of Governors.

The directors of each Federal Reserve Bank also select a person, always a commercial banker, to serve on the Federal Advisory Council, a statutory body consisting of a member from each of the twelve Federal Reserve districts. The Federal Advisory Council consults quarterly with the Board of Governors in Washington and makes recommendations regarding the conduct of monetary policy.

Legal authority is similarly diffused with respect to the *execution* of monetary policy, as the diagram indicates. The Board of Governors has the power to set reserve requirements on commercial bank time and demand deposits, for example, but it cannot set them outside the bounds of the specific limits imposed by Congress (between 3 and 10 percent for time deposits, between 7 and 22 percent for demand deposits).

Open market operations are directed by a body known as the Federal Open Market Committee (FOMC), composed of the seven-member Board of Governors plus five of the Reserve Bank presidents. Since the members of the Board of Governors are appointed by the White House, and the Reserve Bank presidents are appointed by the directors of each Federal Reserve Bank, who are (six of nine) elected by the member commercial banks, the diffusion of authority over open market operations spans the distance from the White House to the member bank on Main Street. In addition, although the FOMC directs open market operations, they are executed at the trading desk of the Federal Reserve Bank of New York by a person who appears to be simultaneously an employee of the FOMC and the Federal Reserve Bank of New York.

Legal authority over discount rates is even more confusing. Discount rates are "established" every two weeks by the directors of each regional Federal Reserve Bank, but they are subject to "review and determination" by the Board of Governors. The distinction between "establishing" discount rates and "determining" them is a fine line indeed, and it would not be surprising if confusion occasionally arose as to precisely where the final authority and responsibility lie.

The Realities of Power

So much for the Land of Oz. Actually, the facts of life are rather different, as the more realistic diagram, on p. 110, illustrates.

By all odds, the dominant figure in the formation and execution of monetary policy is the Chairman of the Board of Governors of the Federal Reserve System, currently Paul A. Volcker. He is the most prominent member of the board itself, the most influential member of the FOMC, and generally recognized by both Congress and the public at large as *the* spokesman for the Federal Reserve System. Although the Federal Reserve Act appears to put all seven members of the Board of Governors on a more or less equal footing, over the past fifty years the strong personalities, outstanding abilities, and determined devotion to purpose of the Chair-

men—first Marriner S. Eccles, then William McChesney
Martin, later Arthur F. Burns, and now Paul Volcker—have
made them rather more equal than the others. As adviser to
the President, negotiator with Congress, and final authority
on appointments throughout the system, with influence over
all aspects of monetary policy in his capacity as Chairman
of both the Board of Governors and the FOMC, the Chairman for all practical purposes is the embodiment of the
central bank in this country.

The other six members of the Board of Governors also
exercise a substantial amount of authority, more so than is
indicated in the formal paper structure of the system, because with the passage of time primary responsibility for
monetary policy has become more centralized and concentrated in Washington. When the Federal Reserve Act was
passed in 1913, it was thought that the Federal Reserve
System would be mainly a passive service agency, supplying
currency when needed, clearing checks, and providing a discount facility for the convenience of the private commercial
member banks. At that time there was no conception of
monetary policy as an active countercyclical force. Open
market operations were unknown and reserve requirements
were fixed by law, with no flexibility permitted. Since then,
of course, the central bank has shifted from passive accom-
modation to active regulation, from the performance of regional service functions to the implementation of national
economic policy. This shift has been accompanied, naturally
enough, by a rise in the power of the centralized Board of
Governors in Washington and a corresponding decline in the
role of the regional Federal Reserve Banks and their "owners," the commercial banks.

It would not be unrealistic to describe the central bank
today as headquartered in Washington, with twelve field

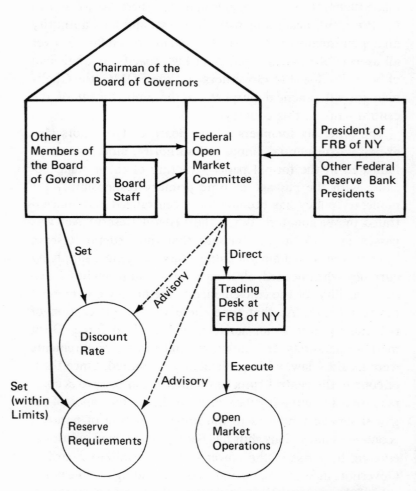

The Realities of Power within the Federal Reserve System

offices located throughout the nation. These field offices may be known by the rather imposing name of Federal Reserve Banks, and they do indeed retain a certain degree of autonomy in expressing their views on the wisdom of various policies. But even so they essentially amount to little more than branches of the Washington headquarters.

Closely related to the Board of Governors in the informal power structure, and deriving influence through that association, is the Board's professional staff of economic experts and advisers. The long tenure in the Federal Reserve System of many senior staff economists, their familiarity with Federal Reserve history, and their expertise in monetary analysis give them a power base that is to a large extent founded on the respect with which they, as individuals, are held throughout the system. Through daily consultation with the individual governors and written and oral presentations before each meeting of the FOMC, staff personnel exert an indefinable but significant influence on the ultimate decision-making process. In fact, in recent years three members of the Board's staff (Robert Holland, Charles Partee, and Lyle Gramley) have been elevated to the Board itself, via presidential nomination. It is also worth noting, by the way, that in 1978 Nancy Teeters became the first woman member of the Board of Governors. The first black member of the Board was Andrew Brimmer, who was appointed in 1966.

Aside from the Board of Governors, its Chairman and its staff, the only other body playing a major role in Federal Reserve policy making is the Federal Open Market Committee, which meets every four weeks in Washington. Of the twelve members on the FOMC, a majority of seven are the Board of Governors themselves. The other five are Reserve Bank presidents. The President of the Federal Reserve Bank of New York is a permanent member of the FOMC, and the other eleven Federal Reserve Bank presidents alternate the remaining four seats among themselves.

The statutory authority of the FOMC is confined to the direction of open market operations, but in recent years it has become the practice to bring all policy matters under review at FOMC meetings. Although only five of the Reserve Bank presidents are entitled to vote at any one time, typically all twelve attend every meeting and participate in the discussion. Thus, potential reserve-requirement and discount-rate changes are, in effect, decided upon within the FOMC, with the twelve Reserve Bank presidents participating in an advisory capacity. The Board of Governors, however, always has the final say on reserve requirements and discount rates if matters should come to a showdown, particularly since legal opinion appears to be that in case of disagreement the Board's power to "review and determine" discount rates overrides the authority of the individual Reserve Banks to "establish" them.

Once the Federal Open Market Committee decides on the appropriate open market policy, actual execution of the policy directive until the next meeting is the responsibility of the account manager at the Federal Reserve Bank of New York's trading desk. He is called the account manager because he manages the System Open Market Account, which includes all of the securities holdings of the Federal Reserve System. Since the FOMC's instructions are often couched in rather broad language, the account manager has to translate these instructions into actual daily purchases and sales of Treasury securities. In the process, at least a modest amount of leeway and personal interpretation is inevitable, as we discuss further in Chapter 10.

Like the account manager, the unique position of the President of the Federal Reserve Bank of New York in the hierarchy also stems from his role and status in the nation's financial center. If he is inclined to use this leverage, as Allan Sproul did a quarter century ago and Benjamin Strong before him, the President of the New York Reserve Bank can mount a substantial challenge even to the Chairman of the Board of Governors. Since such a challenge would have little legal foundation, it would have to be based on the prestige of the presidency of the Federal Reserve Bank of New York and the forcefulness of the man who holds the position. Both Allan Sproul and Benjamin Strong were men of exceptional ability and personality.

But where, in the corridors of power, does this leave the member banks, the directors of each Federal Reserve Bank, and the Federal Advisory Council? Pretty much shut out, if the truth be known.

The member banks do indeed "own" their district Federal Reserve Bank, but such stockholding is mostly symbolic and carries with it none of the usual attributes of ownership. The member banks also have a major voice in electing the directors of their Reserve Bank, but the directors in turn have responsibilities that are largely ceremonial. True, they appoint the members of the Federal Advisory Council, but the Federal Advisory Council serves mostly a public relations purpose and has little to do with actual policy making. The directors of each Federal Reserve Bank also choose the president of their Reserve Bank, subject to the approval of the Board of Governors. But the "subject to approval" clause has meant, in practice, that the most the directors can really do is submit a list of nominees for the position of president. On several occasions, the choice of the directors of a Federal Reserve Bank has not met with approval from Washington; such cases have made very clear exactly where ultimate authority is lodged.

How Independent the Central Bank?

The fact that ultimate authority over monetary policy resides in Washington brings to the fore the relationship between the central bank and the other branches of government also responsible for overall national economic policy—the Congress and the administration, the latter personified by the President.

The Federal Reserve is a creature of the Congress. The Constitution gives Congress the power "to coin money and regulate the value thereof." On this basis, in 1913 Congress created the Federal Reserve as the institution delegated to administer that responsibility on its behalf. Congress requires periodic accountability by the Federal Reserve and has the authority to amend the enabling legislation, the Federal Reserve Act, any time it sees fit.

Essentially, Congress has given the Federal Reserve a broad mandate to regulate the monetary system in the public interest and then has more or less stood aside and let the monetary authorities pursue this objective on their own and to the best of their abilities. Congress has also attempted to minimize interference on the part of the administration by giving each member of the Board of Governors a fourteen-year term, thereby sharply limiting any single President's influence over the board.

This semi-independent status of the central bank is a source of continuous friction. Some members of Congress believe that the Federal Reserve has carried its "independence" much too far. There has been some concern over its freedom from congressional appropriations and its partial exemption from standard government audit, as noted early in this chapter. Also, the Federal Reserve's responsibility on

occasion for tight money and high interest rates has stimulated some intensive questioning at congressional hearings,
including frequent scoldings of Federal Reserve officials by
populist-minded congressmen who get uptight about tight
money.

Others, in Congress and out, have complained that the
Federal Reserve simply has not done a very good job, that
we would all be better off if Congress laid down some guidelines or rules to limit the discretion available to the monetary
authorities in conducting their business. We will discuss such
proposals in Chapter 11.

The relationship between the central bank and the President has also aroused considerable controversy. Many feel
that the Federal Reserve should be a part of the executive
branch of government, responsible to the President, on the
grounds that monetary policy is an integral part of national
economic policy. Monetary policy should therefore be coor-
dinated at the highest level (that is, by the President), along
with fiscal policy, as a component part of the administration's total program for economic growth and stability.

To do otherwise, it is charged, is both undemocratic and
divisive. Undemocratic, because monetary policy is too important to be run by an elite group of experts insulated from
the political process. Divisive, because monetary and fiscal
policy should not work at cross-purposes. Since fiscal policy
proposals are clearly within the President's domain, monetary policy should be as well. A Federal Reserve independent
of presidential authority conflicts with the administration's
responsibility to promulgate and coordinate an overall economic program.

On the other hand, the case for central bank independence
from the President rests on the pragmatic grounds that sub-
ordination of the central bank to the executive branch of

government invites excessive money creation and consequent inflation. The charge that an independent Federal Reserve is undemocratic is countered by the reminder that the central bank is still very much responsible to Congress, which can amend the Federal Reserve Act anytime it wishes. In addition, the President holds regular meetings with the Chairman of the Board of Governors, the Secretary of the Treasury, and the Chairman of the Council of Economic Advisers.

It is feared by many, and not without historical justification, that if the monetary authority is made the junior partner to the President or the Treasury (the fiscal authority), monetary stability will be sacrificed to the government's revenue needs—the government will be tempted to seek the easy way out in raising funds, by printing money or borrowing excessively at artificially low interest rates, in preference to the politically more difficult route of raising taxes or cutting back on government spending. The sole purpose of an independent monetary authority, in brief, is to forestall the natural propensity of governments to resort to inflation.

9

INDICATORS AND INSTRUMENTS

In the good old days, when government agencies told us only what was good for us, the Federal Reserve told us nothing. Does that mean the Fed was engaged in undercover activities —like bugging bank tellers? Quite the contrary, says the Fed. Always reluctant to antagonize the Wizards of Wall Street, the Fed simply wanted to make sure that the financial experts had something to keep themselves busy. And what could serve better than trying to figure out what the Fed was up to? If the Fed told everyone in plain English what kind of monetary policy was on stage and in the wings, what would the multitude of Fed watchers in the financial community do to occupy their time?

Actually, there never was anything cloak-and-dagger about the Federal Reserve. It has always poured forth an alarming volume of reports, pamphlets, magazines, monographs, and books that explained what central banking was all about. Guided tours and speakers were provided free of charge. Fed personnel were always delighted to discuss in detail why and how they did what they did—one, two, or ten years ago. But the *one* thing they were always reluctant to talk about—like central bankers throughout the world—was what they were doing at the moment and what they were planning to do next.

The Fed continues to behave as it always has so far as pamphlets, magazines, and monographs are concerned. But now, under congressional pressure, it must announce its intentions with respect to monetary policy: to be specific, periodically the Fed now announces its money supply targets for the coming year. Nevertheless, Fed watchers in banks and on Wall Street are busier than ever. Evidently what the Fed says and what it does are not necessarily the same thing! So join with us now in a thrilling adventure through the Federal Reserve Forest, as we search for that most elusive of animals: a reliable guide that will tell us what the Fed is really up to. Keep your eyes and ears open and be ever-alert for bear traps, false bottoms, and other unexpected tricks of the trade.

How Important Is the Discount Rate?

To judge by the press, many financial observers rely on movements in the discount rate to indicate the current stance and future course of monetary policy. A change in the discount rate is heralded on the front page of the *New York Times* and solemnly announced in respectful tones on the evening news. It is implied that when the Federal Reserve raises the discount rate, tight money is being ushered in, and when the discount rate is lowered, easy money is entering from the wings.

On the other hand, most Federal Reserve officials and academic economists agree that the discount rate is the *least* powerful of all the monetary instruments, a follower rather than a leader of monetary policy. So what indicators should we study? In order to assess the importance or unimportance of the discount rate and other indicators of central bank actions and intentions, let us first examine discount policy in some detail and then compare it with the other major tools of monetary policy—open market operations and reserve requirements.

One of the primary functions of a central bank, perhaps *the* primary function, has always been to stand ready at all times to provide liquidity to the economy in case of financial stress or crisis. As the ultimate source of liquidity, the central bank is responsible for promptly supplying money on those rare but crucial occasions when the economy threatens to break down for lack of funds. For this reason, the central bank has traditionally been called the "lender of last resort" in emergency situations. In more ordinary circumstances, it also lends funds to banks that are temporarily short of reserves. When the central bank lends, for whatever purpose, the rate of interest it charges is called the discount rate.

The discount rate was considered the main instrument of central banking throughout the nineteenth century and for the first three decades of the twentieth. It reached its apogee in prestige in 1931, when England's Macmillan Committee, somewhat carried away by the splendor of it all, reported that the discount rate "is an absolute necessity for the sound management of a monetary system, and is a most delicate and beautiful instrument for the purpose."

The long tradition behind discounting and the corollary importance of the discount rate stem from the fact that until the mid–1920s it was virtually the only means available to the central bank to accomplish its purposes. Now, of course, with other instruments also at the Federal Reserve's disposal, the relative role of discounting has declined noticeably.

It should be mentioned at the outset that discount policy has two dimensions: one is *price,* the discount rate, the rate of interest the Federal Reserve charges commercial banks when they borrow from the Fed; the other is Federal Reserve surveillance over the *amount* that each bank is borrowing. Thus, one obvious flaw in using the discount rate alone as an indicator of monetary policy is that the rate might remain unchanged while the Federal Reserve employs more stringent (or more lenient) surveillance procedures. Monetary policy could thereby become tighter or easier, even through discount policy, but without any change in the discount rate.

The objective of raising the discount rate is just what the Federal Reserve says it is: to discourage commercial banks from borrowing at the Federal Reserve. When banks borrow from the Federal Reserve, their reserves increase and on that foundation they can expand their loans and investments and thereby the money supply. Less borrowing at the Federal Reserve because of a higher discount rate thus means less bank lending to business, smaller growth in the money supply, and higher interest rates generally.

This process, it should be noted, provides no *direct* connection between changes in the discount rate and changes in market interest rates. The effects of a change in the discount rate are seen as operating through the mechanism of changes in bank reserves and the money supply, just as is the case with open market operations and changes in reserve requirements. (However, as we point out in the next section, the magnitude of the effect on reserves of a change in the discount rate has been minute, compared with the reserve effects of the two other tools available to the Federal Reserve.)

And yet, there does appear to be a connection between the discount rate and market interest rates. As can be seen in the following diagram, a close relationship exists between the discount rate and interest rates on short-term money-market

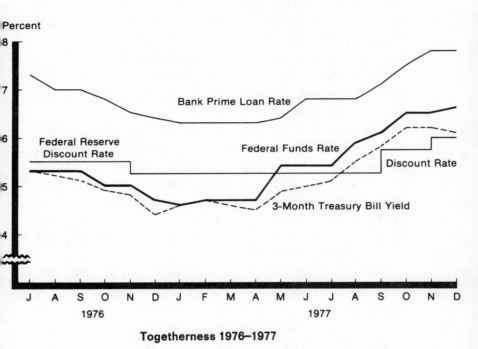

Togetherness 1976–1977

instruments, such as Treasury bills and Federal funds (the rate on overnight loans of reserves between banks), and also between the discount rate and the prime bank lending rate (the interest rate that banks charge their best business customers).

Note that the diagram shows that there is no fixed relationship between the discount rate and other money market yields. Sometimes the discount rate is above the Treasury-bill yield and the Federal funds rate and sometimes it is below them. Moreover, careful examination reveals that changes in Treasury-bill yields typically *precede* changes in the discount rate. Treasury-bill yields rise, probably because of Federal Reserve open market operations, and then—after they have risen quite a while and often quite a bit—the discount rate moves up. Or bill rates fall and then the discount rate is lowered. In other words, a change in the discount rate is likely to come *after* a basic switch in monetary policy has already occurred; it verifies the switch and reinforces it, but does not signal it.

One possible way that changes in the discount rate might directly affect market interest rates is through the "announcement effect" produced when a discount-rate change comes unexpectedly. An unanticipated rise in the discount rate is likely to lead bondholders to expect tight money and higher interest rates (lower bond prices). They sell bonds to avoid capital losses, thus hastening the drop in bond prices and the rise in interest rates.

The key, of course, is that the rise in the discount rate under such circumstances generates expectations regarding future interest rates. But if the public had already observed tightening in the credit markets prior to the change in the discount rate, the actual announcement itself would produce very little reaction. In fact, the bond markets might be relieved of uncertainty, and interest rates might fall.

In any event, the bulk of the evidence suggests that while there may be some cause-and-effect connection between changes in the discount rate and changes in market interest rates, through expectations, for the most part the relationship is indirect—through changes in bank reserves and the money supply. It also bears repeating that typically a change in the discount rate comes after, not before, a basic shift in monetary policy. It confirms what is going on but does not anticipate it. As an indicator, therefore, it is comparable to a fighter who learns his opponent's right cross is on the way when it crashes into his nose.

In an effort to keep the discount rate in closer touch with other short-term rates, there was a change in the administration of the discount rate late in 1970. During the 1960s, changes in the discount rate were made rather infrequently, a pattern that was mirrored by the prime rate charged by commercial banks to their best customers. During the ten years from 1960 until 1970 the discount rate was changed a total of twelve times and the prime rate was changed a total of sixteen times. (In fact, much of the impact of tight money during that period was transmitted to the prime customers of banks by changes in compensating balances—the portion of a loan that must be held on deposit at the bank—that were required of business firms, and by changes in the standards as to who qualified for the prime rate. Thus, even the comovement in the discount rate and the prime rate was somewhat illusory, since the effective prime rate changed even though the posted rate remained fixed.)

To avoid the uncertain announcement effects associated with large and infrequent changes, late in 1970 the Federal Reserve embarked on a course of altering the discount rate more frequently and in smaller steps. During the fourteen months from November 1970 through December 1971, for example, the discount rate was changed eight times, only four less than during the entire 1960–70 period. Similarly, the prime rate was changed a total of twenty-three times during that period, seven more times than during the entire decade of the 1960s.

The discount rate now follows the movements in short-term rates, especially the Treasury bill rate and the Federal funds rate, even more closely than before. It is clear that the

Federal Reserve prefers to get changes in the discount rate off the front pages of the *New York Times* and into the anonymity of the interest rate quotations in the financial section (which happens to be close to the sports pages, allowing you to throw away the first section of the paper). Some commercial banks have tied the prime rate to other short-term rates for similar reasons—so that the prime rate no longer has the appearance of an administered rate but rather moves up and down with impersonal market forces.

Discount Rate versus Reserve Requirements versus Open Market Operations

If changes in the discount rate exert their main effects via bank reserves and the money supply, it is relevant to compare them in this respect with the other tools of monetary policy—changes in reserve requirements and open market operations.

What proportion of member-bank reserves is attributable to the discounting process, to member banks' borrowing the reserves from the Federal Reserve? In 1950, total member-bank reserves were about $17 billion; less than half a billion of these reserves were acquired through the discount process. In 1979, member-bank reserves totaled about $40 billion; about $1.3 billion were due to borrowing from the Federal Reserve.

During the 1950s, 1960s and 1970s, borrowings from the Federal Reserve averaged about half a billion dollars annually. Even at its occasional peak levels, discounting never provided more than 10 percent of total bank reserves and usually the percentage was much less—on average about 2 or 3 percent.

The Federal Reserve does *not* use discount policy as a primary tool for changing bank reserves. For one thing, the initiative for discounting lies with the banks, not with the Federal Reserve. The Federal Reserve can lower the discount rate, but this does not force the banks to increase their borrowings. A change in the discount rate affects only those banks that are in debt to the Federal Reserve, or that consider such borrowing to be a likely source of funds. Many banks never borrow from the Federal Reserve except in dire emergency.

Reserve-requirement changes, on the other hand, have an extremely powerful impact on bank-reserve positions and the money supply. A small change in the required reserve ratio instantly produces a rather large change in bank excess reserves. Because the impact is so powerful, so blunt, so immediate, and so widespread, the Federal Reserve uses its authority to change reserve requirements only sparingly, particularly during tight money periods when increases in reserve requirements would be appropriate.

After all is said and done, the day-by-day standby of monetary policy, in good times and bad, is open market operations. The purchase or sale of government securities can be undertaken in large or small amounts, as the Federal Reserve chooses. The impact is fairly prompt; it is possible to proceed gradually and to reverse field rapidly.

One reason market interest rates change before the discount rate changes is precisely because the Federal Reserve has already been active with open market operations. When the Federal Reserve alters the direction of monetary policy, it is open market operations that typically lead the way. It is also open market operations that do the brunt of the work as the new policy gathers momentum, with back-up support where necessary and appropriate from the discount rate and reserve requirements.

A Pride of Lions, a Gaggle of Geese, and a Plethora of Indicators

Unfortunately, since open market operations are so unobtrusive, the search for reliable indicators of what the central bank is up to becomes more difficult than ever. The discount rate is generally not too helpful a guide to what the Federal Reserve is doing, except as confirmation of a change in monetary policy that has already occurred. A change in the direction of monetary policy can occur without any change in the discount rate, and conversely a change in the discount rate does not normally initiate a change in Federal Reserve policy.

Reserve requirement changes are not of much assistance because they are used so seldom. Paradoxically, open market operations are not very helpful for the opposite reason—they are used too frequently.

Weekly data on Federal Reserve open market operations are released every Friday afternoon and published in Saturday's papers. But the knowledge that the Federal Reserve bought or sold so many government securities during any one week, or even over a succession of weeks, is in itself of limited value; the transactions may have been made simply to offset some "outside" factors that were affecting bank reserves, such as a seasonal inflow of currency, changes in the Treasury's cash balances, or any of a multitude of other possibilities. (You can get more details on some of the mechanics of open market operations—if such things turn you on—in the next chapter.)

Since it is widely understood that weekly data on open market operations alone give an inadequate picture of what is going on, many financial observers rely more on movements in interest rates for clues to the current stance of monetary policy. Of all yields, the ones most quickly responsive to monetary policy are probably the rate on short-term Treasury bills and the Federal funds rate. The Federal funds rate is the rate charged on reserves lent from one bank to another. On any given day, some banks have excess reserves and other banks have reserve deficiencies. There are brokers who bring such banks together to arrange for a loan (called a purchase and sale) from banks with surplus reserves to banks with deficient reserves. The agreed upon interest rate is called the Federal funds rate. It can rise significantly when there are few banks with excess reserves and lots with reserve deficiencies, and it can drop just as precipitously when the reserve rich banks outnumber the poor. Thus it acts as a sensitive barometer of conditions in the reserves market.

However, as reliable indicators of what the central bank is doing, all interest rates have serious limitations. To Monetarists, of course, as we saw in Chapter 4, they are irrelevant. Aside from that, it should be obvious that they are susceptible to change for reasons other than Federal Reserve policy; this makes it dangerous to read them as though they were determined exclusively by the Federal Reserve. The central bank has a substantial influence over the supply of credit, but only limited influence over the demand for it, so that interest rates may fluctuate for reasons that have nothing to do with the Federal Reserve's actions. Tight money generally means a rise in interest rates, but a rise in interest rates does not necessarily mean tight money. Indeed, as we saw in Chapter 4, excessively *easy* money might also produce a rise in interest rates.

Given the shortcomings of all the "orthodox" indicators —the discount rate, open market transactions, and the behavior of interest rates—the Federal Reserve, always helpful, releases a truckload of numbers each Friday afternoon along with the data on open market operations. It presents current statistics on a wide variety of alternative indicators. You can take your pick!

It lists weekly figures on all of the following: the monetary base, total member-bank reserves, the volume of member-bank discounting from the Federal Reserve, free reserves, various measures of the money supply, business loans at large commercial banks, and a few hundred other numbers just for good measure.

All these are self-explanatory except perhaps the monetary base and free reserves. The monetary base is defined as total member-bank reserves plus currency outstanding. Free reserves equals member-bank excess reserves less their borrowings from the Federal Reserve; when borrowings exceed excess reserves, it is usually called net borrowed reserves.

With this smorgasbord of indicators, plus the orthodox ones that are on the back burner, you can select those that best suit your individual taste. As is obvious from Chapter 4, a Monetarist will lean toward the money supply in one form or another, a Keynesian toward interest rates and business loans. An eclectic will stuff himself on a little bit of everything, and if life becomes more complicated that way he has only himself to blame.

Free reserves attained some degree of popularity a few

years ago but have fallen from favor. The main trouble is that a given level of free reserves is compatible with many different levels of the money supply and bank credit. The figure for free reserves has fluctuated within roughly the same limits for the past twenty years, while the money supply and bank credit have grown considerably during that interval.

At the same time as the Monetarists are downgrading interest rates as indicators of Federal Reserve policy, because they are not under the firm control of the central bank, Keynesians are saying the same thing about the money supply—that it is influenced by commercial bank behavior in conjunction with swings in economic activity, and that it can be controlled only imperfectly by the Federal Reserve. For example, as interest rates on bank loans and investments rise (relative to the discount rate) during a business upswing, banks borrow more from the discount window, expand their loans, and increase the money supply. Similarly, as interest rates fall, perhaps because of a slowdown in economic activity, banks repay their borrowings at the Federal Reserve, reduce their loans, and contract the money supply. If it is the central bank that is solely responsible for changes in the money supply, then it is a good indicator of Federal Reserve policy. But if the money supply can change regardless of Federal Reserve intentions, then using it as an indicator is likely to throw you off the track.

In order to save the money supply as an indicator of monetary policy, Monetarists Karl Brunner and Allan Meltzer have marshaled statistical evidence showing that it is Federal Reserve initiative—open market operations and reserve-requirement changes—that is the main cause of movements in the money supply. As a backup, however, they propose the monetary base as an alternative indicator, a first cousin to the money supply but somewhat more directly under the Federal Reserve's thumb.

Other Federal Reservologists prefer total reserves to the monetary base. For still others, including the architects of the Federal Reserve–MIT–Penn model, total reserves must be purged of reserves arising from member bank borrowing at the discount window—leaving us with nonborrowed reserves to chart the course.

By this time, things have clearly gotten out of hand as far as the Monetarists are concerned, and they disassociate themselves from anything further removed from the money supply than the monetary base.

Confused? Read on.

Some Helpful Hints

Where does all this leave someone who is trying to make an honest buck evaluating the posture of monetary policy? Instead of responding with a cliché (as is our custom)—such as "Life is tough for everyone"—we offer a series of helpful hints (HHs) to aid in interpreting Federal Reserve behavior.

1.   Divide the indicators into two groups. One: *the monetary and reserve aggregates*—including the money supply (your favorite flavor), the monetary base, and total reserves. Two: *money market conditions*—especially interest rates on Treasury bills and the Federal funds rate.

2.   Do not conclude that, because there has been an increase in the aggregates, monetary policy is embarked on a wild expansion. The money supply, for example, must in-

crease with a growing economy in order to provide funds for the increased transactions associated with a larger GNP. The money supply has, in fact, increased in every year since 1950 save one (1957), although it can and has declined over shorter intervals (say three or six months).

3. Try to judge whether the aggregates, say the money supply, are growing faster than normal (expansionary policy) or slower than normal (restrictive policy). What is normal? The money supply grew at an annual rate of 4.0 percent during the twenty years from 1955 through 1975. From 1955 through 1965, however, its growth was only 2.2 percent a year, from 1966 through 1975 it was 5.9 percent, and from 1975 through 1979 the growth rate was 6.4 percent. Take your pick.

4. If interest rates are falling at the same time as the aggregates are increasing at a faster-than-normal rate, it is a good bet that the Federal Reserve has embarked on a course of monetary expansion. And if interest rates are rising at the same time as the aggregates are growing at a slower-than-normal rate, it is an equally good bet that the Federal Reserve has begun to exercise restraint.

5. The Federal Reserve publishes the minutes of the FOMC meetings with a thirty-day delay. Read them. If the Federal Reserve decided on increased monetary ease a month ago and your reading of the indicators shows it has not succeeded, look for signs of further easing as the Fed tries harder. If tighter monetary policy was decided upon a month ago and your reading of the indicators shows that the Federal Reserve hasn't succeeded—call your broker and sell (see Chapter 14 first).

Naturally, we assume no responsibility for the misfortunes brought down upon you when following these HHs. But we insist on 10 percent of the profits. For those of you who prefer to construct your own "super indicator" for monetary policy, you are invited to read the next chapter, which explains how to read the directive issued at the FOMC meetings and also treats you to a detailed look at the mechanics of open market operations.

10

THE NUTS AND BOLTS OF
MONETARY POLICY

At 11:15 in the morning of each business day, a long-distance conference call takes place among three men: Peter Sternlight, the manager of the System Open Market Account, who is located in the Federal Reserve Bank of New York; a member of the Board of Governors in Washington, D.C.; and a president of one of the other Federal Reserve banks currently serving on the Federal Open Market Committee. The job of the account manager is to carry out open market operations for the purpose of implementing the monetary policy directive issued at the last meeting of the FOMC. Each morning he reviews the operations planned for the day via the telephone hookup.

Although we have never listened in to what is said during one of these calls, we can make a pretty good guess at the conversation, much as sports commentators are able to surmise what is said at those all-important conferences between the quarterback and his coach in the closing minutes of a game, or the even more important huddle between a pitcher and catcher with men on second and third and none out. It probably goes something like this:

OPERATOR: San Francisco and Washington are standing by, New York. Will you deposit $3.35, please?

NEW YORK: You mean it's our turn to pay? Hold on a minute, operator, we don't seem to have enough change here.

WASHINGTON: This is Chairman Volcker on the line.

NEW YORK: Sorry, there's no one here by that name.

WASHINGTON: No, you don't seem to understand, I'm Chairman Paul Volcker and I want . . .

NEW YORK: Hello Paul, it's Peter. Sorry for the mix-up, but we've just hired a few Ph.D.s to man the phones, and they haven't gotten the hang of it quite yet.

WASHINGTON: I know just what you mean. Say, we've got a problem here. Our staff says the 6½ to 9 percent range for M1B should replace as the main target the 4 to 6½ percent range on M2. Or is it the other way around?

NEW YORK: Frankly, our people have urged me to look at the M3 numbers, trying to hit the fourth-quarter-to-fourth-quarter growth figures, rather than the two-month targets. They say the M1 ball game is over.

SAN FRANCISCO: Hello? Hello? When do we start?

If you think we have exaggerated the potential confusion confronting the Account Manager, a reading of some of the FOMC operating instructions should convince you otherwise. The primary thrust of monetary policy is summarized in the FOMC directive. Let's take a detailed look at how it is formulated and the ways in which it can be interpreted. We can then turn to the open market operations used in carrying it out.

The FOMC Directive

The Federal Open Market Committee meets about once every four weeks. At the beginning of each meeting, the staff of the FOMC, comprised of economists from the Board of Governors and the district Federal Reserve Banks, presents a review of recent economic and financial developments— what is happening to prices, unemployment, the balance of payments, interest rates, money supply, bank credit, and so on. Projections are also made for the months ahead. The meeting then proceeds to a discussion among the committee members; each expresses his views on the current economic and financial scene and proposes appropriate monetary policies.

The FOMC directive, embodying the committee's decision on the desired posture of monetary policy until the next meeting, is voted on toward the end of each meeting, with dissents recorded for posterity. If economic conditions are proceeding as had been expected and the current stance of monetary policy is still appropriate, the previous directive may remain unaltered. If conditions change, the directive is modified accordingly.

In recent years, the FOMC directive has usually contained five or six paragraphs. The first few review economic and financial developments, including the behavior of real output, inflation, monetary aggregates, and interest rates. The fourth or fifth paragraph then turns to a general qualitative statement of current policy goals. For example, at the meeting on February 6, 1979, the goals of the FOMC were set forth as follows:

Taking account of past and prospective developments . . . it is the policy of the Federal Open Market Committee to foster monetary and financial conditions that will resist inflationary pressures while encouraging moderate economic expansion and contributing to a sustainable pattern of international transactions.

While the statement of goals does not contain everything —we know that the FOMC is not trying to eliminate environmental pollution (at least not yet)—it does include virtually every objective of stabilization policy. This general statement of goals is rarely changed significantly. Toward the end of 1975, for example, when in the throes of recession, the phrase "encouraging economic expansion" replaced "inflationary pressures" as the first goal mentioned.

Immediately following this general statement, the directive presents the long-run target ranges for the monetary aggregates that are thought to be consistent with the broadly stated goals. At the meeting of February 6, 1979, the annual targets were stated as follows:

> The Committee agreed that these objectives would be furthered by growth of M-1, M-2 and M-3 from the fourth quarter of 1978 to the fourth quarter of 1979 within ranges of 1½ to 4½ percent, 5 to 8 percent and 6 to 9 percent.

Two sources of flexibility appear in these annual targets. Obviously they can be changed each quarter. In our illustration, the growth rates are calculated from fourth-quarter 1978 to fourth-quarter 1979 but will then be altered to first-quarter 1979 through first-quarter 1980. Moreover, the ranges are rather broad, giving the Fed wide latitude in hitting the targets.

The last order of business in the FOMC directive is to specify the immediate requirements for the implementation of these longer-run objectives. In our by now familiar meeting of February 6, 1979, the specification was as follows:

> In the period before the next regular meeting, System open market operations are to be directed at maintaining the weekly average Federal funds rate at about the current level, provided that over the February-March period the annual rates of growth of M1 and M2, given approximately equal weight, appear to be within ranges of 3 to 7 percent and 5 to 9 percent, respectively.

Now we have a second set of monetary aggregate targets, this time specified for a two-month period. These two-month growth rates are altered, both to take into account "special events" as well as to be consistent with the longer-run objectives. Moreover, the Federal funds rate was used as still another short-run guideline, presumably to help the account manager hit the aggregate bull's eye. Unfortunately, during the past few years, the manager's accuracy leaves much to be desired. Perhaps there are too many numbers and too many targets floating around. It almost guarantees some confusion, as we suggested in our opening conversation.

Changed Emphasis in the Directive

The current emphasis in the directive is clearly on monetary aggregates. It wasn't always that way. In fact, until 1966 the directive to the account manager was couched solely in terms of money market conditions—easier or firmer. Free reserves and short-term interest rates ruled the day, especially the Treasury bill rate and the Federal funds rate.

In 1966, however, the directive was altered to include what was called a proviso clause. The account manager was directed, for example, "to conduct open market operations with a view towards somewhat firmer conditions in the money market, *provided* [our italics] that bank credit was not deviating significantly from projections." At the first meeting in 1970, the monetary aggregates in the directive were expanded to include money as well as bank credit in the proviso clause. At the third meeting in 1970, the monetary aggregates finally were put on a par with money market conditions. The committee expressed a desire to seek "moderate growth in money and bank credit over the months ahead" as well as "money market conditions consistent with that objective." Then, early in 1972, the FOMC added reserves as an operating target along with money market conditions.

Both money market conditions, especially the Federal funds rate, and reserves are supposed to help achieve a desired pattern of growth in monetary aggregates. Now that we know what must be done, let's see how they do it.

The Operating Room

Open market operations are performed in a well-guarded room within a fortresslike building in the heart of the nation's financial center. The Federal Reserve Bank of New York, designated by the FOMC as its operating arm, is located on Liberty Street only three blocks from Wall Street. This location permits Peter Sternlight, the manager of the Federal Reserve System Open Market Account, to be in close contact with the government securities dealers with whom the Federal Reserve System engages in purchases and sales of securities. Every morning of the workweek he meets with one or more of the securities dealers and gets the "feel of the market," as the opening handshakes (firm or limp? dry or sweaty palms?) telegraph whether the market is likely to be a tic tighter or easier. On occasion Sternlight has been known to shock the market by the judicious use of one of those little hand buzzers (the kind you used to be able to get in novelty shoppes).

Feedback from the securities dealers is only one component of the vast array of data and information marshaled by the account manager in mapping his plans for open market operations on any given day. The starting point, of course, is the directive issued by the FOMC at its last meeting. This expression of the proposed stance of monetary policy, together with the more precise range of desired movements in money market conditions and the monetary aggregates, provide the ultimate target for open market operations. Sternlight must still decide, however, how much to sell or buy, to or from whom, and when.

Money market conditions (particularly short-term interest rates) and monetary aggregates are directly affected by the reserves available to the banking system. Each workday morning, a little after 9:30, Sternlight receives a report on the reserve position of the banking system as of the night before. A sensitive indicator of pressure in this market is provided by the Federal funds rate.

A little later in the morning—but before the 11:15 conference call—the account manager is provided with a detailed projection by the research staff. It covers movements in various items that can affect the reserve position of the banking system—including currency holdings of the public, deposits in foreign accounts at the Federal Reserve Banks, and other technical factors. A change in any of these can cause reserves to go up or down and thereby affect bank lending capabilities, interest rates, and growth in the money supply. For example, as the public cashes checks in order to hold more currency, commercial banks must pay out vault cash and thereby suffer a loss in reserves. As foreign accounts at Federal Reserve banks increase—that is, as they present checks for payment drawn against commercial banks—reserves of commercial banks are transferred to foreign accounts at the Fed.

A call is also made to the U.S. Treasury to ascertain what is likely to happen to Treasury balances in tax and loan accounts at commercial banks—deposits of the U.S. government generated by tax payments of the public and receipts from bond sales—and to find out what is likely to happen to Treasury balances at the Federal Reserve Banks, from which most government expenditures are made. As funds are shifted from Treasury tax and loan accounts in commercial banks to Treasury balances at the Federal Reserve, the commercial banking system loses reserves.

By 11:00 A.M. Peter Sternlight has a good idea of money market conditions, including what is happening to interest rates, and of anticipated changes in the reserve position of the banking system. He also knows what the FOMC directive calls for. If the FOMC had asked for moderate growth in reserves in order to sustain moderate growth in the monetary aggregates, and all of the other factors just discussed are expected to pour a large volume of reserves into the banking system, he may decide that open market *sales* are necessary in order to prevent an excessive (more than moderate) expansion in reserves. If, on the other hand, he expects to find reserves going up too little or even declining as a result of these other forces, he may engage in significant open market purchases. It is now clear why knowledge that the Federal Reserve bought or sold so many or so few government securities on a given day or during a given week, in itself, tells us almost nothing about the overall posture or intent of monetary policy.

At the 11:15 conference call with a member of the Board of Governors in Washington and one of the Federal Reserve Bank presidents, Sternlight outlines his plan of action for the day and explains the reasons for his particular strategy. Once his decision is confirmed, the purchase or sale of securities (usually Treasury bills) takes place. The account manager instructs the traders in the trading room of the Federal Reserve Bank of New York to call the thirty-five or so government securities dealers and ask them for firm bids for stated amounts of specific maturities of government securities (in the case of a Fed open market sale) or for their selling price quotations for stated amounts of specific maturities (in the case of a Fed open market purchase). While the Federal Reserve does not engage in open market operations in order to make a profit, it still insists on getting the most for its money, and it is assured of that by vigorous competition among the various dealers in government securities.

It takes no more than thirty minutes for the trading desk to complete its "go-around" of the market and to execute the open market sale or purchase. By 12:30 the account manager and his staff are back to watching the situation and, if necessary, buying or selling additional amounts of government securities to implement the original objective.

Much is left to the judgment of the account manager, even with all of the double-checking with other parts of the Federal Reserve System. By and large, Peter Sternlight receives high marks for his job, despite the errors that inevitably enter any human undertaking. He is also a very pleasant fellow. There are some, however, who would have him, as well as (or especially) the FOMC, replaced by a computer, an automatic telephone, and a disembodied voice that periodically calls out orders to buy or sell $200, $300, or $400 million worth of government securities. The reasons for such an Orwellian prescription for the Federal Reserve are discussed in the next chapter.

Fed Strategy: A Summary

Before ending this chapter let's pause a moment and survey the terrain. After so much on the intricacies of Fed policy making, the details have taken over and we are in danger, to coin a phrase, of losing the forest for the trees.

The ultimate purpose of the Federal Reserve is to influence total spending and GNP. But it has no way of directly altering GNP, so it has to exert its influence indirectly—through the supply of money and credit and various interest rates, mostly medium-term and long-term rates. However, these variables—let's call them the Fed's intermediate objectives— are not directly under the Fed's control either. So it has no choice but to aim at an *operating target,* perhaps several different ones, hoping that if it hits these operating targets they will eventually nudge the intermediate objectives and thereby get the job done.

This game plan is illustrated schematically in the accompanying chart. Notice the distinctions between operating targets, intermediate targets and ultimate objectives. Much of

The Fed's Game Plan

the confusion regarding Fed policy arises because these distinctions are ignored.

Notice also what is included in the concepts you will often encounter in the financial pages of your newspaper: the monetary aggregates, money market conditions, and the reserve aggregates.

The *monetary aggregates* are intermediate targets; the phrase includes M1A, M1B, M2, and M3. Other intermediate objectives are bank credit, total credit, and medium-term and long-term interest rates.

Money market conditions are one set of possible operating targets; the phrase refers to free reserves and money market interest rates—especially the Federal funds rate and to a lesser extent the three-month Treasury bill rate.

The *reserve aggregates* are another group of possible operating targets; the phrase includes a wide variety of bank reserve measures, such as the monetary base, total reserves, and so on. The chart above summarizes the arithmetic relationships among the various reserve measures. Interestingly, the last of these—namely, free reserves—is usually considered an indicator of money market conditions rather than as one of the reserve aggregates.

In recent years, the Fed has been putting its plan into operation this way (more or less): It specifies its intermediate objective in terms of a desired range for monetary growth over the year—say an increase in M1B of from 5 to 8 percent. Then it sets an operating target for bank reserves that it figures will produce this rate of monetary growth—say an increase in total reserves or perhaps in nonborrowed reserves of from 4 to 6 percent over the year. Simultaneously, it sets another operating target—the Federal funds rate—that is thought to be consistent with the desired rate of increase in reserves.

MONETARY BASE (= total reserves + currency outside banks)
Minus Currency outside banks
_____
= TOTAL RESERVES

Minus member bank borrowing from the Fed
_____
= NONBORROWED RESERVES

Minus required reserves
_____
= FREE RESERVES (or, if negative, NET BORROWED RESERVES)

Relationships Among Alternative Reserve Measures

The Federal funds rate has been used by the account manager as an indicator of the state of bank reserves. If reserves are growing too rapidly, the Federal funds rate will fall below target, signaling the account manager to intervene and drain reserves by open market sales. Alternatively, if reserves are growing too slowly, the Federal funds rate will rise above target, alerting the account manager to intervene and supply reserves by open market purchases.

This is the way it was until October 1979, when the Federal Reserve shifted its emphasis away from the Federal funds rate as an operating target, turning its attention to reserves instead. Whether this shift in favored operating targets is temporary or permanent is uncertain. And that cannot help but confuse matters for Fed-watchers.

Armed with these details, you can now return to the task of the last chapter: constructing an ideal indicator of Fed policy. If you come up with a winner, let us know.

11

SHOULD A ROBOT REPLACE THE FEDERAL RESERVE?

Some Monetarists, most notably Milton Friedman, have abandoned countercyclical stabilization policy altogether. They never had any use for fiscal policy to begin with, and the issue of time lags in the impact of monetary policy has led them to jettison countercyclical monetary policy as well. In Chapter 5, we noted that time lags do indeed make the implementation of monetary policy potentially hazardous.

"Countercyclical" monetary policy means leaning against the prevailing economic winds: easy money in recessions, to get the economy on the move again; tight money when there is a boom, to slow it down. In its most naive form, however, countercyclical monetary policy tends to ignore the complications bred by time lags.

Assume that the Federal Reserve forecasts a recession due six months from now. If the forecast is correct, and if a current expansion in the money supply would have an impact six months hence, well and good. But what if the Federal Reserve's crystal ball is not that clear, and it is more than a year before the main impact of today's monetary policy is reflected in the economy? Then the effects of today's expansionary monetary policy are likely to be felt *after* the economy has passed the trough and is already on its way up.

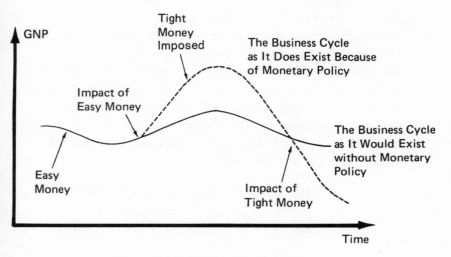

**Friedman's Alleged Perverse Effects of
Countercyclical Monetary Policy**

As the accompanying diagram illustrates, the impact of today's easy money may exacerbate tomorrow's inflation. This is Milton Friedman's explanation for the rampant inflation of 1969; the rapid rate of growth in the money supply in 1968, intended to forestall recession, lit the fuse of the inflationary time bomb that exploded the following year. Tight money will have similarly delayed effects; it may be imposed with the best of intentions, to curtail a boom, but its real impact, being long delayed, might accentuate a recession. And this occurred in its most reckless form in late 1974, so the argument goes. Excessively tight money was aimed at curtailing the rampant inflation; it precepitated the 1975 recession in the process. Monetary policy is a destabilizer rather than a stabilizer!

On these grounds—the precarious nature of economic

forecasting and the alleged length, variability, and unpredict-
ability of the time lags involved—Friedman and some other
Monetarists have given up on orthodox monetary policy.
Friedman argues that the economy has been and is now
inherently stable, and that it would automatically tend to
stay on a fairly straight course if only it were not being
almost continuously knocked off the track by erratic or un-
wise monetary policies. Conclusion: quarantine the central
bank. The best stabilization policy is no stabilization policy
at all. Hasn't it all been said before:

> They also serve who only stand and wait.
>
> JOHN MILTON

Rules versus Discretion

What Professor Friedman proposes instead is that the Federal Reserve be instructed by Congress to follow a fixed
long-run rule: Increase the money supply at a steady and
inflexible rate, month in and month out, year in and year out,
regardless of current economic conditions. Set the money
supply on automatic pilot and then leave it alone.

The specific rule would depend on the definition of the
money supply adopted. Actually, the particular number
itself is not so important to Friedman as the restriction
that once it is decided upon it be left alone thereafter. No
tinkering!

The constant growth rule is intended to keep prices stable
and employment high by allowing aggregate demand to grow
secularly at the same rate as the growth in the economy's real

productive capacity (due to growth in the labor force and increased productivity). It is also supposed to compensate, according to Friedman, for a long-term gradual downtrend in velocity—although, in fact, velocity has done nothing but rise since the end of World War II, and from all indications will continue to do so.

Such a rule, it is claimed, would eliminate forecasting and lag problems and therefore remove what Friedman sees as the major cause of instability in the economy—the capricious and unpredictable impact of countercyclical monetary policy. As long as the money supply grows at a constant rate each year, be it 3, 4, or 5 percent, any decline into recession will be temporary. The liquidity provided by a constantly growing money supply will cause aggregate demand to expand. Similarly, if the supply of money does not rise at a more than average rate, any inflationary increase in spending will burn itself out for lack of fuel. Anyway, any discretionary deviations by the central bank would interfere with the natural course of the economy and only make matters worse.

The United States Congress has been impressed enough to come part of the way toward a Friedman-type rule, in preference to allowing the Federal Reserve to rely entirely on its own judgment and discretion. In March 1975, both the House of Representatives and the Senate passed House Congressional Resolution 133, which instructed the Federal Reserve to "maintain long-run growth of the monetary and credit aggregates commensurate with the economy's long run potential to increase production." It also required that the Fed report quarterly to Congress on its target monetary and credit growth rates for the upcoming twelve months. In November 1977, these provisions were incorporated into the Federal Reserve Act itself.

The Friedman position is based on a number of pillars,

each supported by mounds of statistical evidence produced by Friedmanities. However, very little is really known about the length and variability of the time lags. Such evidence as there is, and there is not much, is extremely mixed, as we saw in Chapter 5. Serious research on the subject is only in its early stages, and no consensus is apparent among economists who have worked in the area.

It is ironic—or instructive—that in the final analysis the extremists from both camps, Monetarist and Keynesian, have collectively ganged up on the Federal Reserve. The extreme Monetarists want to shackle it, because their concern with time lags leads them to believe it is both mischievous and harmful. The extreme Keynesians want to subordinate it to fiscal policy, because they think it is either useless or lethal.

In the middle, squabbling but finding more common cause than they had thought possible, are the moderates: moderate Monetarists, who believe that the forecasting-lag problem is not so great as to negate all the potential stabilizing effects of monetary policy; and moderate Keynesians, who believe that monetary policy probably does change interest rates and/or the availability of credit and that those changes, along with fiscal policy, probably do influence spending decisions in the right way at more or less the right time. While one group concentrates mainly on the money supply and the other primarily on credit conditions, they are nevertheless in agreement that some form of countercyclical monetary policy is necessary and, on balance, beneficial.

It seems clear, after all is said and done, that central banking is still at least as much art as science. We simply do not yet know enough to legislate an eternal rule, or even a rule for the next six months, that the Federal Reserve must follow under any and all circumstances. When we do know that much, the Federal Reserve will know it too, and if they are rational they will follow it regardless of whether it has been enacted into law.

Meanwhile, for better or worse, we appear to have no alternative but to rely on our best knowledge and judgment in the formulation of monetary policy. We can only try to make sure that the decision-makers are able and qualified people with open minds and the capacity to learn from experience.

PART IV

*Fiscal Policy
and Debt Management*

12

FISCAL POLICY VERSUS

MONETARY POLICY

The promoter of a match billed as Fiscal Policy versus Monetary Policy would surely be able to call this encounter the Main Event for the Heavyweight Title. Twenty-five years ago, however, such a contest would not have made even the preliminaries in the Featherweight division. A forfeit would have been declared in favor of fiscal policy. The reason? It was generally believed that monetary policy was unable to defend itself.

The dramatic resurgence of monetary policy since the 1950s rivals the most classic of comebacks. A quarter century ago, monetary policy was relegated to the subservient role of sweeper before the chariot of the Champion. Its functions were to keep bank reserves plentiful and the market for government securities firm, so that interest rates could remain low and nothing impede the right of way of the Great Man. Fiscal policy, alone, in all its glory, would promote full employment, stabilize prices, ensure economic growth, and eliminate poverty. The reader who thinks that this might be an exaggeration, which it probably is, should reread some of the more exuberant literature typical of that era.

Today they march to a different tune. Although some die-hard fans of fiscal policy still decry each move of the monetary authorities, calling every punch a foul and every feint unfair, their enthusiasm is not what it once was and their ranks have dwindled with the passage of time. Government economists now place monetary policy on an equal footing with fiscal policy in the pursuit of national economic objectives. Some academic economists even go so far as to argue that monetary policy should be *the* instrument of economic stabilization, that the impact of fiscal policy is negligible, at best. As we indicated earlier, much of the controversy centers about the debate between the Monetarists and the Keynesians.

How Fiscal Policy Works

According to the Monetarists, a change in the money supply will alter aggregate spending and GNP by a predictable amount, since the velocity of money is quite stable. Thus they contend that monetary policy is a much more effective instrument than fiscal policy.

Keynesians, on the other hand, are skeptical about the reliability of the relationship between the money supply and GNP. As they view it, a change in the money supply can alter aggregate spending only to the extent that it first changes interest rates or the availability of credit, and then only if business or household spending is sensitive to those changes. There is no direct link between the money supply and spending. Put briefly, the relationship between the money supply and GNP is seen as tenuous and variable, since fluctuations in the velocity of money may counteract changes in its supply.

In Keynesian eyes, changes in government spending or taxation—the primary tools of fiscal policy—*do* have a direct and fairly predictable impact on GNP. An increase in government spending raises GNP immediately. It also induces additional "multiplier effects" via a GNP-consumption-GNP link. As GNP rises because of an initial injection of government expenditure, consumers receive more income; they spend a fraction of this increased income, which causes GNP to go up even further. For example, if government spending rises by $10 billion, income (or GNP) automatically goes up by $10 billion. Of this larger income, consumers will then spend a predictable fraction, say four-fifths, or $8 billion. Since spending by A is income to B, GNP goes up by this $8 billion as well. Of this, consumers then spend another four-fifths, or $6.4 billion. By now, GNP has gone up $24.4 billion. Eventually this process will come to a halt as the successive increments in income and spending become smaller and smaller; but the end result will be an increase in GNP by some multiple of the original increase in government spending.

Changes in tax rates are seen as having a similar multiple impact on GNP. If tax rates are lowered, consumers are left with more disposable income. They spend a predictable fraction of this, causing a rise in GNP, which in turn induces additional consumer expenditure. Conclusion: to bring about an expansion in spending and GNP, we should increase government spending and/or lower tax rates—that is, create a budget deficit. Anti-inflation policy would call for the opposite: reduce government spending and/or raise tax rates—that is, create a budget surplus.

It is important to note the central role of this GNP-consumption-GNP relationship in the Keynesian "multiplier" analysis. If consumer spending does not respond to changes

How to Score (Old-Timers' Day)

Monetarist Power Sweep

Milty Friedman hands off to J. S. Mill—who streaks down the right sideline behind a big block (actually a clip) by Swifty Irving Fisher that completely upends Big Tommy Malthus.

Keynesian Long Bomb

J. M. Keynes hits Poor Paul Samuelson with a TD pass—fantastic blocking by the unsung heroes of the front line, led by Bob Solow, Alvin Hansen, and Elton John (betcha didn't know he was a closet Keynesian).

in income, tax-rate changes would not affect spending or economic activity and the "multiplier effects" would be minimal.

Changes in government spending and/or tax rates can be implemented in many different ways. Government spending can be changed via military expenditures, outlays for education, urban renewal, farm price supports, medical research, the space program, or for any other specific government program. Tax receipts can be altered by changing the corporate income tax, the personal income tax, the investment tax credit, or any specific excise or sales tax.

While the impact of a change in any one of these tax or expenditure categories can be made virtually identical with a change in any other one, insofar as the arithmetic effect on GNP is concerned, profound social implications flow from which particular tax or expenditure program is or is not altered. For example, if we are experiencing substantial unemployment and a low rate of economic growth, and fiscal policy is decided upon as the appropriate remedy, a choice arises between lowering taxes and raising government spending. If we lower tax rates, the expansion in GNP will be brought about by private spending. On the other hand, if we increase government spending, this will give us more government services as well as more private purchases. Which alternative we choose should depend on the volume of government (social) services we want.

Going still further: if we decide that we should increase government spending, should it take the form of more money devoted to curbing environmental pollution or an expansion in urban renewal? When we are faced with inflationary pressures, should we cut back military expenditures or antipoverty programs? These issues involve social problems and policies that go far beyond the bounds of economics.

Measuring Fiscal Policy

Until now, we have discussed expansionary and contraction-ary fiscal policy in terms of deficits and surpluses in the federal budget. A budget deficit is expansionary and a budget surplus is contractionary. However, just as many widely used indicators of monetary policy are less than adequate (see Chapter 9), so also are there serious limitations to using the *current* deficit or surplus as a guide to the stance of fiscal policy.

The measurement problem stems from the fact that tax receipts, and hence the size of the deficit or surplus, vary passively with GNP. Congress sets tax *rates,* not receipts; receipts then go up and down with GNP. Given the level of government spending, when GNP rises tax receipts automat-ically increase and surpluses are automatically created (or deficits reduced). When GNP falls tax receipts decline and deficits automatically result. Thus, it is impossible to draw any meaningful conclusions regarding the stance of fiscal policy by comparing a budget surplus in one year at one level of GNP, with a deficit in another year at a *different* level of GNP.

For example, the existence of a deficit during a recession suggests, at first glance, that fiscal policy is expansionary. It may be, however, that the tax structure is so steep that it drives income (and thereby tax receipts) down to reces-sion levels. A deficit may thus actually be the result of a *contractionary* fiscal policy. The tax cut of 1964 was enact-ed primarily on the basis of such thinking; its intention was to reduce the "fiscal drag" on the economy. It was argued that the overly restrictive tax structure—with taxes rising too rapidly as GNP went up—made it virtually impossible for a rise in GNP to make any sustained headway.

The budget concept that *is* useful as an indicator of the posture of fiscal policy is called the full employment budget. The main problem in comparing deficits or surpluses in year X with year Y is that there are different levels of GNP in both years. As the diagram indicates, the idea of the full employment budget eliminates this problem by sticking to one concept of GNP, namely the full employment GNP. The full employment budget is defined as what the federal budget surplus (or deficit) *would be,* with the expected level of government spending and the existing tax structure, *if the economy were operating at the full employment level of GNP throughout the year.*

This calculated measure, the full employment budget, can be used to evaluate the effects and the performance of fiscal policy more meaningfully than the actual state of the budget, whatever it might be. Indeed, as an indicator of fiscal policy, the full employment budget is a much less ambiguous policy measure than any we thus far have been able to produce for monetary policy.

As an illustration, in 1962 GNP was well below its full employment potential. As the diagram indicates, a low level of GNP produces a poor tax harvest and, consequently, a deficit in the actual budget. Nevertheless, fiscal policy was hardly expansionary. In fact, it was quite the opposite; if GNP had been at the full employment level, or close to it, tax revenues would have risen so greatly that the *full employment budget* would have had a substantial surplus. Conclusion: the fundamental stance of fiscal policy was restrictive, not expansionary, and one reason for the high level of unemployment in 1962 stemmed from fiscal policy—even though the actual budget showed a deficit.

Thus, in a rare example of fiscal bravery, a tax cut was

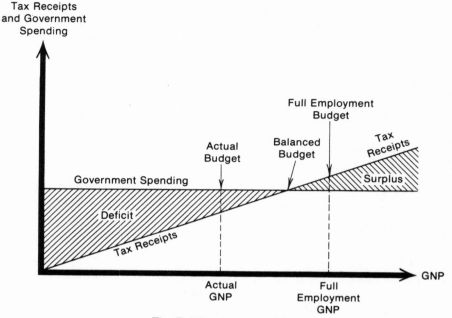

The Full Employment Budget

passed by Congress in 1964 despite the existence of a current budget deficit. A reduction in tax rates swings the tax receipts line (in the diagram) downward and diminishes the full employment surplus. An increase in government spending also shrinks the full employment surplus. A tax-rate increase or a drop in government spending, both of which are restrictive actions, enlarge it. It is clear that changes in the full employment budget reflect basic *discretionary* changes in fiscal policy, as contrasted with movements in the actual budget that can be the *passive* result of fluctuations in GNP. In fact, an expansion in GNP due to a tax cut will succeed in lowering the size of the actual deficit.

All of this violates the most sacred canons of "traditional" (or pre-Keynesian) finance. According to the maxims of "orthodox" finance, an actual deficit is a signal to immediately set about balancing the budget by *raising* tax rates and/or *decreasing* government spending—this promptly drives GNP lower, thereby creating an even *larger* deficit, which makes matters worse all around.

Financial Aspects of Fiscal Policy

The fiscal policy mechanism described above is not the whole story. This is recognized by both Keynesians and Monetarists. The total impact on GNP of an expansionary fiscal policy cannot be fully ascertained until the method of financing government deficits is specified. Similarly, the net effect of a reduction in government spending and/or increases in tax rates cannot be fully calculated until the disposition of the surplus is taken into account.

When GNP goes up as the result of deficit spending, the public's need for day-to-day transactions money rises along with it. If the supply of money does not increase simultaneously, the public will find itself short of cash, will presumably sell off some financial assets in order to try to get additional money, and will thereby drive up interest rates. This so-called "crowding out" effect may inhibit private investment spending and home-building, partly offsetting the expansionary impact of the government's spending.

But a budget deficit can be financed in either of two ways. For one, the government might simply print money to finance itself. Since this is often frowned upon in the best of circles, its twentieth-century equivalent is used instead: the Federal Reserve buys the bonds that are sold by the government and in the process brand-new checking accounts are created for the government. If this is done, the increased supply of money will probably be sufficient to satisfy the enlarged need for money and interest rates will not rise. In this case, there will be little or no offset to the expansionary impact of the deficit spending, and GNP will be able to rise without interference from the monetary side.

Alternatively, the deficit might be financed by the sale of government securities to the public. If this is done, however, the pressure on financial markets is actually intensified, since the increase in the supply of new bonds on the market drives up the rate of interest even further. The sale of government securities will "crowd out" private borrowers, and the consequent decline in investment spending will offset an even larger portion of the increased government spending. The net effect, according to the Keynesians, is still expansionary, although less so than in the case of money-financed deficits.

In any event, regardless of details, the important point is that the execution of fiscal policy is inextricably mixed up with monetary implications. The two cannot be separated.

The Monetarists versus the Keynesians

The Keynesian position is that any fiscal action, no matter how it is financed, will have a significant impact on GNP. Keynesians do not deny that interest rates are likely to rise as GNP goes up, unless new money is forthcoming to meet cash needs for day-to-day transactions. Thus, they admit that a deficit financed by money creation is more expansionary than one financed by bond sales to the public, and that both are more expansionary than increased government spending financed by taxation. However, Keynesians do not believe that the decrease in private investment spending caused by higher interest rates (the "crowding out" effect) will be great enough to offset fully the government's fiscal actions. They think that the net impact on GNP will be significant, and in the right direction, regardless of what financing methods are used.

One reason for this conclusion is that higher interest rates are seen as having dual effects. They may reduce private investment spending, but they may also lead people to economize on their cash balances, thereby supplying part of the need for new transactions money from formerly idle cash holdings. Put somewhat differently, even if a deficit is not financed by new money, the velocity of existing money will accelerate (in response to higher interest rates) so that the old money supply combined with the new velocity will be able to support a higher level of spending and GNP.

The Monetarist view, on the other hand, is that unless a budget deficit is financed by new money creation it will not alter GNP. In order for GNP to rise, the money supply must expand. If a fiscal deficit is financed by printing money, it will indeed increase spending and GNP. But according to the Monetarists, it is not the deficit that is responsible—it is the additional money. Furthermore, a deficit is a very clumsy way to go about increasing the money supply. Why not simply have the Federal Reserve engage in open market operations? That would accomplish the same purpose, a change in the money supply, without getting involved in budget deficits or surpluses.

As the Monetarists see it, a fiscal deficit financed in any other way—as by selling bonds to the public—will not affect aggregate GNP. True, the government will be spending more. But others will wind up spending less. The "crowding out" effect is total and complete. Net result: no change in total spending or in GNP. The rise in government spending will *initially* increase GNP. However, this will increase the demand for cash for transactions purposes and drive interest rates up, and bond sales to finance the government's expenditures will drive rates up still further. The public will be buying government bonds and financing the government, instead of buying corporate bonds and financing business firms. The rise in interest rates will reduce private investment spending by as much as government spending is increased, and that will be the end of the story. Government fiscal policy, unaccompanied by changes in the supply of money, merely changes the proportion of government spending relative to private spending.

Anti-inflationary fiscal policy encounters similar objections from the Monetarists. An increase in tax rates that generates a fiscal surplus reduces private income and consumer spending. If the government destroys or simply holds the money, the tax revenues it has collected over and above its expenditures, then the surplus is accompanied by a reduction of the money supply in private pockets. Both Keynesians and Monetarists would agree that this is anti-inflationary, although for different reasons—the Keynesians because of the direct fiscal impact on consumer spending, with the tax increase reducing people's take-home pay, and the Monetarists because of the contraction in the money supply.

But if the government uses the surplus to retire part of the national debt, the funds flow back into the economy. The government retires debt by buying back its bonds. Bond prices are driven up, interest rates fall, and private investment spending increases. Keynesians would argue that GNP will still decline, that the debt retirement is a minor ripple on a huge wave. Monetarists, however, would say that private investment spending will increase until it replaces the cutback in consumer spending, leaving no net effect whatsoever on GNP.

As we stressed in Chapter 4, the confrontation between fiscal and monetary policy can be decided only by resort to empirical evidence. The Keynesians claim that the power of fiscal policy was demonstrated by the success of the 1964 tax cut in bringing the economy up to a high level of employment. The Monetarists contend that fiscal policy alone is useless and that it was the rapid expansion of the money supply during the months preceding the tax cut that did the job. They also point to the failure of the 1968 tax surcharge to stop inflation. The Keynesians respond by asserting that acceleration of the war in Vietnam undid the impact of the 1968 tax increase.

Frustrated, let us turn to Federal Reserve's model for a decision. The accompanying figure shows the simulated response in nominal GNP (left side) and real GNP (right side) to a $10 billion expansion in government expenditure. In each of the pictures there are three lines, each representing alternative monetary policies accompanying the expansionary fiscal policy. The solid line shows the effect with a monetary policy that keeps the three-month Treasury bill rate unchanged. That assumption implies an expansion in the money stock to accommodate rising demand as GNP goes up. The dotted line assumes a monetary policy that keeps bank reserves (but not necessarily the money supply) unchanged. The dot-dash line simulates the results with a constant money stock.

It is evident from the pictures that this last monetary policy causes a substantial amount of crowding out, as we would expect. The fixed money stock policy forces rates of interest to rise as GNP increases and this cuts off investment

Evidence of Crowding Out from the Federal Reserve Model

Nominal GNP

Billions of $, Annual Rate

— Bill Rate Unchanged
---- Reserves Path Unchanged
—·— Money Supply Unchanged

Quarters

Real GNP

Billions of 1972 $, Annual Rate

Quarters

spending. Note, however, that there isn't complete crowding out of nominal GNP, although in the right-hand picture there is complete crowding out of real GNP after about two years.

The multiplier effects of government spending are much more expansionary with the two more accommodating monetary policies. Thus the Fed model confirms the crucial role of money for the size of the fiscal policy multipliers. But the Fed model maintains that complete crowding out does not take place even with a fixed money stock assumption.

The Monetarist model of the Federal Reserve Bank of St. Louis is less wishy-washy than its sparring partner: An increase of $1 billion in the money supply raises GNP by over $5 billion after one year, while a similar increase in government spending has *zero* impact on GNP over the same time period. An increase in government spending raises GNP after six months, but by the time a year has elapsed, other types of spending have been crowded out to offset the expansion in government expenditures. What other types of spending? On this the St. Louis model is silent, just as it is silent on the transmission mechanism through which money affects spending. Indeed, it is this agnosticism on the transmission process and the surprising result with respect to fiscal policy that make the St. Louis model incomprehensible to many Keynesians.

Who gets the verdict has implications far beyond flattering the egos of economists with vested intellectual interests on opposite sides of the fence. If we are in a recession and use easy money to raise GNP, interest rates will fall and private investment and home-building will expand. On the other hand, if we use fiscal policy—lowering tax rates or increasing government spending—consumer spending or social services will be favored instead.

If we are in a boom and want to reduce aggregate spending, tight money will hit housing hard; tight fiscal policy probably will not. If a vibrant housing industry is important for national social and economic welfare—on the theory that the American Dream consists of each citizen owning his own house with a well in the backyard—perhaps we should rely mainly on easy money to stop recessions and mainly on tight fiscal policy to halt inflation.

A rational overall stabilization policy would evaluate all of these elements, and more, before embarking on a course of action. There are likely to be other side effects, some desirable, others undesirable. Often political considerations will be involved as well. It is difficult, for example, to raise taxes in an election year. Not to mention the influence that various pressure groups, both business and labor, are likely to bring to bear on such decisions.

In any case, the importance of *both* fiscal and monetary policy, and the numerous interrelations between them, make it plain that there can be no clear-cut winner. If either fiscal policy or monetary policy is declared the victor, to the neglect and subjugation of the other, it is we who will be the losers.

13

SHOULD WE WORRY ABOUT THE
NATIONAL DEBT?

"Personally," said President Eisenhower, in his State of the Union Message in 1960, "I do not feel that any amount can properly be called a surplus as long as the nation is in debt. I prefer to think of such an item as a reduction in our children's inherited mortgage."

In the same vein, Senator Harry F. Byrd, Sr. pondered the $275 billion national debt in 1955 and gloomily predicted: "The debt today is the debt incurred by this generation, but tomorrow it will be debt on our children and grandchildren, and it will be for them to pay, both principal and interest."

Debt worriers are fond of statistical computations. We now have a national debt of some $800 billion (in the form of marketable and nonmarketable government securities, held by the public and by government agencies) and a population of about 220 million. Conclusion: every man, woman, and child in this country owes about $3,635 whether they know it or not. Every newborn infant starts life not only with a pat on the back but also with a $3,635 share of the national debt hanging over his or her head.

Agonizing over the size of the public debt is one of our major national preoccupations. Is the situation really all that bad? Are the debt worriers right when they warn us that, by passing on a national debt of $800 billion, we are burdening future generations with a weight that will be almost impossible for them to bear? Are they correct in cautioning us, with stern voices, that we are penalizing those as yet unborn by forcing them to pay for our own vices and follies?

The National Debt Equals the National Credit

The national debt is essentially the net result of past and present fiscal policy, mostly past. It is the sum of all past deficits, less surpluses, in the federal budget. A budget deficit requires that the government either print money or borrow to cover the deficit, and most modern governments choose to borrow (that is, sell government securities). As a result, we acquire a national debt, embodied in the form of government bonds; the total of government securities outstanding *is* the national debt. It is increased by every additional deficit we incur and finance by issuing more bonds.

If the national debt is a debt, we must owe it to someone. Indeed we do—we owe it mostly to ourselves. Most of our government's bonds are internally held, that is, they are owned by citizens of the United States. Thus, while we the people (as the United States) *owe* $800 billion, we the people (as owners of government securities) are simultaneously *owed* close to the same amount. A government bond is, after all, an asset for whoever buys it.

All evidences of debt must appear on *two* balance sheets, and government securities are no different from any other IOU in this respect. Every IOU appears on the balance sheet of the debtor, as a liability; but it also turns up, not surprisingly, on the balance sheet of whoever is holding it, its owner, this time as an *asset*. Thus, every liability necessarily implies the existence of a financial asset owned by someone else. For the same reason, every *financial* asset implies a corresponding liability on the part of someone else.

This accounting gem has interesting ramifications. It means, for one, that merely creating money cannot, in and of itself, make a country richer, a conclusion that always pleases conservatives. After all, money is a financial asset, which implies that somewhere else there is a corresponding liability. If liabilities go up as rapidly as assets, the country as a whole (including both the government and the private sector) can be getting no richer.

Most of our money is in the form of demand deposits, which are liabilities of banks. The part of our money that is in the form of coin or currency is a liability of either the United States Treasury or the Federal Reserve, depending on which agency issued it.

Thus merely creating money can hardly make a nation richer, no matter how much it creates. To become richer— to increase its net worth—a country must increase its output of *real* assets, its production of real goods and services. As conservatives like to point out, if we want to become wealthier, we must work harder and produce more. Printing money, per se, will not do it.

By the same token, however, exactly the same logic also implies that another favorite conservative incantation is equally false: namely, the belief that increasing the national debt makes a country poorer. Government bonds are liabilities of the government but are financial assets to whoever owns them. If the national debt increases, someone's financial assets go up as much as the government's liabilities. If domestically held assets rise along with liabilities, the country as a whole can be getting no poorer.

The very term *national debt* is thus a half-truth. If it is a domestically held debt, it could just as well be called the *national credit.* Both labels are half-truths. As with all liabilities, it is *both* a debt (to the borrower) *and* a credit (to the lender).

To become poorer—to reduce its net worth—a country must reduce its holdings of real assets, curtail its production of *real* goods and services. Increasing the national debt, no matter how high, cannot in and of itself make a country poorer so long as it is owned internally. (Actually, about $125 billion of our $800 billion national debt is held by foreign citizens and institutions.)

Nor does an increasing national debt, just because of its size, impose a burden on future generations. As long as the debt is held internally, neither the interest nor the principal represents a dead weight on the backs of our children and grandchildren. The taxes that must be raised to pay the interest are merely transfers from one group within the economy, the taxpayers, to another group, the bondholders. Future generations inherit tax liabilities, but they also inherit bonds and the right to receive the interest on them.

Even if the debt had to be paid off, future generations, as inheritors of the bonds, would be making payments of the principal to themselves. In fact, of course, the federal debt never has to be fully repaid any more than does the debt of any going concern, public or private. As parts of the debt come due, they can be repaid with fresh borrowings. Continuous refinancing is typical of the modern successful corporation, because confidence in the company's ability to earn future income makes holding its bonds both safe and profitable. Similarly, confidence in the continuing viability and taxing power of the federal government eliminates the need for net repayment of principal, either currently or in the future.

The Real Burden of the Debt: I

Does this mean, then, that the debt worriers are completely off the track? Not quite, and therein lies the story of the *real* burden of the debt as contrasted with the imaginary burden. In the first place, holdings of government bonds are not evenly distributed among the population. Some of us have more than our $3,635 share, much more; and some have less, much less. Thus current interest payments on the debt, while "only" an internal transfer from taxpayers to bondholders, may create problems of legitimate concern to the public. If taxpayers are largely from the lower and middle income groups, while bondholders are primarily in the upper income brackets, then the tax collection → interest payment transfer will increase the inequality of income distribution. Little is known about the pattern of interest payments on the government debt according to income of the recipient. This transfer *may,* therefore, interfere with social objectives of reducing income inequality.

Furthermore, if the federal debt grows at a faster rate than GNP, tax rates may have to be increased in order to meet interest payments. Higher tax rates may reduce work incentives. If so, production falls and overall economic well-being decreases. In the United States, however, the national debt has actually declined, quite substantially, as a proportion of our gross national product. In 1945, the national debt was about 130 percent of GNP; in 1955, 70 percent; in 1965, 45 percent; and in 1979 it was 35 percent.

Even if the debt falls as a proportion of GNP, if interest *rates* go up sufficiently then tax rates may have to be raised to meet the interest payments, thus again possibly reducing work incentives. Interest rates have indeed risen since 1945, but nevertheless the interest "burden"—interest charges as a proportion of GNP—has not increased. Over the past thirty years, annual interest payments have been stable at between 1½ and 2½ percent of GNP, with the most recent figure hovering at 2 percent.

The Real Burden of the Debt: II

Aside from the possible income-redistribution and work-incentive problems associated with interest payments on the national debt, there is one way in which the debt might impose a burden, a cost, on future generations. This involves not the interest, but the principal itself.

As we noted above, a country will become poorer only if it reduces its output of real assets, its ability to produce real goods and services. In this very meaningful sense the wealth of future generations can be measured by the real capital stock they inherit, the real productive capacity of the economy we bequeath to them. A smaller capital stock permits less production, hence less consumption. A larger capital stock enables the economy to produce more, hence consume more.

Assume that the economy is already operating at a full capacity rate of production and that the budget is balanced. Whereupon the government increases its spending, financing its additional expenditures by sufficient new *taxation* to forestall inflation. In this case, the increased use of resources by the government comes primarily at the expense of consumption. Consumers, left with less after-tax income, have to cut back their spending by as much as government spending has been stepped up.

Alternatively, under the same initial circumstances, assume that the additional government spending is *debt-financed* rather than tax-financed, and that a tight monetary policy is used along with debt-financing to prevent inflation. Now interest rates will rise and the increased use of resources by the government will come primarily at the expense of investment instead of consumption. The higher interest rates will release resources from private investment for use by the government, with investment spending cut back by as much as government spending has been increased.

As a result, the production of new plant and equipment will be curtailed, and future generations will consequently inherit a smaller capital stock. Future productive capacity is lower than it might have been. In this limited sense, the "burden" of debt-financed current government expenditure is transferred to future generations.

Two qualifications are necessary. First, note that the argument assumes we start from a full capacity rate of production, roughly a full employment level of GNP. If the additional government spending were to take place during a recession, when there are idle resources available, then there would be no "burden" on future generations, no matter how it was financed. During a recession there are unemployed resources that can be tapped, so the government can increase its spending without anyone else reducing theirs. There would be no reason to permit a rise in interest rates, since the danger of inflation would be minimal, and an expansion in spending and GNP would be beneficial to all.

Under such circumstances, the future capital stock is not diminished. In fact, if the government's deficit spending succeeds in getting us out of the recession, the future capital stock will probably be *enlarged.* Thus increasing the national debt during a recession, instead of imposing a burden on future generations, is actually doing them a favor.

Second, the "burden" argument totally ignores what the government spends the money on. Assuming full employment, if the government's expenditure is for current consumption purposes—such as subsidizing inexpensive lunches for Congressmen or schoolchildren—then total capital passed on to the future is indeed reduced. But if the government builds highways or dams, or increases any type of capital asset that raises future productivity, the increased investment by the government replaces the decreased investment by private business. Future generations will inherit the same capital stock, except more will be in the form of public capital and less in the form of private capital.

Moving from theory to reality, the fact of the matter is that a significant part of our public debt stems directly from World War II military spending. In 1941 our national debt was $65 billion, and in 1945 it was $280 billion. Most of these expenditures occurred during a period of full employment. Yet few would call this a burden passed on to the future. Without it, we might well have had no future.

The Nuts and Bolts of Debt Management

Given a national debt of $800 billion, its day-to-day management has implications for the functioning of financial markets and for economic stability. How can the debt be refinanced most smoothly when portions of it come due? How much of the debt should be in the form of short-term Treasury bills, how much in the form of long-term Treasury bonds?

The dimensions of the Treasury's debt-management chore can best be appreciated by realizing that about $230 billion of the debt comes due every year and must be paid off. How? By refinancing it, of course—that is, by borrowing $230 billion from someone else. The Treasury can replace the maturing issues with new short-term Treasury bills, or with intermediate- or long-term bonds, thus providing some elbow room for altering the maturity structure of the debt.

What are the objectives of day-to-day debt management? One goal is to minimize the interest cost of the debt to the taxpayers. But this can hardly be the only objective. If it were, the Treasury could minimize the interest cost—indeed, reduce it to zero—by simply printing money and buying back all the outstanding securities. That is, it could replace its interest-bearing debt (bills and bonds) with its noninterest-bearing debt (money). Obviously, the Treasury does not "monetize the debt," because to do so would probably result in massive inflation, and the Treasury also has the objective of managing the debt to promote economic stability.

These two objectives often dictate opposite policy actions. Minimizing the interest cost suggests that when we are in a recession, and interest rates are low across the board, the Treasury should refund its maturing issues with new long-term bonds, thus ensuring low interest payments for itself well into the future. During boom periods, on the other hand, when interest rates are typically high, the Treasury should refinance by selling short-term issues, Treasury bills, so the government does not have to continue paying high rates after yields have fallen to more normal levels.

Stabilization objectives call for just the opposite policies.

When we are in a recession, the last thing we want to do is to raise long-term interest rates, which is precisely what pushing long-term securities onto the market is likely to accomplish. Boom periods, when we *do* want to raise long rates, are when we should sell long-term bonds.

Thus the objective of minimizing interest costs dictates lengthening the maturity structure of the debt (more long-term bonds relative to short-term bills) during recession periods and shortening the maturity structure during boom periods. For purposes of economic stabilization we should do the opposite—try to shorten the maturity structure during recessions and lengthen it during prosperity.

A complication that makes it difficult to lengthen the maturity structure of the federal debt is the archaic 4¼ percent legal ceiling on government bond interest rates. By virtue of a law passed in 1917, the Treasury is not allowed to pay more than a 4¼ percent interest rate on bonds with seven or more years to maturity. Since long-term market interest rates have generally been well above 4¼ percent in recent years, the Treasury has been unable to offer competitive yields on long-term securities and thus has had no choice but to borrow via shorter-maturity issues. (In a daring break with tradition, Congress grabbed the bull by the tail and faced the situation squarely; it modified the law and permitted the Treasury to issue up to $27 billion of bonds at rates above 4¼ percent.)

Debt-management policy must be administered in coordination with monetary and fiscal policy. If minimizing the interest cost is the primary goal of the Treasury, then monetary and fiscal policy will have to take appropriate action to offset this counterstabilization debt policy. If economic stabilization is the primary objective of debt management, then the monetary and fiscal authorities can take this into account and reduce the forcefulness of their own actions.

Coordination between the monetary and debt-management authorities is also essential on a continuing basis because of the vast magnitude of the Treasury's frequent refunding operations. When the Treasury refinances a large volume of maturing issues and decides to replace them with longer-term issues, it often needs help from the central bank. If the Federal Reserve is pursuing a tight money policy, for example, it will often become less aggressive and resort to a policy of keeping an "even keel" in the bond markets as the date of a refinancing approaches. In effect, the central bank will mark time for a few weeks while the Treasury goes through the mechanics of the refunding operation. It is difficult enough for the Treasury to roll over so much debt without being forced to cope with additional complications resulting from actions of the monetary authorities.

Monetary policy, fiscal policy, and debt management are often considered the three primary tools of stabilization policy. In practice, however, debt management has typically been the runt of the litter. Perhaps that is just as well. Given the power of monetary and fiscal policy to implement national economic goals, perhaps debt management can make its most significant contribution by successfully accomplishing the more limited but not unimportant task of continuously refinancing a very large volume of government securities without unduly disturbing the nation's financial markets.

PART V

Of Stocks and Intermediaries

14

DOES MONETARY POLICY AFFECT

THE STOCK MARKET?

Any civic or social club program chairperson knows that if it is announced that next week's meeting will feature a renowned speaker on "The Crisis in America's Cities," hardly anyone will show up. But if the announcement states that the topic will be "The Outlook for the Stock Market" and mentions a speaker no one ever heard of, the hall will be packed. It would be hard to find a subject that intrigues people more than the stock market. Everyone knows about stocks: how they go up, and how they can make you rich. Fifty years ago everyone knew about stocks: how they go down, and how they can make you destitute.

Why do stock prices go up and down? Not so much particular stocks, like IBM or Xerox, but why does the entire stock market soar or shudder, with all stocks more or less rising or falling together?

It is a fact of life that the total supply of stocks in existence is more or less fixed. What changes is not so much the number of shares lying around—in vaults, under mattresses, and concealed between the pages of the family Bible—but the price of each.

For example, at the end of 1979 the market value of all the publicly held shares of stock in existence amounted to something like $1,000 billion. In the early 1960s it was about $500 billion, and in the early 1950s less than $200 billion. And yet in the past twenty-five years corporations have raised relatively little money by issuing new stock, perhaps $150 billion or so at most. This means, and the word has obviously gotten around, that almost all of that $1,000 billion—probably at least $850 billion of it—represents price appreciation of existing shares.

The fact that the total supply outstanding is relatively fixed does not, of course, imply that the amount offered on the market need be fixed. People who have bought, and even some who haven't, can always sell. Thus in recent years stocks have been drifting out of the hands of individual investors, who on balance have been selling, into the plush suites of institutional investors, who have been buying. In 1960 pension funds, mutual funds, insurance companies, and other institutional investors held about 15 percent of the market value of outstanding shares; now they hold about 30 percent. But 70 percent or $700 billion is still held by individuals, about 25 million of them, and each and every one is out to make a killing.

Strangely enough, given the widespread interest in the stock market, economists have generally had very little to say about it. The most popular postwar college textbook, Paul Samuelson's *Economics,* is estimated to have sold over three million copies since it first appeared in 1948. Considering the royalties accruing to so popular an author, and a leading economist in the bargain, one would think he might have accumulated both the wherewithal and the trained experience to discover at long last the secret of what makes the market tic. But if Paul has found out, he isn't telling! The latest edition of *Economics* contains only nine pages on the stock market (out of 861).

Some economists are less reticent than Professor Samuelson about letting us in on why stock prices fluctuate. Their explanations have ranged from the influence of sun spots on people's emotional behavior to the conspiratorial machinations of shadowy figures in high places. However, the explanations that are of most interest to us here deal with money and monetary policy.

Is it true, as some claim, that the elusive clue to movements in overall stock prices is found in changes in the money supply? Or does the secret lie, as others believe, in changes in monetary policy in general? If the former are correct, and to some extent the latter, perhaps all the paraphernalia with which market analysts now so laboriously wrestle for signs of the future can be put aside; the best tout sheet might turn out to be the weekly member bank reserve statistics.

A Money Supply View of Stock Prices

The belief that fluctuations in the money supply provide the key to movements in stock prices is based on a series of cause-and-effect hypotheses that contain elements of both Monetarist and Keynesian thinking. In its simplest form, the reasoning is as follows: when the Federal Reserve increases the money supply at a faster than normal rate, the public, finding itself with more cash than it needs for current transactions purposes, spends some of its excess money buying financial assets, including stocks. Since the supply of stocks is more or less fixed, especially in the short run, this incremental demand raises their price. Some stocks will go up more than others and some may go down, depending on the prospects for particular companies, but overall the *average* of stock prices will rise.

Or the transmission process might be somewhat more complex, but with similar results. The increase in the money supply may first lead the public to step up its *bond* purchases, thereby raising bond prices. Higher bond prices imply lower interest rates. With bonds yielding less, some potential bond purchasers are likely to switch over to the now relatively more attractive stock market. The demand for stocks expands because their substitute, bonds, has become more expensive—just as the demand for Yamahas will expand when their alternative, Hondas, become more expensive (not to mention the Suzuki.)

Or it could be an even more roundabout process. The larger money supply leads to lower interest rates, more investment spending, more consumer spending, a higher GNP, and along with it larger corporate profits. Enlarged corporate profits spur stock purchases and higher stock prices.

In any case, the result is the same. Whether the chain of causation is direct, from the money supply to stock prices, or indirect, through the bond market and interest rates, or through GNP, an increase in the money supply is seen as accelerating the demand for stocks, leading to higher stock prices.

Conversely, decreases in the money supply—or increases at a slower rate than necessary to provide for the transactions needs of a growing economy—leave the public with shortages of funds. Result: among other things, a cutback in stock purchases—again, either directly or because, with higher interest rates, bonds become more attractive buys, or because corporate profits decline as GNP falls. This reduced demand for stocks lowers their prices.

Conclusion: a rapidly expanding money supply leads to higher stock values; inadequate monetary growth leads to a bear market. Persuasive as the underlying reasoning may seem, all too frequently the facts simply do not bear it out. Evidently, too many other crosscurrents simultaneously impinge on the stock market, such as business expectations and political developments. Like so many other single-cause explanations in economics, this simplified view of stock price determination contains too much truth to ignore but not enough to make it very reliable in the clutch.

Consider 1929, and the couple of years before and after. From mid-1927 to mid-1928, the money supply increased by 1.6 percent; from mid-1928 to mid-1929, it increased by 1.2 percent. The stock market, meanwhile, going its merry way, *doubled.*

In the next two years, from mid-1929 to mid-1931, the money supply contracted by about 5 percent each year. If the stock market was merely reacting to changes in the money supply it was by all odds the biggest overreaction in history, because the proverbial bottom dropped out and the market promptly lost all the gains it had made in the previous two years and then some.

Furthermore, it is not at all clear precisely what is cause and what is effect. Did the market crash in 1929 because, among other things, the money supply contracted? Or did the money supply contract because the market crashed (as banks called speculative margin loans and demand deposits were wiped off the books)? The latter explanation is as logical as the former.

The 1929 market collapse, as many see it, was due to a number of interrelated factors: an unwarranted mood of euphoric optimism prior to the crash, excessive speculative activity, fundamental weakness in underlying business conditions, and so on. The money supply, if it influenced the break at all, did so only as one among many causes.

None of which is meant to imply that the money supply was or is unimportant. If it had been rapidly and forcefully restored to its 1929 level by 1930, or even 1931, the depression initiated by the stock market collapse would probably not have been either as severe or as long as it turned out to be. That the Federal Reserve stood by, wringing its hands, while the money supply declined by 30 percent from 1929 to 1933 undoubtedly intensified and prolonged what we now call the Great Depression. But that is a very different thing from saying that movements in the money supply caused or could have given one even a vague idea of the heights or the depths to which stock prices went from 1927 to 1931. As a matter of fact, most of the drop in the money supply occurred *after* 1931; by that time, however, the market was too weary to do much reacting, either over or under.

To come closer to the present, in 1940 the stock market fell 15 percent even though the money supply was then rising 15 percent (on top of a similar rise the year before). In 1962, again, the market tumbled despite an increasing money supply. And in 1973–74 the stock market fell by more than 40 percent, even though the money supply increased by 11 percent over that two-year period.

On other not infrequent occasions, however, it is true that declines in stock prices *were* preceded or accompanied by declines in the rate of growth of the money supply, as in 1957, 1960, and 1969. And often increases in stock prices were indeed associated with increases in the growth of the money supply, as in 1967, 1968, and 1975.

In at least some of these instances, however, both stock prices and the money supply might conceivably have been reacting to a third causal force, perhaps an upturn in busi-

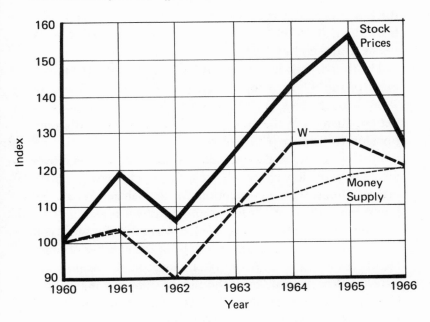

Stock Prices and Other Variables, 1960–1966

ness conditions stimulated by the outbreak of war ( ) peace ( )—check one—a spurt in consumer spending, or something else. An improvement in business conditions, regardless of cause, typically leads to an expansion in business loans at banks, a larger money supply, brighter profit prospects, and thereby higher stock prices. As the history of business cycles indicates, such upswings (or downturns) are capable of generating a cumulative push that can work up considerable momentum, carrying *both* the money supply and stock prices along with it.

The accompanying chart provides some idea of the pitfalls involved in reading a cause-and-effect relationship into two sets of statistics simply because they move together. The thick line indicates the movement of stock prices, annually, from the end of 1960 through the end of 1966, using stock prices at the end of 1960 as the base (= 100).

The thin dashed line, on a similar index basis, is the movement of the money supply annually, also from the end of 1960 through the end of 1966. Over this particular six-year period, changes in the money supply clearly bore little relationship to turning points in stock prices.

Finally, the chart also includes a third line (W). Its movements are obviously closely related to changes in stock prices. Almost without exception, the line labeled W and the line tracing stock prices move up and down together.

Cause and effect? The line labeled W, make of it what you will, is an annual index (1960 = 100) of the number of times members of the old Washington Senators baseball team struck out each year, over the period 1960 through 1966. (Source: The Sporting News's *Official Baseball Guide and Record Book,* Annual, 1960–66.) For at least these years, evidently, an investor trying to forecast turning points in the stock market would have been better off spending his time reading the box scores instead of the money supply figures.

Monetary Policy and Wall Street

Once we expand our horizon to encompass more than the money supply alone, there seems to be agreement that monetary policy, in general, frequently does have a considerable influence on the stock market. The consensus appears to be that it is by no means the only influence, and often is overshadowed by other forces and events; nevertheless, it is widely believed that on balance monetary policy has had a substantial effect on stock prices at times in the past, especially since the mid-1960s, and is likely to continue to do so in the foreseeable future.

This is quite aside from the power of the Federal Reserve to set margin requirements on stock purchases. In an attempt to prevent a repetition of the speculative wave, financed heavily with borrowed funds, that carried the market to dizzy heights in 1928 and until the Fall of 1929, Congress in the 1930s authorized the Federal Reserve to impose margin (or minimum downpayment) requirements on the purchase of stocks. If the margin requirement is 100 percent, then 100 percent cash must be put up and no borrowing at all is permitted. If the margin requirement is 80 percent, that much of one's own cash must be put up when buying a security and only the remaining 20 percent can be financed by borrowing from a bank or a broker. Of course, you could always finance the entire amount by borrowing from your brother-in-law and no one would be the wiser (except perhaps, in the long run, your brother-in-law).

High margin requirements probably have helped restrain speculation in stocks, particularly by those who could least afford it. Nevertheless, if the Federal Reserve had only this device to influence the market, it would be relying on a weak reed indeed. Margin requirements are 100 percent at Santa Anita and Hialeah racetracks, but at last report speculative activity by those who could not afford it as well as by those who could appeared unimpaired.

The impact of overall monetary policy on stock prices stems not so much from the Federal Reserve's power to set margin requirements as from its influence over the money supply, the entire spectrum of interest rates and financial markets, and current and expected business conditions. It is in the recent past, rather than twenty or thirty years ago, that the effects of monetary policy on stock prices are most clearly visible. The credit squeezes of 1966, 1969, and 1974 are prime examples.

During 1966, for instance, the money supply increased at a slower than normal rate. Bankers, businessmen, and the general public, carried away by skyrocketing interest rates, labeled the episode the Great Credit Crunch of 1966. Credit availability was sharply curtailed and interest rates on fixed-income securities soared. Stock prices tumbled about 20 percent during the first ten months of the year, despite booming business conditions—a rather clear indication of the potency of tight money, when applied vigorously, in affecting stock prices.

The easy money policy that prevailed during 1967 and most of 1968 was correspondingly accompanied by a rapid and lengthy upturn in the stock market. Reimposition of exceedingly tight money in 1969, however, was followed by a prompt collapse of stock prices. The Dow-Jones Industrial Average plunged from 985 in late 1968 to the 630 level in mid-1970, when it finally began to turn around.

In 1974 we again had tight money, as interest rates rose even higher than in 1966 and 1969. The prime rate at commercial banks, for example, hit what was then a record high of 12 percent in mid-1974. And stock prices, which had already fallen 20 percent in 1973, fell another 30 percent in 1974.

During the three decades from the early 1930s to the early 1960s, the reaction of the stock market to monetary policy was less prompt and less predictable than it has recently been. Stocks frequently seemed to go their own way during those years, regardless of what the central bank was doing. Not so any more; since the mid-1960s there is a rather clear cause-and-effect relationship between the general stance of monetary policy and movements in stock prices. There are two reasons for this change.

First, the central bank has recently acted with more authority than it did previously. In retrospect, during the 1950s and early 1960s, when the Federal Reserve was just testing the air after almost twenty years of virtual hibernation, a wiggle in long-term bond rates would cause it to beat a hasty retreat. It was afraid to probe too far for fear of starting a recession. An increase in interest rates on long-term government bonds from 3½ to 3¾ percent was considered a hazardous venture.

The Credit Crunch of 1966, however, gave the monetary authorities a different perspective. Prices fell on long-term government bonds to the point where effective interest rates approached 5 percent—not so high by later standards, but the equivalent of Mount Everest then—and yields on some intermediate-term Treasury bonds went over 6 percent. The economy thrashed and strained, but it did not collapse. It proved to be more resilient than many had supposed.

However, something else did happen. For the first time in a generation, many investors became aware that such things as bonds existed. And that, under certain conditions, they were more attractive additions to one's portfolio than stocks. The rise in bond interest rates (which means a fall in bond prices) thus had repercussions in the stock market; some individual and institutional investors held off buying stocks, or sold some they had, and bought bonds instead, thereby driving stock prices down.

In theory, the prices of stocks and bonds *should* move together in precisely that way, since they are substitutes for each other in investor portfolios just as Yamahas and Hondas are on the highway (with or without monkey bars and sissy bars). As we noted earlier in this chapter, if the price of bonds falls (implying higher interest rates), some buyers will switch out of stocks and into the now relatively more attractive bonds—thus causing the price of stocks to fall too. For similar reasons, if bond prices rise, stock prices should rise also.

However, during the 1950s this relationship did not hold very closely. For most of that decade, interest rates on bonds were slowly rising, cautiously adjusting upward from artificially low war and postwar levels. Slowly rising bond interest rates imply slowly falling bond prices. Stock prices, on the other hand, were ebullient during most of the decade.

With yields on bonds and stocks now at more realistic levels relative to each other, the sympathetic relationship between them has reasserted itself and they are likely to continue to move together in the future. From now on, when the Federal Reserve bangs bonds around, stocks are likely to get a nosebleed.

The *second* reason monetary policy affects stock prices more today than twenty or thirty years ago is simply that the Federal Reserve has made believers out of many former skeptics. If the Federal Reserve is ineffectual, who cares? But if monetary policy is effective in influencing the course of the economy, then a lot of people care a great deal. Today, many more financial analysts and observers of economic trends are persuaded that the central bank can achieve its announced objectives, or at least come reasonably close, than thought so a few decades back.

Monetary Policy Expectations and Stock Prices

Indeed, the pendulum appears to have swung so far in recent years that expectations about the immediate future course of monetary policy have now become one of the main topics of conversation among stock market analysts. Every week stock market participants anxiously await the release of the Federal Reserve's latest money supply figures.

If the figures show that the money supply is growing *faster* than the Fed's announced guidelines—say the Fed is aiming to increase the money supply by 4 to 6 percent annually, but the weekly figures reveal that in fact it has been increasing by 9 percent—then Wall Street concludes that the Fed will soon be *tightening* to get the money supply back on track.

Alternatively, if the figures show that the money supply is growing *more slowly* than the Fed's announced guidelines— again say the Fed is aiming to increase the money supply by 4 to 6 percent, but this time the weekly figures reveal that in fact it has been increasing by only 1 percent—then Wall Street concludes that the Fed will soon be *easing* to get the money supply back on track.

Views on Wall Street are mixed as to precisely what such figures imply for stock prices. If the money supply has been growing faster than the Fed's target, so that tightening is in order, then some see this as heralding a fall in stock prices, but others view it as signaling an upturn. Those who see tighter money as precipitating a fall in the stock market reason that tighter money means higher interest rates (lower bond prices); this will make bonds relatively more attractive than stocks, resulting in lower stock prices as well. On the other hand, others see tighter money as signaling an upturn in stock prices on the logic that inflation has been bad for stock prices; tighter money will stop inflation, which in turn will eventually bring interest rates down and thereby stimulate higher stock prices.

The same divergence of views exists for the implications of easier money. If the money supply has been growing more slowly than the Fed's target, so that easing is in order, some see this as likely to produce higher stock prices. They reason that easier money means lower interest rates (higher bond prices); this will make stocks relatively more attractive than bonds, resulting in higher stock prices. Others, however, come to the opposite conclusion. They see easier money as fueling inflation, which in turn will eventually bring higher interest rates and thereby depress stock prices.

By and large, the first group (tighter money will depress stock prices, easier money stimulate them) seemed to hold the predominant opinion in the early seventies. But as inflation accelerated during the decade, the second group gained adherents (tighter money will stimulate stock prices, easier money depress them).

Both groups, however, had their problems (and so have we). One problem is difficulty in interpreting the weekly Federal Reserve statistics, which are often ambiguous. One money supply measure may overshoot the target at the same time as another money supply measure undershoots it. Which measure should be used? Or the money supply may overshoot the target on the basis of the past month's data but undershoot it on the basis of the past two or three months' data. Which time span should be used?

Not to mention the potentially biggest problem of all: the Federal Reserve may have changed its target! There is a one-month delay between meetings of the Federal Reserve's Open Market Committee and release to the public of what transpired. If the Fed changed its money supply target from a 4–6 percent annual growth rate to 1–3 percent, then 1 percent is right on target and does not imply future easing. Someone who acts as though it does imply future easing could be making a serious mistake.

But then whoever said making money in the stock market is a snap!

15

WHAT IS FINANCIAL

INTERMEDIATION?

Financial intermediation played an important role, it is said, in permitting monetary velocity to rise during the 1950s. Financial *dis*intermediation, on the other hand, has been a significant factor in aggravating periodic tight money conditions. The words are big, but the process, it turns out, is commonplace and familiar. It is so ordinary, in fact, that we can add to those who have been talking prose all their lives, and were not aware of it, the millions who have been engaged in some aspect of financial intermediation or disintermediation, and did not realize it.

Financial intermediaries are nothing more than financial institutions—such as commercial and savings banks, savings and loan associations, credit unions, pension funds, insurance companies, and the like—that act as middlemen, transferring funds from ultimate lenders to ultimate borrowers. They borrow from Peter in order to lend to Paul.

What are some of the differences and similarities among financial institutions? What do they do? Why do they exist?

There is really very little difference between savings and loan associations and mutual savings banks in terms of what they do and how they operate. Both are frequently referred to as "thrift institutions." They tend to specialize in mortgage lending. Savings and loans are more familiar to many people since there are about 5,000 of them and they are spread throughout the nation. On the other hand, there are only about 500 mutual savings banks because they are chartered in only seventeen states, mostly in the Northeast. Both of them used to differ from the country's 15,000 commercial banks in that they did not, strictly speaking, offer checking account services. However, in recent years they have started offering payment orders that are essentially checking accounts. In the near future, federal and state laws are likely to be changed to permit them to acquire a wider variety of assets as well, in which case they will become virtually indistinguishable from commercial banks.

Life insurance companies, as the name implies, insure people against death, with premiums based on mortality statistics. These premiums are used to buy corporate bonds and stocks and mortgages, especially on industrial properties. Property and casualty insurance companies are the folks who insure homeowners against burglary and fire and insure car owners against theft and collision. With the premiums they receive—big ones from those under twenty-five—they buy high-grade municipal and corporate bonds and blue-chip stocks.

Pension funds provide individuals with a systematic plan to contribute funds during their working years, to be paid out after they retire (called an annuity). Pension funds invest most of their money in stocks and corporate bonds. Mutual funds enable the small saver to buy corporate stock and if you want to get your money back you don't have to wait until retirement, since you can sell your mutual fund shares any time you want (although not at any price you want). Money market mutual funds are a special variety: they pool the funds of small savers and invest in high-yielding, short-term assets. Credit unions and finance companies are at the other end of the financial spectrum: they help individuals spend now and pay later by extending consumer loans.

What all financial intermediaries have in common is that they acquire funds by issuing their own liabilities to the public (savings deposits, savings and loan shares), and then turn around and use this money to buy financial assets (stocks, bonds, mortgages) for themselves.

Because these institutions exist, savers who do not want to hoard their cash under a mattress, but who feel hesitant about purchasing corporate bonds or stocks or mortgages because they feel that these assets are perhaps too risky or too illiquid, are given a third alternative. They can "purchase" savings deposits or savings and loan shares. In that way, they can hold a relatively safe and quite liquid financial asset, yet still earn *some* interest income. At the same time, corporations and potential home-owners can still sell their bonds, stocks, and mortgages—to the financial intermediaries rather than to the original savers themselves. Financial intermediaries, in brief, "intermediate" between original savers and final borrowers.

Financial intermediation is precisely the above process: savers depositing funds with financial institutions rather than directly buying bonds or mortgages, and the financial institutions, in turn, doing the lending to the ultimate borrowers. *Dis*intermediation is the reverse: savers taking funds out of deposit accounts, or reducing the amounts they normally put in, and investing directly, in their own names, in market securities such as stocks and bonds.

Financial Intermediation Lowers Interest Rates

Interest rates on securities (bonds, stocks, mortgages, and so forth) must compensate lenders for the risks inherent in owning them—risks such as potential capital losses due to interest rate fluctuations, possible default, illiquidity, and so on. In other words, the borrower must pay the lender for parting with the most liquid of all assets, money, and holding in its place a relatively illiquid and possibly risky security.

Financial institutions are in a better position than individuals to bear and spread the risks of security ownership. Because of their large size, intermediaries can diversify their portfolios and minimize the risk involved in holding any one security. They are experts in evaluating borrower credit characteristics. They employ skilled portfolio managers and can take advantage of administrative economies in large-scale buying and selling.

For these reasons, they can afford to receive lower yields on their assets and will accept them if they have to. Competition among financial intermediaries forces interest rates to the lowest level compatible with their evaluation of the risks of security ownership. These yields are lower than if the same securities were held by individual investors, unable to minimize their risks so efficiently.

Looked at in another way, financial institutions also help to reduce the demand for money, thereby contributing to lower interest rates. People hold money both for day-to-day transactions and for safety, because of the riskiness of stock or bond holding (relative to cash). But such intermediary liabilities as savings deposits and savings and loan shares are also safe, as safe as money and virtually as liquid. Indeed, they are so safe and liquid that they are often called near-monies or money substitutes.

With such safe and liquid assets available and earning interest to boot, people will have less desire to hold money itself. They can be almost as liquid (and also earn some interest) if they substitute savings deposits in place of some of their cash holdings. The money that people release and deposit in financial intermediaries will be used, in turn, by the intermediaries to buy bonds, mortgages, and so on. Thus additional money enters the bond market and bond prices are bid up (interest rates drop). The net effect of financial intermediation is to lower interest rates.

There are several ways of looking at this process. We have just seen that the demand for bonds goes up. With a given supply of bonds, the increased demand drives bond prices up. Alternatively, we have also seen that the demand for money falls. Since the supply of money remains unchanged (it is determined by the Federal Reserve), this means that the supply of money is now greater than the demand, which tends to lower interest rates. Still another indication of intermediation is revealed by the behavior of velocity. Spending on goods and services can be increased when intermediary liabilities rise, as formerly idle cash is made available to finance ultimate borrowers. And when spending (GNP) goes up, while the money supply does not, an increase in velocity results.

The growth in financial intermediaries has been spectacular in the last thirty years. Time and savings deposits in commercial banks have grown from $30 billion at the end of World War II to over $600 billion, and savings and loan shares have increased from less than $10 billion to over $500 billion. At the same time we have experienced a general *increase* in the level of interest rates. This does not necessarily contradict what we have said above. If all other factors had remained the same, the growth in intermediation should have reduced interest rates. But, of course, all other factors have not remained the same.

Both the money supply and intermediary liabilities have been growing, providing us with increased liquidity. However, this has been more than absorbed by the rise in GNP, which has increased the demand for cash for transactions purposes. The net effect has been that the increase in the demand for liquidity has outpaced the increase in the supply of liquidity, so that interest rates have risen. In light of the great rise in GNP since World War II, what is surprising, and must be attributed in large part to the growth of intermediation, is that the rise in interest rates has not been considerably greater.

It is worth noting that since financial intermediation tends to lower interest rates, or at least moderate any increase, it has been highly beneficial to our rate of economic growth. A high rate of economic growth requires a large volume of real investment. The lower the rate of interest that ultimate borrowers must pay, the greater their expenditure on real investment is likely to be.

The beneficial effect of intermediation on economic growth can also be seen from the viewpoint of risk-bearing. Intermediaries are better able than individuals to bear the risks of lending out capital. As was previously stressed, ability to diversify, economies of scale, and expertise in lending account for this comparative advantage of institutions over individuals. As financial intermediaries own a larger and larger portion of the marketable securities outstanding, the subjective risk borne by the economy is lowered, interest rates are reduced, and more real investment takes place. Funds are channeled from ultimate lenders, through intermediaries, to ultimate borrowers more efficiently than if the intermediaries did not exist.

Intermediation and Monetary Policy

One of the earliest confrontations between modern Monetarists and Keynesians arose during the 1950s. It focused on the influence of financial institutions, such as savings and loan associations and savings banks, on the efficacy of monetary policy. Since savings deposits could not have checks written on them at that time, they were not part of the narrowly defined money stock (M1B). But they seemed sufficiently close to demand deposits to warrant the question: Should monetary policy be concerned with such nondemand deposit liabilities of financial intermediaries in gauging the impact of monetary policy?

Recent changes in regulations have blunted much of the debate. Some savings deposits now have direct checking privileges while others can be automatically transferred to checking accounts. The distinctions between commercial banks, savings and loans, and savings banks are less pronounced than they once were. Nevertheless, the controversy survives in the form of the various definitions of money that we encountered back in Chapter 2. Let's go to the original source of the debate and then see what lessons can be drawn.

John G. Gurley and Edward S. Shaw of Stanford University wrote a series of articles in the mid-1950s that eventually became known as the Gurley-Shaw thesis. They emphasized that the deposit liabilities of savings and loan associations, savings banks, and other financial intermediaries are, after all, not much different from the demand deposit liabilities of commercial banks, even though we generally call only the latter "money." It is true that we can spend demand deposits, and that we cannot spend a savings and loan share without cashing it in first. But cashing it in is a simple matter, easily accomplished; thus savings and loan shares and savings deposits, whether at commercial banks or at savings banks, are for all practical purposes almost as liquid as demand deposits.

Gurley and Shaw conclude that since these near-monies are outside the jurisdiction of the Federal Reserve, they make the successful execution of monetary policy difficult. Controlling liquidity only through the narrowly defined money supply will not work very well, since liquidity can also be provided by near-monies. For example, assume the Federal Reserve reduces the narrowly defined money supply to inhibit spending on real and financial assets to help fight inflation. Interest rates on securities rise. Now the intermediaries go into action. Aware of the higher yields and the profits they imply, savings and loan associations raise the rate they offer on deposits in an effort to attract more funds, which they can then invest in the higher-yielding securities. The increase in deposit rates induces some individuals to put more funds in savings banks, savings and loan associations, and so on. Financial intermediation shifts into high gear.

The individuals switching money to the intermediaries may use funds they formerly had invested directly in securities, thus rebuilding their liquidity; they also may use what were idle money balances, now coaxed out of hiding by the attractive rates posted and widely advertised by the inter-mediaries. As long as the latter occurs to some extent, there will be a net expansion in the demand for market securities (by the intermediaries), a consequent moderation in the rise in interest rates, and—most important of all—the channeling of previously idle money balances into the eager hands of ultimate borrower-spenders.

The behavior of financial intermediaries therefore partially offsets the impact of monetary policy on interest rates. Rates still rise as a result of tight money, but less than they would have without the intermediaries. The Fed has difficulty in controlling inflation because it can't control nonbank finan-cial intermediation and the creation of near-monies.

The Gurley-Shaw hypothesis, first developed in the mid-1950s here and at about the same time in England by the Radcliffe Committee, seemed vindicated by the experience of the 1950s and early 1960s. At that time, tight money invari-ably was accompanied by the mobilization of idle balances, an expansion in intermediation by financial institutions other than commercial banks, and consequent financing of the boom by these intermediaries. Debate raged as to whether the Federal Reserve should have the power to set reserve requirements for savings banks and savings and loan associa-tions, and congressional hearings were held to explore ways to solve the problem.

But perhaps the problem solved itself, or was solved acci-dentally, because the tight money periods of 1966, 1969, 1973–74, and 1979–80 told a different story.

Disintermediation

During the tight money episodes of 1966, 1969, 1973–74, and 1979–1980 market interest rates rose to what were then record levels, but the expected financial intermediation did not take place. Deposit rates did not go up as rapidly as open market rates on securities—and savers, instead of shifting funds *to* financial intermediaries, shifted them *out.* Individuals removed funds from savings accounts and put the money directly into corporate, municipal, and government securities. Financial *dis*intermediation!

This behavior put the intermediaries under severe pressure. With substantial withdrawals and minimal inflows of new funds, their profit position was threatened, their solvency was endangered, and their ability to lend evaporated. They reacted as financial institutions will—by pulling in their horns, trying to retrench, and running to Congress for help. In other words, they aggravated tight money conditions instead of, as before, ameliorating them.

What happened? What unraveled the Gurley-Shaw thesis?

Market rates went so high so fast that the intermediaries, for both internal and external reasons, could not raise the rates they paid depositors high enough or fast enough to stay competitive. Disappointed depositors drowned their sorrows by going out and buying high-yielding open market securities on their own.

Two reasons prevented the intermediaries from adjusting their deposit rates sufficiently to stay competitive with open market rates. *Internally,* they felt they could not afford to. The assets of most intermediaries are predominantly long term; most were bought some time ago, at considerably lower yields. The average rate of return is thus heavily weighted by the past. The purchase of new, higher-yielding securities will only slightly increase the overall yield on the total portfolio. On the other hand, if they increase their passbook savings deposit rates to attract new money, they have no choice but to pay the new higher rates to *all* passbook savings depositors.

In 1966 and again in 1969, 1973–74, and 1979–1980, market rates moved up so far and so rapidly that most financial institutions felt, after a brief attempt to stay in the race, that it was too costly to continue. They had, to put it bluntly, been priced out of the market.

But there was another reason why they did not stay in the race, an *external* one. Some intermediaries—perhaps the better managed ones—were all for posting higher passbook savings deposit rates and going after new business. But they couldn't. The legal deposit rate ceilings, imposed by the Federal Reserve, the Federal Home Loan Bank Board (charged with supervising savings and loan associations), and other supervisory agencies prevented them from raising deposit rates further once the maximum limits had been reached.

Indeed, in mid-1966 the deposit-rate ceilings were actually rolled back to lower levels, forcing many institutions that had posted higher interest rates to reduce them. With market rates still rising, it is no wonder depositors withdrew their money and went directly into the securities markets.

Deposit Rate Ceilings

The Federal Reserve sets the legal maximum interest rates —through what is known as Regulation Q—that commercial banks are allowed to pay on their time and savings deposit liabilities. The maximum interest rates that savings banks and savings and loan associations may offer depositors are also regulated.

If these ceilings are set above going deposit rates, they are inoperative and irrelevant. But once deposit rates push up against the ceilings, they tend effectively to inhibit intermediation by preventing financial institutions from competing against open market securities for funds. To the extent that disintermediation results, open market yields will rise even higher than otherwise.

For this reason, when we are in a period of tight money and the regulatory authorities fail to raise Regulation Q and the comparable regulations over the other intermediaries (or actually lower the ceilings, as they did in 1966) they are making monetary policy even more restrictive. Raising Regulation Q and its counterparts, as was always done prior to 1966, is viewed as an easing sign.

This may seem a bit peculiar—considering the lowering of an interest rate to be a sign of tightness, the raising of a rate a sign of ease. Once the intermediation process is recognized, however, it is clear that a lowering of Q induces financial disintermediation, and thereby higher market interest rates; while an increase in Q promotes financial intermediation, and thereby lower market interest rates, especially long-term rates.

An increase in Q tends to make bank time deposits more attractive than competing, highly liquid, short-term financial instruments, such as Treasury bills. This may raise short-term interest rates on Treasury bills, as people and corporations shift from bills to deposits. But as the intermediaries, in turn, buy long-term financial assets with the funds, long rates tend to fall. Since investment spending by business firms is related primarily to long-term rates rather than short rates, the entire process is expansionary.

Regulation Q emerged rather late as a tool of monetary policy. When the Federal Reserve Act was passed in 1913, it contained no provision of any sort fixing maximum permissible interest rates that banks could pay on their time and savings deposits. At that time, this was not considered an appropriate area of regulation. Twenty years later, in 1933, Congress instructed the Federal Reserve to set such rate ceilings on commercial banks. However, the ceilings were always raised to higher levels whenever they became troublesome—until 1966. At that time, similar rate ceilings were imposed on competing thrift institutions and, instead of being raised, they were *lowered.*

The 1933 provision was enacted on the grounds that excessive interest-rate competition for deposits during the 1920s had undermined the soundness of the banking system. It was believed that competition among banks for funds had driven deposit rates up too high. To cover their costs, banks acquired high-yielding but excessively risky low-quality assets. This deterioration in the quality of bank portfolios, it was said, contributed to the collapse of the banking system in the early 1930s. Abolition of interest rate competition for deposits, by setting rate ceilings, was seen as rooting out the basic element weakening the banking system. Similar arguments were responsible for the imposition of comparable ceilings over other intermediaries starting in 1966.

This analysis is open to serious question. In retrospect, it is not at all clear that the historical experience on which Regulation Q was based was correctly interpreted at the time the legislation was enacted. Interest rates on bank time and savings deposits actually declined during the 1920s, and thorough investigation since has failed to substantiate any appreciable deterioration in the quality of bank assets during that period.

With respect to the early 1930s, what was once interpreted as a banking collapse due to mismanagement by commercial bankers now appears to be much more a case of banking collapse due to inadequate *central* banking. There is widespread agreement today that, had the Federal Reserve stepped in promptly and vigorously, the greater part of the banking debacle of the early 1930s could have been avoided.

Enthusiasm for Regulation Q probably reached its peak during the 1966 credit squeeze. One member of the Board of Governors of the Federal Reserve System went so far as to say that "Regulation Q was the cutting edge of monetary policy." Why did holding deposit rates down via Regulation Q become so popular?

In its crudest form, the reason for wanting to elevate deposit rate ceilings to the heavy artillery in the arsenal of monetary policy appears to be as follows. Monetary policy, as traditionally employed, frequently results in sharply higher interest rates. Such higher rates produce unpalatable side effects, such as a larger interest burden on the national debt, political repercussions, and possible distortions in the distribution of income, to mention only a few. It would be so much nicer if monetary policy could achieve its purposes without such side effects. Regulation Q to the rescue. Monetary policy without higher interest rates. Monetary policy without tears.

A somewhat more charitable interpretation would run

along the following lines. The main objective of the central bank is to control the extension of bank credit. Regulation Q reinforces the bite of monetary policy by encouraging depositors to shift their funds *out* of commercial banks when market rates rise above the ceilings. This curtails the ability of banks to extend further credit and thereby reinforces the traditional instruments of monetary policy. (Notice that while the line of thinking in the previous paragraph involves keeping interest rates *low,* the argument in this paragraph is precisely the opposite—it involves *high* market interest rates as the inducement for financial disintermediation.)

By the time the 1969 credit crunch arrived, however, the banking system had devised numerous ways to soften the impact of Regulation Q; prevented by the rate ceilings from attracting deposits, bankers invented alternative sources of funds. They established holding companies that in turn issued commercial paper, borrowed funds from their European branches, and tapped a wide variety of other nondeposit sources to acquire lendable funds.

The lesson has become clear. Once the financial community recovered from the shock, it learned how to adjust to rate ceilings by locating and cultivating alternative (non-regulated) sources of funds. The Federal Reserve then had to try to plug these leaks by new regulations, mainly special reserve requirements against these new sources of funds. What the Federal Reserve Bank of New York described as a "cat and mouse game" became the primary preoccupation of both commercial and central bankers. The effect of rate ceilings has become primarily the diversion of funds *around* the regulated areas and into those that are not (yet) regulated; the ceilings do not affect the aggregate flow of funds as much as they alter the course they take.

Because of these shortcomings, the Federal Reserve has

started to rely somewhat less on the disintermediation effects of Regulation Q's deposit rate ceilings. In 1970 it eliminated the ceilings on large-size ($100,000 and over) negotiable certificates of deposit that mature in less than three months, in order to ease money market pressures stemming from the collapse of the Penn Central Railroad. Certificates of deposit (CDs) are distinguished from passbook savings deposits in that they are held by business firms as well as by individuals and they have a specific maturity date, say three or six months; large-size CDs are also negotiable—that is, the depositor can sell the CD before maturity, much as you can sell a stock or a bond. In 1973 the Fed eliminated the ceilings on the longer maturity large-size CDs.

Equally important, especially in forestalling disintermediation during the tight-money episode of 1979–1980, was a newly permitted six-month money market time certificate that commercial banks and thrift institutions were allowed to issue starting in mid-1978. The interest rate on these is tied to the Treasury bill rate, so that depositors could receive high money market yields without withdrawing their funds from the depository institutions. They can merely shift their funds for six months in the same bank or savings and loan association from a passbook savings account to a money market time certificate. So far, however, these are not permitted in denominations below $10,000, leaving smaller depositors out in the cold.

Money market mutual funds were the private sector's answer to this under-$10,000 gap. With large depositors able to get the benefits of high money market rates, there was room for ingenuity and innovation on behalf of small depositors. This ingenuity was provided, beginning in the early seventies, by money market mutual funds: they gather together the funds of many small savers, in batches as small as $1,000 and

$2,000 and then proceed to buy high-yielding large-size CDs and other money market instruments, such as commercial paper, in denominations of $25,000, $50,000, and $100,000. By pooling their funds, small savers are thus able to gain access to money market yields that Regulation Q would otherwise prevent them from realizing. Remember, however, these money market funds are not insured by any Federal agency. Nevertheless, by early 1980 the money market mutual funds had grown to over $40 billion in total assets.

Thus, deposit rate ceilings have unwittingly changed the face of many of our financial intermediaries. These ceilings have also served as a competition-inhibiting element within our financial system, as we discuss in the next chapter.

16

THE STRUCTURE OF THE
COMMERCIAL BANKING INDUSTRY

Commercial banks are the most important financial institutions in the United States. At the start of 1980 they had total assets amounting to $1,350 billion, compared with $580 billion for savings and loan associations, $430 billion for life insurance companies, and $160 billion for savings banks. An industry this size, particularly one so intimately involved with the monetary and payments system, clearly occupies a key role in the functioning of the economy.

Is the banking industry so structured as to best provide the financial services needed by a changing and growing economy? For example, do borrowers who are refused a loan at one bank generally have other viable options open to them, other banks to which they can turn? Similarly, are the opportunities open to depositors sufficiently varied to give them an array of choices with respect to deposit terms and yields, so that they can shop around for those that best fit their particular circumstances? In other words, is there enough competition in banking to make it a dynamic and innovative industry, responsive to private needs and public goals?

Deposit Rate Ceilings Again

Probably the most competition-inhibiting element in banking at the present time is our old friend Regulation Q, the legal prohibition against banks paying depositors more than a specified maximum interest rate on time and savings deposits. As noted in the previous chapter, interest rate ceilings were enacted in 1933 on the questionable premise that excessive rate competition for deposits had undermined the soundness of the banking system.

Whatever the logic of such ceilings in 1933, after thousands of bank failures, there are far fewer grounds for continuing them today, in the considerably different environment of the 1980s. Bank failures are now rare—over the past quarter century they have averaged less than six a year—and those that have occurred have generally been attributable not to competitive pressures but to embezzlement or similar fraudulent practices. In any case, the reason so few banks have failed is not due to Regulation Q but to the existence of the Federal Deposit Insurance Corporation. By insuring deposits under the auspices of the federal government, the FDIC has successfully eliminated the "run on the bank" by frightened depositors that invariably culminated in a bank failure in the 1920s and early 1930s.

What Regulation Q *does* do is effectively prevent aggressive, well-managed banks from offering depositors more attractive interest rates than the bank next door. Aggressive banks that would like to compete for funds by bidding more for deposits have been legally prohibited from doing so, which also means, of course, that depositors have simultaneously been deprived of the enlarged options that more vigorous price competition among banks would offer them. It is true that banks have been known to give away toasters, radios, and a two-year subscription to *Playboy* in order to attract savings deposits. But how do banks reach those who don't eat bread, can't stand the radio, and have foresworn serious reading?

In addition, Regulation Q discriminates against the small saver. Regulation Q rate ceilings have been lifted entirely from large-size certificates of deposit ($100,000 and over), but limits are still imposed on the interest rates small savers can get. In the early 1980s, for example, the most a small depositor could legally get on a passbook savings account at a commercial bank was 5¼ percent, although large depositors were getting about three times as much. When frustrated small depositors tried to shift over to higher-yielding Treasury bills in 1970, joining the crowd in financial disintermediation, the U.S. Treasury showed whose side *it* was on by promptly raising the minimum Treasury bill denomination from $1,000 to $10,000.

Closely related to Regulation Q on time and savings deposits is the legal prohibition against banks paying any interest at all on *demand deposits*—in effect, a demand-deposit interest rate ceiling set at zero. The reasoning behind this legislation, which was also enacted in 1933, is similar to that behind the ceiling on time and savings deposits—as are the objections to it.

The right to deal in checking accounts evidently has some value. If it did not, commercial banks would not be so eager to get them and savings banks and savings and loan associations would not be lobbying for the right to do the same. Under such circumstances, it is reasonable to expect that if competition were unfettered some bankers would bid, via interest payments, to attract demand deposits. As matters now stand, this source of funds is acquired at no cost, which is nice for bankers but not so nice for depositors. Actually, banks do compete for demand deposits by providing their customers with checks that have their names and sometimes even pretty pictures on them. This certainly costs the banks money. But wouldn't we all be better off if the banks offered us cash instead—in the form of interest payments? Some people might prefer money over art, strange as that might seem.

One function of financial institutions is to offer as broad as possible a spectrum of liabilities, thereby enlarging the options available to potential depositors. At present, because of the zero interest rate ceiling on demand deposits, there is a gap in the alternatives—the option of an interest-bearing demand deposit. If any depositor wants that option and any bank wants to provide it (and all indications point to a yes answer to each), both would presumably be better off were they permitted to come to terms.

Branching and New Entry

While deposit interest rate ceilings are probably the most important factor restraining competition in banking today, they are run a close second by the network of laws and regulations regarding branch banking and new entry into the industry.

With over 14,000 commercial banks in the United States, there appears to be, on the face of it, a high degree of robust competition. However, closer scrutiny reveals that a large percentage of banks are very small institutions, with less than $25 million in deposits per bank. Indeed, fully half of the banks in the country are that small. Most of them are located in small, one-bank towns.

If this large number of very small banks were the product of natural evolution, it would indicate that the optimum (low cost) size bank is probably a very small institution, with less than $25 million in deposits. Their large numbers would attest to their competitive viability.

However, the reason there are so many very small banks in this country does not have much to do with their successful adaptation to changing economic needs or their innovative capabilities. It is simply because most of them are *sheltered* from competition by state antibranching statutes, to which the federal banking authorities defer. Many very small banks would be unable to remain in business were a large bank to open up a branch next door. The fact that in many states the large bank is legally prohibited from doing so is what permits many small banks to survive—and to saddle their communities with high-cost banking.

About one-third of the states, mostly in the Midwest, permit only unit banking—that is, no branch banking is allowed at all. Another third of the states, mostly in the East, allow only some limited form of branching. The remaining states, largely in the West, permit unlimited statewide branching. *Federal regulations require that a federally chartered bank abide by the branching laws of the state in which it is headquartered, and interstate branching is prohibited everywhere.* About half of the banks in the country are located in the unit-banking states, where the average bank size is only about one-fifth that in unlimited branching states.

Thus it is state antibranching statutes, not economic circumstances, that are the principal determinant of the number of banks in the United States. The fact that there are over 14,000 commercial banks bears witness to the *absence,* not the presence, of vigorous competition. If there were fewer banks, and more of them were close to optimum size, the general public would be better served.

Most state legislatures that have maintained strict anti-branching statutes have done so in the face of considerable evidence that branching would be more efficient and more viable than many small independent unit banks in providing the financial services needed by a dynamic economy. This has become more important with the introduction of large-scale computerized technology into banking; even present, not to mention future, technology cannot be utilized advantageously by small unit banks, where the costs are too great because volume is too small. However, the political influence of the banking industry on the state level has repeatedly outflanked the interests of the (unorganized) general public, a process that has been facilitated by the tactic of playing on the deep-seated American fear of bigness, especially in banking.

Closely related to the branching issue is that of new entry into the banking industry. By law, both federal and state banking authorities typically evaluate a number of conditions before chartering a new bank. These include the adequacy of its capital structure, the general character of its management, its future earnings prospects, and the convenience and needs of the community it proposes to serve. (Further, the well-known liquidity index is given due consideration: namely, the number of state legislators on the bank's board of directors multiplied by the number of Little League baseball teams it proposes to sponsor.)

Few would dispute the necessity of maintaining standards of capital adequacy, or the need for determining that the management of a proposed new bank, and their backers, are honest people, without underworld connections. (Not to mention the desirability of a rating higher than 3π on the liquidity index.) But the other two elements in the screening process, the future earnings prospects of the proposed new bank and the convenience and needs of the community in which it would be located, in effect shield existing banking institutions from the rigors (and vitality) of competition more than they serve the interests of the public at large.

The purpose of both an earnings prospects criterion and a convenience and needs criterion is said to be the prevention of bank failures. But measures that insulate all banks from the slightest chance of failure are also measures that inhibit risk taking, discourage financial innovation, circumscribe management decision making, and stifle the benefits to the general public that can flow from competitive rivalry. These are high costs to pay, particularly when federal deposit insurance protection has eliminated the widespread distress that bank failures formerly caused.

Do the Giant Banks Pose a Monopoly Threat?

So far we have emphasized that there are probably too many very small banks in the United States, too small for efficient operation. What about the other end of the scale: the approximately two dozen Giant Banks, each of which has over $5 *billion* in deposits? This handful of banks, one-tenth of 1 percent of all the banks in the country, holds one-fourth of all the banking system's deposits. Do these couple of dozen giants pose a clear and present monopoly danger?

Opinions differ on this, of course, but at this stage in history the giant banks appear to be more benign than malignant. Not because they are particularly generous, home-loving, or patriotic—at least no more so than any of us—but simply because, large as they are, they still face sufficient competition to keep them in line. Close on their heels are another two dozen banks with deposits between $3 and $5 billion, and close behind *them* come another hundred banks with deposits between $1 and $3 billion.

The monopoly threat is further ameliorated in this country by legislation that forbids banking and industrial operations by the same firm. In some other countries—Japan is the outstanding example—giant banks are affiliated with giant manufacturing firms under common ownership, representing a vast concentration of economic power. If Chase Manhattan Bank, Xerox, and IBM could merge into a huge combine, as is permissible in Japan (where they are called *zaibatsus*), then we would really have something to worry about.

None of the above should be taken to advocate complacency. Advances in technology are likely to increase the optimum size of bank in the future, as well as generate powerful economic incentives for mergers between banks and other kinds of business—especially with those involved in data transmission and communications. Nevertheless, so long as existing antitrust statutes are enforced, fears of the dangers of banking monopoly appear to be unrealistic—at least for the time being.

PART VI

Money and National Priorities

17

FINANCIAL RESOURCES, REAL RESOURCES, AND NATIONAL PRIORITIES

As the United States has encountered serious social problems in the past decade, many have urged that we need a major reordering of our national priorities. What is being said is that we have to do something to alleviate poverty, urban blight, crime, pollution, and so on. Typically, that is the end of the story, except for apocalyptic visions of what is likely to happen if *something* isn't done. No attempt is made to quantify what has to be done, however.

What dollar amounts are involved? Who will foot the bill? Priorities are by nature relative; if some are raised higher, then mustn't others be dropped lower? Should a reordering be accomplished via tax changes or selective credit policies?

Quantifying Reordered Priorities

Aside from the direct reduction of poverty, which we shall return to later, there appears to be widespread concern about the need to: (a) improve mass transit in urban and suburban areas; (b) curb environmental pollution; (c) provide better housing for low-income families; (d) improve police protection, law enforcement, and the judicial and penal systems generally; (e) upgrade the quality of education, particularly that available to minority group children; and (f) better the quantity and quality of medical research and health care, especially by increasing its availability to the aged and to low- and middle-income groups.

It has become abundantly clear that none of these problem areas can be resolved simply by spending more money, any more than purely military means ever succeeded in resolving the Vietnam quagmire. "Spend more money" is a first cousin to "Send more troops." It is equally true, however, that improvements cannot realistically be expected unless more money is indeed spent. At present, estimates of the dollar amounts needed to make significant headway in these areas are little more than guesswork (and even less thought has been devoted to least-cost methods of realizing objectives). Nevertheless, some crude calculations can give a rough idea of the financial magnitudes involved. Take out your pencil, because here come some numbers.

Conservative estimates require the following *additional* spending: $10 billion a year (1980 prices) to improve mass transit; $20 billion a year more to make meaningful progress toward pollution control; $20 billion a year more for low- and middle-income housing; $25 billion additional annually for law enforcement and judicial-penal reform; $30 billion annually toward nationwide school reform; and another $30 billion a year for appropriate health care and medical research. This package adds up to a total of $135 billion *a year* more for these purposes than we, as a nation, are currently spending.

How does this stack up against existing priorities? In 1979, for example, 64 percent of our $2,370 billion national output was in the form of consumer goods and services, 11 percent was capital goods (business investment spending), and 5 percent went for federal defense. These are the Favored Priorities: they command 80 percent of our total output of goods and services. The remaining 20 percent of GNP are the Ugly Duckling Priorities—state and local government spending (13 percent), housing (5 percent), and federal nondefense purchases of goods and services (2 percent).

Almost all of the $135 billion a year, or 6 percent of 1979's GNP, needed to *reorder* priorities falls into the Ugly Duckling class—in the main, they are either state and local government functions, housing, or federal government nondefense functions (either by tradition or because of default on the part of the private sector). A meaningful reordering of national priorities implies taking *6 percent* of our national output away from the Favored Priorities and moving it over to the Ugly Ducklings. A real reordering of priorities, as opposed to liberal lip service, is clearly no trivial matter.

A Growth Dividend

Many advocates of reordering priorities think that it can be done with little pain, that a normal "growth dividend" will magically supply all the needed $135 billion. They are not altogether wrong. Growth will help, but alone it is not enough. As economists have observed time and again, there is no such thing as a free lunch—you always wind up paying for it, in some way.

Economic growth refers to the ability of our economy to expand its productive capacities over a period of time. Most forecasts for the coming decade anticipate a real growth rate averaging no more than 4 percent a year. If realized, this would yield additional real output averaging about $95 billion a year every year during the rest of the 1980s. But the process of growth does no more than make about $95 billion of additional resources available every year, which are then up for grabs. If state and local spending, housing, and federal nondefense spending—the Ugly Ducklings—continue to receive the same shares of the pie as they do now, which total 20 percent, then growth alone will provide only 20 percent of the $95 billion annual expansion in output for those purposes, or an incremental $19 billion a year every year.

At best, then, a growth dividend could contribute only $19 billion the first year, $38 billion the next year, $57 billion the year after that, and so on. It would take seven years to reach the requisite $135 billion, and by that time neglect would have swollen the required amount. While we may not preach "instant gratification," neither do we endorse "benign neglect."

Deliberate Resource Reallocation

If we are truly to reorder priorities, we thus have no choice but deliberately to use governmental policies to *reallocate* some resources. If the Ugly Duckling Priorities are to get more, some of the Favored Priorities will have to get less. The only questions are what to cut and by how much.

A favorite starting point for radical surgery is usually business plant and equipment spending. Let the giant corporations pull in their belts; aren't they already too big? Hit the Fat Cats where it hurts, below the pocketbook. But this approach is likely to be self-defeating. (Sorry about that.) Unless business firms continue to build and improve their plant and equipment, productivity will falter and the 4 percent growth rate in GNP will be one more unfulfilled prophecy. The result would be a smaller-than-$19-billion annual growth dividend, thereby compounding our difficulties.

This leaves federal defense (5 percent of GNP) and consumer spending (64 percent) as the only candidates left for contraction. (So what else is new?) To realize a reordering of priorities, it all comes down to not *whether* to cut back on defense and/or consumer spending, but *how* and in what proportions. If national defense absorbs the entire decline, then consumer spending can remain unaffected. But national security requirements may prevent meaningful reductions in the defense budget, and then consumer spending will have to take the brunt of the squeeze. Given reordered priorities and reasonably full employment, every additional dollar spent on guns will mean a dollar less for butter (the old guns-and-butter problem that helped Paul Samuelson sell millions of copies of his textbook).

All of this suggests that consumer spending will indeed have to be curbed if we are to feed the Ugly Ducklings. This could be undertaken through a variety of governmental measures, including most prominently higher tax rates (don't laugh—pretty soon you may be paying your share) and selective credit controls. We look at both of these methods in the remainder of this chapter.

Reordered Priorities Mean Higher Taxes

The standard way to influence total consumer outlays is by varying tax rates—lowering them to encourage, and raising them to discourage, consumer spending. Higher tax rates thus emerge as the painful counterpart of reordered priorities. It is precisely here that the American public's desire for a true reordering of priorities meets its severest test, because any significant restraint on consumer spending must necessarily imply higher taxes on middle-income families. As a practical matter, reduced consumption simply cannot be accomplished primarily by increasing taxes on business or the wealthy.

Higher business taxes are likely to inhibit investment rather than consumer spending. But business investment in new plant and equipment, as emphasized above, is needed for an adequate growth rate. Despite recent questioning of some of the by-products of economic growth, the fact remains that it is still the most important single generator of usable resources.

"Soaking the rich" is no answer either. Raising taxes on the rich, say on those with annual incomes over $100,000, might be justifiable on grounds of equity but it is not likely to go far toward the objective of reducing consumer spending. The rich do not account for that much consumer spending in the first place, and of all taxpayers they would be the most likely to react to higher taxes by cutting back their saving rather than their spending. Nor, of course, can any help be expected from reducing the consumption of those already at or close to the subsistence level.

The conclusion is inescapable: A large share of the cost of reordered priorities (less consumption) will have to be borne (in taxes) by middle-income families; it is they who comprise the bulk of the population and who do most of the consumer spending.

An alternative to explicitly higher tax rates is the *implicit* tax imposed through inflation. Increased spending on the Ugly Ducklings, without reductions in either defense or consumer spending, is likely to strain the economy's productive capacity and drive prices higher. The result generally is to contract most the consumption of those least able to protect themselves, such as the elderly and others living on fixed incomes and fringe workers in nonunionized employment.

Finally, there is the direct attack on poverty per se. This is somewhat different from the kinds of things we have mentioned so far. Pollution control, upgrading the quality of education, and so forth, involve the shifting of resources from one category of spending to another. The objective of income maintenance programs, on the other hand, is not to direct spending to particular uses, but to direct income to particular persons; the main effect would be a redistribution within the total of consumer spending, from upper income groups toward lower.

It has been estimated by the Census Bureau that direct action to bring all Americans up to the subsistence level, via some plan of family allowances or negative income taxes, would cost about $15 billion a year. Again, this would have to be financed in substantial part by taxes on middle-income families, because that is where most of the income is.

Can Selective Credit Controls Help?

Taxes hurt. You have to dig into your pocket—aggravating your tennis elbow. They may also inhibit work incentives, as we saw in Chapter 13, reducing aggregate production and economic well-being. Politicians, long aware of the unpopularity of higher taxes, have sought a less painful way to reorder national priorities.

Selective credit policies are the politicians' favorite alternative to taxation in reallocating resources among different uses. Such policies include prohibitory regulations regarding certain uses of credit, such as consumer credit and real estate credit controls; favored legal status to lenders who make certain types of loans, such as the favorable tax treatment received by savings and loan associations as a quid pro quo for their concentrating on mortgage lending and the line of credit at the Treasury granted to the Federal National Mortgage Association in exchange for operating a secondary market in mortgages; and interest rate subsidies to certain categories of borrowers for making particular kinds of expenditures, such as students who are borrowing from banks to finance their education and poor families who are taking out mortgages to finance the purchase of homes.

This list only scratches the surface of the myriad of selective credit policies currently on the books in the United States. At last count, there were over fifty general categories of federal credit programs in operation, and that count did not include either the usury laws or the regulations imposed on financial institutions to channel credit into particular uses, such as the portfolio restrictions on savings and loan associations and the various legal lending limits imposed on commercial banks.

New selective credit policies are, in fact, being proposed all the time. For example, Andrew Brimmer, a former member of the Board of Governors of the Federal Reserve System, has suggested that banks be required to have different reserve ratios on various categories of loans—higher ratios to discourage unfavored types of loans and lower ratios to encourage favored types.

At this point it is appropriate to ask at least four questions: (1) How are selective credit policies supposed to work? (2) Do they in fact work successfully? (3) What's wrong with them? (4) Why are they so popular?

A Catechism on Selective Credit Policies

QUESTION: *How are selective credit policies supposed to work?*

ANSWER: Their objective is to encourage (or discourage) a particular type of real expenditure—say, housing or consumer durable goods expenditures—by increasing (or decreasing) the volume of credit directed to such activities and/or by making the terms of credit (interest rates, downpayments) easier or more stringent. One obvious prerequisite for the effectiveness of selective credit policies is that there be a close relationship between a specific type of credit and a particular category of real expenditure. For example, as long as the purchase of a home is closely related to the availability of mortgage credit, it is possible to encourage housing by inducing lenders to make mortgage loans rather than other types of loans. As lenders devote more funds to mortgages and less, say, to business loans, the interest rate on mortgages should fall in relation to the rate on business loans, and people will thus be encouraged to take out mortgages and buy new homes.

But that is not the only way to use mortgage money. What if someone already has enough cash to buy a home and is ready to spend it for that purpose regardless of mortgage terms? The availability of cheap mortgage money then induces him to take out a mortgage to finance his home—freeing his other funds for more serious endeavors, like a six-month tour of the world's sunniest beaches.

A selective credit policy will be most effective in redirecting real resources when there is a rigid dollar-for-dollar relationship between a specific type of credit and a particular category of expenditure. To the extent that there is some slippage—that is, as long as the expenditure can be financed in other ways or the specific type of credit can be used differently—the effectiveness of the selective credit policy is impaired.

Many selective credit policies are imposed on only one sector of the financial markets. The portfolio restrictions imposed on savings and loan associations, for example, limit their assets essentially to government bonds and mortgages. Another example is Brimmer's proposal that commercial banks have different reserve requirements on different types of loans. Such selective credit policies increase the flow of credit to the favored uses only so long as other (unrestricted) lenders in financial markets do not counteract their behavior. For instance, if Brimmer's proposal were enacted and the reserve requirement against mortgage loans were low while the reserve requirement against consumer installment loans were high, banks would find it profitable to divert more funds to mortgages and less to consumer installment credit. Initially, mortgage rates would decline and consumer credit rates would go up. This is precisely the desired objective of the selective credit policy. *But* the reaction of other institutional lenders, such as life insurance companies, might then be to make fewer mortgage loans and to expand credit to consumer installment loans, which will ultimately tend to offset the impact of the selective policy. As long as this offset is incomplete, however, selective credit policies on only a few sectors of the credit market can successfully divert some funds into favored uses.

QUESTION: *Do they in fact work successfully?*

ANSWER: Under most circumstances, selective credit policies do seem to work. Imposing regulations and controls does appear to succeed in diverting credit into desired channels. Furthermore, borrowers do tend, for the most part, to use certain types of credit for specific types of real expenditures. But as we saw near the end of Chapter 15, in our discussion of Regulation Q, participants in financial markets are very creative when it comes to circumventing regulations. The very success of selective credit controls is likely to sow the seeds of their ultimate failure. If consumers cannot get credit from banks to finance the purchase of automobiles because, say, the banks are preoccupied with sewage bonds of local municipalities, then the auto dealers will arrange the necessary financing. How? Most probably through the auto manufacturers, who can float bonds in the capital markets and use the proceeds for anything they want, including extending loans to potential customers.

QUESTION: *What's wrong with selective credit policies?*

ANSWER: For one thing, as indicated in the preceding paragraph, their effectiveness tends to wear out with the passage of time. Another drawback is that the real costs of such programs are obscured by the financial maze. The unavoidable fact of life is that there is no such thing as a free lunch—when we are already close to full employment, the cost of more resources in education or housing has to be fewer resources available for other things. This lesson is brought home loud and clear when taxes must be raised to deter the other types of expenditure, with the proceeds going to the favored groups.

But favoring some borrowers (and thereby in effect squeezing others out of the credit market), while less direct than taxation, has similar social costs—less of something else. If politicians are not aware of these costs (and the proliferation of credit programs makes it doubtful that they are), then the indiscriminate use of selective credit policies tries to favor everyone and everything and winds up producing nothing.

QUESTION: *Why are selective credit policies so popular?*

ANSWER: Partly because they don't *seem* to be as painful as taxation. Those who are unable to buy new cars because they can't get financing are likely to blame fate or the world in general, while those who can't buy them because they have so little left after taxes are likely to blame the politicians in power. Also, more positively, selective credit policies do have the attractive feature of making the private sector an active partner in the process of redirecting resources. The government only provides the incentive—an interest subsidy, insurance for the lender against default, or some other feature. The bulk of the funds are still channeled through nongovernmental institutions.

The scope of activities currently receiving favorable treatment in the credit markets extends from exports and foreign economic development to community redevelopment and higher education. Housing, however, stands head-and-shoulders above all other activities as the spending category receiving the most credit favors. In the next chapter we explore the housing situation in detail, with special reference to the impacts of monetary policy and selective credit programs on home-building.

18

DOES TIGHT MONEY DISCRIMINATE

AGAINST HOUSING?

Countercyclical monetary policy has often been accused of having "discriminatory" effects on the housing market. It is argued that tight money has its greatest impact on residential construction. In boom periods, when money is tightened and interest rates rise, home-building gets strangled. Subsequently, in recessions, when money eases and interest rates fall, home-building zooms ahead at an unnaturally rapid pace.

As a result, employment in the construction industry is unstable; workers try to even out their incomes over time by restrictive entry requirements and work rules; and entrepreneurs are discouraged from mechanization and modernization. All of which, it is alleged, leads to lower productivity in the housing industry than elsewhere in the economy. We are in the last half of the twentieth century but still building homes as though we were in the first half of the nineteenth. Low-cost housing seems impossible to construct and rents across the board, on both new and existing dwellings, are higher than they need be.

Is home-building indeed that fickle? If so, why? Can anything be done about it? *Should* anything be done about it? What role is there for selective credit policies?

The Truth about Housing

On the basis of the evidence, the contention that home-building is a foul-weather friend is difficult to deny. When GNP is bursting at the seams, construction tends to slacken; during downturns in overall business activity, the housing industry tends to expand. Of all the components of GNP, the record indicates that residential construction has experienced the greatest cyclical variability during the postwar years.

The accompanying chart traces residential construction as a percent of GNP from 1951 through 1977. The shaded areas represent periods of recession in general business conditions, from the peak of the boom at the start of the shaded area to the trough of the recession at the end.

Home-building typically starts up during, or in some cases shortly after, a recession. On the other hand, during those years of highest overall employment and bubbling prosperity, usually accompanied by tight money, which are typically the years just *before* the shaded areas, residential construction is generally taking a nosedive. These boom periods are the very years when other kinds of spending, for example, consumer durables and business plant and equipment, are generally at or near their peak. But housing does not follow suit. As resources turn to making automobiles, television sets, and machine tools, the construction of homes takes a back seat.

Why? What causes these fluctuations in the housing market, fluctuations that appear to be so closely related to the actions of the central bank?

New Housing Expenditures as a Percent of GNP, 1951–1977

The Instability of Supply

During periods of tight money and rising interest rates, the supply of funds to the mortgage market is drastically curtailed. This sharp reduction in funds available for home financing can be traced primarily to the inability of the major mortgage lenders, savings and loan associations and mutual savings banks, to compete for funds as interest rates rise. As we saw in Chapter 15, when interest rates rise during a period of tight money these institutions can compete for funds only so long as they can continue to move their deposit rates up in tandem with market rates. But two reasons prevent them from doing so for very long.

First, the assets of these institutions are primarily long term. Only a small portion of their portfolio turns over during any one year. Hence, when interest rates go up, they can receive a higher yield on only a small portion of their assets. Some of these financial institutions thus find it too costly to raise their deposit rates by as much as the increase in yields on government, municipal, and corporate bonds. Second, while many of the better-managed institutions might be willing to raise their deposit rates to maintain their inflow of funds, after a while they are prevented from doing so by the legal interest rate ceilings imposed on deposit rates.

As market rates continue to advance, but deposit rates at savings institutions do not, savers—potential depositors—start to find it more attractive to invest their funds directly in the capital markets, rather than depositing them in savings and loans or savings banks. Financial disintermediation!

Since individual investors are not large mortgage lenders, funds that might well have gone into the mortgage market had they been deposited in a savings and loan association now move directly into stocks or bonds. The supply of funds available for mortgage lending dries up. This occurred most dramatically in 1966, when the savings and loan associations and savings banks lost funds not only to direct investment but also to the commercial banks, and again in 1969, 1974, and 1979–80 when all deposit-type financial institutions (including commercial banks) were hard hit by financial disintermediation.

All this is only half the story. Another side of the coin, the nature of the *demand* for mortgage loans, also contributes to the instability of residential construction.

The Sensitivity of Demand

In Chapter 5 we noted that residential construction spending appears to be much more sensitive to changes in interest rates than any other category of expenditure. In the Federal Reserve's econometric model of the economy, a one percentage point increase in long-term interest rates reduces housing demand by $3 billion after one year, while business plant and equipment spending is reduced barely half a billion dollars.

Why is the demand for housing so much more sensitive to changes in interest rates than other kinds of spending? There are probably two major reasons. First, interest is a much greater proportion of total outlay in home-buying than it is in shorter-lived investments such as inventory investment or the purchase of manufacturing equipment. The longer the investment period—that is, the longer the money will be tied up in the investment—the larger interest costs loom as an element in total costs. As we noted in Chapter 7, if you buy a $50,000 home and obtain a mortgage for the full amount at 9 percent interest for thirty years, you will be paying $93,000 in *interest alone.* If the mortgage rate rises to 10 percent, this will add an additional $12,000.

Second, the demand for housing is probably more sensitive than other kinds of spending to interest rate changes because it is families that are undertaking the investment rather than business firms, and families can more easily postpone such expenditures for a year or two. Business firms also invest in long-lived projects—heavy machinery, physical plant, and so on—in which interest costs bulk as large as they do in housing. But corporations face competitive pressures from rival sellers and frequently have no choice in the matter; often they must either make improvements and additions quickly or else risk losing their share of the market.

The reaction of home buyers to changes in interest rates thus reinforces the reaction of potential suppliers of mortgage money. When rates fall or rise, home buyers revise their spending plans and lenders rethink their allocation of funds. Result: feast or famine in the building industry.

Fannie Mae and Her Friends

Since housing is high on our list of national priorities and since it is, in part, the government's use of countercyclical monetary policy (producing wide swings in interest rates) that causes instability in the housing industry, there has been considerable governmental effort to reduce the variability of home-building. Almost all this effort takes the form of selective credit policies designed to ameliorate the impact of tight money on housing.

The *F*ederal *N*ational *M*ortgage *A*ssociation, more widely known as Fannie Mae, is a government-sponsored institution that buys mortgages when there is a shortage of private funds. Fannie is aided in the purchase of mortgages by her cousin (so she says), Ginnie Mae (*G*overnment *N*ational *M*ortgage *A*ssociation), which is part of the Department of Housing and Urban Development. Ginnie guarantees the timely payment of interest and principal on pools of mortgages known as "GNMA Pass-Throughs." Things get even more interesting when we introduce another government-sponsored agency, the Federal Home Loan Bank System, which makes loans to savings and loan associations—permitting them to borrow in large amounts to offset declines in deposits during periods of tight money. Now that, by itself, isn't so interesting, except that the Federal Home Loan Bank System was given a subsidiary by Congress in 1970—namely, the Federal Home Loan Mortgage Corporation, which also buys mortgages during periods of tight money. Still not especially interesting? But wait. Wall Street, which handles the securities that these agencies issue to finance their purchases of mortgages, has dubbed the 1970 addition to the mortgage-market fan club, Freddie Mac. Are the Wall Streeters just male chauvinist pigs, or do they know something about these three that can only be discussed behind closed doors and drawn curtains?

All these government and government-sponsored agencies are very active during periods of tight money. During 1969 and 1974 both Fannie Mae and the Federal Home Loan Bank System pumped large amounts of funds into the mortgage market in an effort to mitigate the downturn in housing. Their success is somewhat debatable.

There has been much concern in the money and capital markets, however, over the growth of federal credit programs. As we saw in the previous chapter, if one use of credit is favored some other use will have to be cut back. As federally sponsored agencies bid for funds in the credit market by issuing their own securities (in order to buy mortgages), other borrowers without federal backing are squeezed out. It is those who are squeezed out (the squeezees) who bear the burden of tight money and higher interest rates.

Should this massive federal credit effort be made to stabilize the mortgage market? It is not such a bad thing, once you think about it, for the economy to have a foul-weather friend. The fact that housing has slackened during boom periods has taken some of the extreme inflationary pressure off the boom. Equally important, the prompt revival of housing during recessions has made our postwar recessions much less severe than they might otherwise have been. From the point of view of the housing industry, its instability has caused serious problems; but from the point of view of the overall economy, it has been, at least to some extent, a blessing.

Congress, if one is to judge by its procreation of mortgage credit programs, has decided that some other sector of the economy (but not housing) should bear the brunt of anti-inflationary monetary policy. It has implemented its decision by selective credit policies aimed at sheltering housing. It could have chosen a quite different route: namely, to prevent inflation the medicine could be tight fiscal policy (high tax rates and cutbacks in government spending) instead of tight money. If that were done, interest rates could possibly remain relatively low across the board, and the rate ceilings, being irrelevant, would not interfere with the flow of mortgage funds. In a sense, home-building would be favored by a tight fiscal policy in much the same way it is hurt by a tight monetary policy. (Consumer and government spending would probably be penalized most by a tight fiscal policy, leaving home construction relatively unaffected.)

Congress, in its infinite wisdom, has opted for maintaining tight monetary policy *cum* selective credit programs rather than tinkering with tax rates and government expenditures during periods when anti-inflationary policy is the rule. Perhaps Congress knows something we don't about Fannie Mae and her friends. Or could it be vice versa?

19

EQUAL OPPORTUNITY IN BANKING:

THE CASE FOR AND AGAINST

JOB QUOTAS

In recent years, equal employment opportunity for women and minorities has become a declared objective of national economic policy. How can we best provide such equal job opportunity in banking, as well as elsewhere? One view is that job quotas would be a useful instrument toward this end, but this position is challenged by others who believe just as firmly that quotas would be more harmful than helpful.

Indicative of current polarization on this issue, the authors of this book hold opposite opinions on the subject of quotas. While we have been able to reconcile our differences on everything else, when it comes to quotas we find ourselves unable to agree. So in this chapter only we have to present our views separately. After reading both sides, you can come to your own conclusion (as you should on everything, anyway).

I. THE CASE FOR JOB QUOTAS (RITTER)

Job quotas have been advocated as a means of boring through the encrusted prejudice that, long after passage of the 1964 Civil Rights Act, still restricts employment opportunities for women and minorities. To get their "fair share" of jobs, proponents want quotas established, requiring that women and minorities be employed in virtually all occupations and at virtually all levels in rough proportion to their percentage distribution in the local labor force.

In reaction, angry opposition has arisen from employers, unions, ethnic groups, and religious organizations, almost irrespective of their "liberal" or "conservative" views on other issues. They maintain that hiring should be based solely on individual qualifications, that promotion should depend strictly on individual merit, without regard to a person's race, color, sex, religion, or national origin. Indeed, in executive suites and union halls, job quotas are usually considered a subject fit only for ridicule ("How about a quota in professional basketball for people less than six feet tall?").

Who is right? Are job quotas based on race or sex more likely to enhance equality of opportunity or destroy it?

Employment Patterns in Banking

The pattern of minority and female employment in the banking industry has been so widely publicized in recent years, that a brief recapitulation of some of the major findings is sufficient.

On the basis of 1966 data, Governor Andrew Brimmer of the Federal Reserve Board reported that only 4 percent of the jobs in banking were held by blacks, although they comprise about 10 percent of the population. In addition, one-third of those blacks who did work in banks were concentrated in the service workers category (janitors, and so on), even though service worker jobs are but a small fraction (5 percent) of total employment in banks. Further, among those blacks who were in white-collar bank jobs, almost none were at the professional or managerial level, although a fifth of all white-collar bank jobs fall into that classification. With respect to women, the pattern was somewhat different: almost all were white-collar workers, but hardly any above the office and clerical worker level (whereas half of the male white-collar workers in banks were in professional and managerial positions).

A later investigation (1971) by the Council on Economic Priorities revealed some improvement since the mid-1960s, but not enough to make more than a marginal change in the basic picture. Minorities were still concentrated disproportionately in service and clerical jobs, women still in clerical jobs. Relatively few of either were in professional or managerial positions (although more women are executives in banking than in any other industry).

Data for 1974—the most recent available—show that minorities represent 16 percent of the work force in banks but have only 5 percent of the professional or managerial positions. Women make up two-thirds of the work force in banks but have only one-fifth of the higher-ranking jobs. There appears to have been some progress in the late seventies and the early eighties, especially in the larger banks in the larger cities, but there is still a long way to go before we reach true equal employment opportunity for all.

Unfair Demand or Unqualified Supply?

By itself, the fact that minorities and women are concentrated disproportionately in lower-echelon bank jobs, if they are employed at all, does not prove that banks discriminate unfairly against them—just as the difficulties small businessmen have in getting bank loans when money is tight do not prove unfair bank discrimination against them. Banks give priority to their most creditworthy customers; since small businesses are more prone to default than larger ones, when funds become scarce small firms are likely to feel the pinch most. The pattern of employment in banking may similarly reflect, at least in part, a scarcity of women and minorities *qualified* to perform managerial or executive functions.

In other words, the present composition of employment in banking may be due to supply shortages as much as or more than demand biases. A similar argument has been made by many universities—they claim that try as they might they simply cannot find many female or minority group Ph.D.s to staff their faculties. Observation does confirm that banks and colleges seeking qualified women or minorities for higher-echelon positions have frequently encountered supply shortages, particularly in the past few years.

Why should this be? One does not have to look far, of course, to find the answer. Blacks and Puerto Ricans, to take two glaring examples, generally grow up in slum neighborhoods, go to grossly inferior schools, encounter majority group hostility at an early age, and learn in countless ways that the cards are stacked against them. In such an environment, childhood and adolescence involve not growing up but being ground down.

With respect to bank employment, two levels of discrimination are therefore relevant. One is job discrimination, prejudiced demand; the other is general environmental discrimination, ultimately responsible for shortages of qualified supply. Even if every bank in the country suddenly were to become an equal opportunity employer in fact as well as name, this would have little bearing on general environmental discrimination inflicted on minorities *before* they ever enter the job market. Given the prevalence of environmental discrimination, it is hardly surprising that a sudden reduction in job discrimination should find comparatively few minority group members ready for careers in banking.

It is not particularly fruitful to try to unravel which is more responsible for the present employment profile in banking—job discrimination that shrinks the demand for women and minorities, or general environmental discrimination that eventually shows up in the guise of unqualified supply—since it is necessary to reduce discrimination at both levels before significant improvement can occur in the composition of bank employment. Less job discrimination alone will lead only to unfillable demands for women and minorities, and less environmental discrimination alone will lead only to more college-educated typists and tellers.

The conclusion is obvious: A *multipronged* antidiscrimination program is necessary. Not so obvious is the key role, within this context, that job quotas can play.

Public Policy: Rhetoric or Numbers?

Governmental measures intended to expand equal employment opportunity include: (1) general rights legislation; (2) a variety of special-purpose manpower training programs (Neighborhood Youth Corps, Job Corps, New Careers); and, most recently, (3) promotion of "affirmative action" programs, setting forth "goals" and "timetables" for hiring and advancing women and minorities.

At first, opposition to "affirmative action" was neither more nor less vocal than opposition to any proposed remedy for discriminatory employment practices. Antagonism escalated, however, as soon as government officials—under pressure from minority groups—suggested that employers and unions move beyond general goals and actually specify the *number* of women and minorities they planned to admit at various levels over a scheduled time period. The reaction was vehement. The *New York Times,* for example, speaking for many who had previously approved of "affirmative action" programs, warned of "the danger of turning the government's fair employment goals and timetables into covert quotas," and commended those government officials who had shown awareness of the "peril" (editorial, October 12, 1972).

General goals—in the form of "good faith and effort"—evidently meet with widespread approval. But when the goals are made more specific, their content concrete in the form of numbers, then approval rapidly shifts to opposition. Any numerical employment goal can always be expressed as a quota, and vice versa—that is, an employment objective can be expressed in terms of so many workers (a goal) or in terms of a certain percentage of a company's work force (a quota).

Thus, when quotas are denounced, what is really being condemned is the evolution of a *general* goal into a *quantitative* one. Since it is difficult to implement, enforce, or even evaluate a goal until it is quantified, apparently "affirmative action" programs are acceptable to many when they affirm but not when they act.

Fortunately, the United States Supreme Court has taken a meaningful stand in favor of action as well as affirmation. The landmark 1978 *Bakke* decision, for example, permits colleges and universities to treat race and minority status as a positive factor in the admissions process. Colleges and universities can not establish "quotas" or guarantee a specific number of places for minority students and women, but they can set "numerical goals" in rough and general terms. Similarly, the 1979 *Weber* decision upheld affirmative action programs designed to correct past discriminatory practices as manifest in racial imbalances in employment, and the 1980 *Fullilove* v. *Klutznick* decision explicitly endorsed the power of Congress to take racial status into account in awarding federal contracts.

Opposition to job quotas and quantitative goals can be classified under three headings:

1. You Can't Fight Human Nature—the objective of equal employment opportunity is misguided.

2. The Private Sector Can Take Care of It—the objective is worthy, but it lies outside the legitimate scope of governmental intervention.

3. You're on the Right Track But the Wrong Road—the objective is worthy, and government intervention to achieve it is desirable, but job quotas and numerical goals are not the proper means to use.

You Can't Fight Human Nature

To many, the whole idea of equal employment is misguided. By virtue of thousands of years of Darwinian natural selection, combined with the blessings of free enterprise, employment and responsibility already are distributed in accordance with talent and ability. The people on top are there because they can do the job, and those in the middle and on the bottom are there because that's where they belong. Men are men and women are women. Whites are white and blacks are black, and Puerto Ricans and Chicanos shouldn't be here to begin with. If people would only learn their place and do their job properly, we'd all be better off.

It is difficult to argue logically against this position. In effect, it speaks for itself.

The Private Sector Can Take Care of It

To others, the objective of equal employment opportunity is worthy, but it lies outside the legitimate scope of governmental intervention. The problem, it is said, can best be resolved by leaving it to the initiative of the private sector. But the private sector, left to its own devices, has not eliminated discrimination. And in this day and age, it is difficult to imagine any general principle that would bar the government from the pursuit of equal employment opportunity, while at the same time permitting the present scope and depth of government involvement elsewhere in the economy.

In fact, federally supervised job quotas would do no more

than combine three well-established areas of federal activity. Government actions directed toward employment in general have been well accepted since the Employment Act of 1946, as have government activities regarding discrimination in general since the Civil Rights Act of 1964 (not to mention the Fourteenth Amendment of 1868). And government quota-setting is nothing new either—witness crude oil import quotas, farm acreage allotment quotas, and immigration quotas, to name but three.

The Federal Reserve Act itself contains not one, but two quotas. With respect to the Board of Directors of each Federal Reserve Bank, directors by statute specifically represent banking interests, commercial interests, and the general public. With respect to the Board of Governors in Washington, membership is limited to no more than one governor from a Federal Reserve District, and the Board's composition must also reflect "fair representation" of the country's financial, agricultural, commercial, and industrial interests.

You're On the Right Track but the Wrong Road

More typical of objections to job quotas and numerical goals is the widely held view that while the objective of equal employment opportunity is worth pursuing, and governmental intervention to achieve it desirable, nevertheless these are not the proper means to use: hiring and promotion should *always* be determined by individual merit, *never* on the basis of racial, religious, sexual, or nationality criteria. Governmental antidiscrimination measures should be confined to general civil rights legislation, manpower training programs, and the like.

At the outset, a distinction should be drawn between means and ends, between the methods used to achieve objectives and the objectives themselves. And it should be made clear that proponents of job quotas *also* seek hiring and promotion based on individual merit. The real dispute is, therefore, not about objectives, but about the most effective means of reaching them. Can equal job opportunity, based on individual ability, be more realistically attained with or without the use of quotas? Opponents of numerical goals argue that their very use subverts equal opportunity, by substituting racial, sexual, or nationality criteria in place of individual merit.

In more general terms, the issue is whether *any* ultimate objective can ever be achieved through means that apparently contradict it. In such general terms, without specific reference to employment, it should be clear that ultimate objectives indeed *are* frequently realized via methods that on the surface appear contradictory. Men fight to preserve peace, surgeons amputate to maintain life, families consume less (this year) to consume more (next year), and banks sacrifice earnings (in the short run) to increase earnings (in the long run). Sometimes it works and sometimes it doesn't. In the final analysis, each individual case can only be decided on the basis of its unique circumstances.

The Merits of Quotas

With specific reference to equal employment opportunity as an objective, the merits of job quotas and quantitative goals as a means toward that end are more persuasive than generally realized:

1. It is popular to be for job "goals" for minorities and women, and against "quotas." But, as noted, a quota is nothing more than a quantitative goal. Only by attaching numbers to a goal can it be assessed as to its reasonableness, implemented according to a time schedule, evaluated on the basis of performance, and enforced objectively. In practical terms, the only goals that are operational—in contrast to rhetorical—are quantitative ones.

2. The main reason for proposing job quotas—requiring that women and minorities be employed, in virtually all occupations and at virtually all levels, in rough proportion to their percentage distribution in the local labor force—is not to start the use of racial, sexual, or nationality criteria in employment, but to stop it. Job quotas are not advocated in a vacuum. They are advocated as an antidote to the widespread implicit quotas that already exist, quotas that already employ racial, religious, and sexual criteria—but use them *against* minorities and women.

Proposed quotas are typically judged by comparing them with ideal conditions, wherein everyone is hired and promoted strictly on the basis of individual merit. But such a comparison is misleading; in the real world at the present time those ideal conditions simply do not exist. The realistic comparison is between the informal, quietly administered quotas that currently protect entrenched privilege and restrict opportunity; and formal, mutually established, and government-enforced quotas that would break down such barriers and expand opportunity. To be against opportunity-expanding quotas today because one has been opposed to opportunity-restricting quotas in the past is like taking a stand against the scalpel because one is opposed to the dagger.

3. It is frequently argued that quotas will reduce efficiency and thereby raise costs. It is not immediately apparent, however, why job quotas should be any more efficiency-inhibiting than many other widely accepted employment practices—such as, for example, seniority in the factory and tenure in the classroom, both of which involve employment criteria other than individual ability. Seniority in the factory favors longtime employees, although newer ones may be more productive; tenure in the university protects the jobs of older professors, although younger ones may be better teachers and more capable scholars. Why is it that seniority and tenure are not opposed with the same intensity as employment goals for minorities and women?

4. Job quotas are no panacea. They cannot do the job alone. They are obviously most directly applicable in counteracting job discrimination (prejudiced demand). But their effectiveness is minimized without a corresponding diminution in general environmental discrimination, to expand the supply of qualified women and minorities.

General environmental discrimination is not directly susceptible to treatment by job quotas. More relevant are other governmental policies that would meaningfully upgrade the quality and quantity of low-income housing, radically improve inner city public school systems, expand federally sponsored job training programs, and so on. Even here, however, job quotas have indirect implications: once established, they would put many who have traditionally lobbied against such programs in a position where, for the first time, they have a financial stake in their success. If hiring and promotion were quota-influenced, for example, business firms would be more directly concerned with the quality of ghetto schools. And if blacks and other minorities were not such a disproportionate percentage of the unemployed, public policies to reduce both aggregate and structural unemployment would probably be more vigorously pursued.

Put somewhat differently, as matters stand the costs of both job discrimination and general environmental discrimination are now borne entirely by those who are discriminated against. Job quotas would force a more equal sharing of those costs among the population as a whole. The more widely the costs are distributed, the more likely that the political process will generate real pressures to eliminate the underlying discrimination.

5. In summary, the main reason for imposing job quotas is the prevalence of already existing discriminatory practices. The ultimate objective of quotas is equality of employment opportunity, elimination of discrimination, and thus their own demise. When there is no more discrimination, there will be no more need for quotas.

Quotas per se are neither good nor bad, any more than nuclear energy, drugs, or money can be said, per se, to be good or bad. Some quotas restrict opportunity and some expand it. Even among those that expand it, the desirability of any particular quota system cannot be evaluated in the abstract. It depends, in each instance, on the reasons for establishing it; the alternatives to it; its applicability to the particular type of job, occupation, or profession; and its specific provisions, including the time schedule set for its targets to be reached. These are the concrete issues that deserve serious consideration, within realistic contexts, not whether quotas in the abstract are "right" or "wrong." It would be ironic if such matters continue to be dismissed out of hand by invocation of the very ideal that they could help make a reality: hiring and promotion based, in fact as well as principle, on individual merit—regardless of race, color, sex, religion, or national origin.

II. DON'T DO IT WITH QUOTAS (SILBER)

There are good quotas and bad quotas—good for me and bad for you; good for banking, but bad for basketball; good for financial institutions, bad for football. To those advocating quotas to redress imbalances in the employment of "minority groups" in banking and financial institutions, I respond with an equally disturbing proposal: quotas to rectify imbalances in the employment of "minority groups" in football or basketball. The minority groups are quite different in each case and are necessarily defined within a very specific context. Blacks and women (at 51 percent of the population, obviously not a real minority) are the *relevant* minority groups as far as the business world is concerned, while in the sports world the underprivileged are skinny kids with glasses.

That is a ridiculous analogy. Everyone knows that basketball demands certain skills. Requiring 25 percent (or whatever the relevant number is) of all professional basketball players to have such *irrelevant* characteristics is certain to do at least three things: destroy the incentive of some to invest their own time, money, and effort to develop the requisite basketball skills; penalize those who have already done so;

and lower the quality of the product that is offered the public.

Most quotas are bad—they introduce the same type of distortions and inequities as the ones just ridiculed. And yet, there are "good" quotas of which we are very proud—one man, one vote; equal radio and TV time for candidates to public office; 100 percent of all children under sixteen must be in school. And there are quotas that are quite necessary —100 percent of those without driver's licenses cannot sit behind the steering wheel. Quotas that set a floor, a minimum percentage, for minority employment in banking or any other industry do not fall into the category of either proud quotas or necessary quotas. They are bad quotas that must be resisted in favor of other means of redressing the evils of any type of discrimination.

The Need for Government Intervention

The rationale of a free market economy, as opposed to one that is centrally planned, rests on the foundation that the decisions of what to produce, how, and for whom, are best made within a competitive environment, with each individual free to "do his own thing" based on the information he receives from the price system. This is not the place to go into the elegant proofs of efficiency of the price system. Let us assume it is so, just as we can also assume that discrimination by sex, race, or religion is bad, and that it exists.

There are situations, of course, when the price system is faulty, and here government intervention is called for. The price system, for example, rewards each individual according to the quality of his or her own performance. But what if my actions also benefit others? If I educate myself, I benefit because of increased future earnings, but others benefit because I am literate and because I behave more civilly (presumably). The solution—encourage literacy and civics via free public education. Similarly, if my actions injure others, the price system is also modified. I may be able to afford a car—but if I drive it without knowing how, others may be killed. The solution—the motor vehicles bureau and licensing.

Another type of intervention comes in the form of "it's good for you even though you don't know it." In general, consumers buy what they like, and that's why the price they are willing to pay is a good measure of the value of the product. But under some conditions the government suspends the price system to "give us what is good for us" (can we ever get too much of a good thing?)—free milk to schoolchildren rather than a dime to buy whatever they like.

In some areas the price system is eliminated completely. In politics, unlike economics, the quota is one man, one vote, not one dollar, one vote. The price system has been eliminated because of philosophical and ethical principles inherent in the democratic form of government.

Finally, the government intervenes when free competition is prevented from operating: when prices don't reflect consumers' desires—they are set by monopolists; or when an individual is not rewarded according to the quality of his or her own performance (or is denied access to the requisite education or training)—because of artificial barriers to entry.

This last category justifies government intervention in the form of antitrust legislation and antidiscrimination laws. Quotas for minority employment must be justified in this context if they are to be accepted as a legitimate form of government interference with the market.

There is surely no philosophical or ethical principle that would *require* women or blacks to make up 27.3 or 42.6 percent of middle management positions in banking; there is only the principle that they have the opportunity to do so. *Equality of opportunity is the watchword, not equality of result.* Similarly, while there might be benefits to some if women or blacks make up a minimum portion of the banking industry, there are others who might be hurt. Discrimination by race, sex, or religion must be eliminated, but the use of minority employment quotas is just a means toward achieving that goal, certainly not an end in itself. It must be justified as the best means toward that end, or fall by the wayside in favor of some other mechanism for setting things right.

The Economics of Quotas

It would be hard to find an economist who prefers the long-run results of minimum employment quotas to an effectively implemented set of antidiscrimination laws. The solution to monopoly power is to break it up via antitrust legislation, not to give other firms similar market strength. The analogy to discrimination in employment is perfect; the solution is effective implementation of antidiscrimination laws and not perpetuating the discrimination ethos by quotas for each section of the population. In the extreme, that solution approaches the most abhorrent of them all—the caste system in India.

Quotas are more popular among noneconomists, especially politicians, or political-minded economists. The reasons are not hard to find. Quotas seem to be a quick way to achieve the objective of equal employment treatment of races, ethnics, and sexes. They also are beloved by politicians because they don't cost anything in federal or state budgets; they don't create the need for taxes. One doesn't have to be from Missouri to be suspicious of quick solutions that don't have any apparent costs. And in this case the doubts are well founded.

Quotas impose real costs on society which are very difficult to measure but are there nevertheless. One serious drawback, therefore, of minimum employment quotas compared with other antidiscrimination tools is that we cannot measure their real cost. An intelligent government program must be evaluated in terms of costs versus benefits. When taxes are imposed to implement a program, they are a straightforward measure of costs. When they are compared with the benefits of the program, it is possible to decide if people are better off without (both the taxes and the program). Not so with quotas.

Minimum employment quotas impose at least two categories of costs. First, there is the direct cost to a bank of training less qualified applicants for a job. The barriers to entry that create the problems of discrimination in employment stem, in part, from inferior educations provided by ghetto schools and by the social mores characteristic of our society. While there still may be many who are merely "standing at the gates waiting to get in," a significant problem involves removing the legacy of discrimination that began further back in the chain. Retraining, reeducating, and rehabilitating (the three R's) the relevant minority groups is certainly a cost that will be incurred. There is no reason for such costs, stemming largely from the failure of society as a whole, to be borne by individual banks or other firms.

But even if individual banks are at fault (because they set up artificial barriers) and are willing to redress the legacy of discrimination and absorb the cost of the three R's, there is an even more significant, if less obvious, set of costs imposed by quotas. Those who have already invested time, money, and effort to acquire the requisite training and skills will be deprived of their expected returns by administrative fiat. Furthermore, incentives that are a crucial component of a free market economy, insuring that resources are used in the best possible way, will be destroyed. A bank may appear magnanimous in its willingness to absorb the costs of breaking down discriminatory practices. But in reality, it is absorbing only a small fraction of the costs; it shifts the remainder onto society as a whole (reduced incentives), and it also burdens innocent bystanders with the pecuniary and nonpecuniary costs of having prepared themselves for a productive role in the economy, only to be denied access under the rubric of justice to others.

One can certainly argue that a bank in violation of antidiscrimination laws should be fined, and rather severely (treble damages?). But the question of who should bear the full costs of removing discrimination by race, sex, or religion is quite another matter. A clear case can be made for society as a whole, since discrimination and unequal opportunity are perpetrated by many institutions and at different stages. That suggests distributing the costs via the best vehicle governments have yet devised—taxation. Joseph Pechman, a tax expert from the Brookings Institution, emphasizes that the objective of any tax system is to distribute the cost of government fairly; whatever the shortcomings of the tax system, there is no better way for us to proceed.

A less popular case can be made for the group that benefits most to bear the costs of removing discrimination. While collective action is necessary to remove discriminatory practices, those who are the objects of discrimination stand to gain most from their removal, hence they should bear the greatest portion of the costs. This suggests self-help organizations, lobbying groups, economic boycotts, and so on, in order to force society to eliminate discrimination. The cost of change in such instances is borne primarily by the minorities, not by society, and there is sufficient precedent for such self-help groups organized by many different minorities in their fight for equal rights.

None of the arguments suggests that the costs ought to be imposed on those who have already invested time, money, and effort in acquiring skills. Nor do they suggest that the costs should come in the form of reduced incentives. In fact, the optimum type of government intervention in such matters comes when individual incentives are left unimpaired. *There is a reasonable case for using the tax system to distribute the costs, and a less reasonable case for using the benefit principle, but there is no case at all for using a haphazard, inequitable, and inefficient mechanism such as quotas.*

The Political Economy of Quotas

Alexander Hamilton, the first Secretary of the Treasury, unwittingly made the best case for minimum employment quotas for minorities. In particular, he argued for tariffs or quotas on foreign goods in order to protect "infant industries" in the young American economy. While interference with free trade via tariffs causes inefficiencies, it may be justified in order to permit an industry to get started; once started, it will be able to hold its own without protection. The tariff is just a temporary measure which will be suspended when the industry grows up. Similarly, minimum employment quotas, so the argument goes, are a temporary means for getting minorities started in heretofore "foreign" occupations. Once the barrier is broken, quotas will be removed and minorities will fend for themselves.

Paul Samuelson provided the best commentary on protecting infant industries via tariffs or quotas: history reveals that most such cases produce perpetual infants. Once imposed, quotas are almost impossible to remove; while they are justified as *short-run solutions* they are transformed, via political realities, into *long-run institutions.*

Quota-lovers simply cannot be taken seriously when the minimum employment quotas for minorities are put forth as a temporary means to achieve the lofty goal of nondiscrimination by race and sex. In fact, it is paradoxical that quotas should be used in this context, since that is the very thing we are trying to root out. They are proposing minimum quotas to destroy maximum quotas (no blacks or women). Aside from the reasonable proposition that minimum employment quotas should be just as illegal as maximum quotas (anyone living in an apartment house readily recognizes that one person's floor is someone else's ceiling), they also perpetuate the race and sex differences they seek to overcome. As long as there are other means to achieve the objective, one need not adopt methods of tenuous legality and dubious morality.

The Right Way

What means should be used to redress the evils of discrimination? The best solution is vigorous enforcement of the antidiscrimination laws in education and employment. Great strides have already been made in this regard. As far back as 1971, Governor Andrew Brimmer of the Federal Reserve Board presented a study to the NAACP and said, "it is also clear from the above analysis that blacks who are well-prepared to compete for higher paying positions in the upper reaches of the occupation structure have made measurable gains." Brimmer goes on to point out, however, the continued underrepresentation (less than their 11 percent of the total population) of blacks in well-paying "prestigious" occupations. But Brimmer's data also reveal that the gains made between 1960 and 1970 were substantial: an increase of over 50 percent (from 4.4 to 6.9 percent of total employment) in white-collar professional and technical work, and an increase of over 40 percent (from 4.8 to 6.8 percent of total employment) in the craftsmen and foremen category of blue-collar workers. Special note is made of progress in communications, banking, and insurance. While Brimmer's data have not been updated, there is good reason to believe that similar gains continued through the 1970s.

As an aside, it should be noted that I am using employment percentage numbers with great reservation, fully cognizant of their serious limitations in proving or revealing anything about discrimination. There is little reason to expect each ethnic group to be represented proportionately in all occupations. While intelligence may be normally distributed in the population, we do not, cannot, and should not assume that occupational choice is unaffected by family background and social interrelationships.

We can certainly do more in implementing antidiscrimination statutes. But it must be done on an individual, case-by-case basis. The speed with which individual violations are heard and adjudicated is of great importance. Government funds must be spent to set up "human rights commissions" and to streamline hearings of individual cases. The existence of quick access to the courts, accompanied by stiff pecuniary penalties to those found guilty, will help employers and others recognize the futility and potential costs of setting up artificial barriers.

Efficient and effective judicial review is not costless. Indeed, one of the advantages of this mechanism is that we know what it costs. It has none of the drawbacks of quotas and it militates against their perpetuation.

A case might also be made, not only to destroy discriminatory practices, but to help *all* those at the poverty level to overcome their lack of skills so that they can become more productive members in the economy. Manpower retraining programs, subsidies, or tax credits to employers who retrain those who are unemployed or those whose incomes are below a certain level can be instituted. But care must be taken *not* to tie eligibility to race, sex, or ethnic background. Information about such programs should be distributed widely and frequently, not only to black ghettos, but to all potential participants. Despite the stereotyped notions of who is poor, they aren't all or even mostly black. The others deserve as much or as little retraining and preferential treatment as the minorities currently in the public eye.

Knowing how much the antipoverty-discrimination programs cost in terms of foregone tax revenues (in the case of tax credits) and/or increased budget expenditures is a prerequisite for intelligent government intervention. We then can tell how much we are willing to give up for such matters. We are also able to distribute the costs equitably, via taxation. *Quotas sweep the costs out of sight, but not out of society.* Quotas appear to have the advantage of producing quick results, but they may not be much faster than an appropriate level of budget expenditure or tax relief. Every proponent of quotas submits a timetable, knowing full well that the shorter the horizon the greater the distortions and inequities. The types of programs listed here can match that timetable with an appropriate level of expenditure, only now we'll know what it really costs.

However appealing to those clamoring for action, quotas in banking and in every other industry hide the true costs, create inequities in the process, cause short-run and long-run misallocations compared with other solutions—and may not be any quicker in achieving the goal of equal employment opportunity.

PART VII

International Finance

20

MONEY IN INTERNATIONAL

FINANCE

The United States has had a deficit in its international balance of payments almost every year since 1949, which, as everyone knows, is a Bad Thing. As a result we have lost more than half of our gold, and *this,* it goes without saying, is an even more Serious Matter. We were the proud owners of 700 million ounces of gold in 1949, and now we have only about 275 million ounces left.

What to do?

An international "balance of payments" is an accounting record of all payments made across national borders. For each country it shows the payments made to foreigners and the receipt of funds from them, in the same way that a family might keep a record of all its expenditures and receipts. Americans make payments to others, for example, when we import foreign goods, buy foreign securities, lend to other countries, build factories on the outskirts of London or in the suburbs of Rome, or travel abroad on our summer vacations. On the other side of the ledger, we take in money when foreigners pay us for our exports, buy our stocks or bonds, build television factories in Illinois, or visit the Grand Canyon.

A deficit in our balance of payments is no different from

a deficit in a household's budget. It means that we have been paying out more money abroad than we have been taking in, possibly because we have been importing more than we have been exporting, or because more Americans are visiting Paris and London than foreign tourists are taking in the sights of Yonkers and Yazoo City. Foreigners thereby accumulate more dollars than they need for their payments to us, and in the ordinary course of events—at least prior to 15 August 1971—many of these dollars were presented to the United States Treasury with a polite but firm request that they be exchanged for gold. Until 15 August 1971 the Treasury stood ready to honor, promptly if not happily, all official foreign requests at the rate of one ounce of gold for every $35 tendered, but on that date President Nixon got tired of paying out so much gold and called the whole deal off.

A nation can hardly run balance of payments deficits forever (although the United States does seem determined to prove otherwise). Sooner or later, after all, a country has to pay for its imports, and to do that it has to get the money from somewhere—for example, by borrowing from abroad or by selling some of its own products to others (i.e., by exporting). To that end, a number of suggestions are constantly made to cure our chronic deficit—to stop paying out more than we take in. One remedy that has often been proposed by many in the international financial community, and occasionally echoed by some here at home, is old-fashioned discipline, otherwise known as the time-honored hickory stick treatment.

The Discipline of the Balance of Payments

Balance of payments disciplinarians believe that to spare the rod is to spoil the child. Their recommendations as to how we should go about restoring equilibrium in our international accounts are appropriately strict. The Federal Reserve should administer the hickory stick by contracting the money supply and raising interest rates until tight money succeeds in reducing GNP and lowering wages and prices. It is difficult to estimate how much unemployment this might involve—perhaps 15 or 20 percent of the labor force, at a minimum.

With a depression-level GNP, the incomes of Americans would be so low that we would be hard put to afford such "luxuries" as travel abroad and the purchase of so many foreign products. In addition, there would be effects stemming from the change in prices here relative to prices abroad. With lower costs and prices in the United States, foreign goods become relatively more expensive, which discourages Americans from buying so many Volkswagens and Japanese transistor radios, thus reducing our imports. The lower price tags here would similarly encourage foreigners to buy more of our now cheaper goods and services, thereby expanding our exports. Less imports and more exports: we will be paying out less money abroad and taking in more, thus reducing and possibly eliminating our balance of payments deficit.

At the same time, it is expected that purely financial flows would reinforce these effects. The higher interest rates that tight money induces here would bring in some foreign money seeking our attractive-yielding securities, and domestic money that had formerly been invested in foreign securities would presumably now return home to buy bargain-priced American stocks and bonds.

This is called Defending the Dollar. Obviously it is not a pleasant process, involving as it does tight money to induce substantial unemployment—large enough to wring lower wages and prices out of the economy—and a shrinking GNP. It is clear that it is based on the well-known Rocky Marciano Principle, that the best defense is a good offense: we defend the dollar by attacking the economy.

For those of you too young to remember, Rocky Marciano (Rocco Francis Marchegiano) was the world heavyweight boxing champion from September 1952 until he retired undefeated in April 1956. He never learned to box very well, but he didn't have to. He had forty-nine professional fights and won all of them, forty-three by knockouts.

Professor Marciano thus takes his place in the Annals of Economics, right behind Professor Phillips, of Phillips Curve fame (see Chapter 6) and Professor E. J. Finagle, discoverer of Finagle's Law ("Inanimate objects are out to get us"). Of course, like all firm discipline, the Marciano Principle is administered reluctantly and only for our own good. Rest assured, it would hurt the Federal Reserve more than it would hurt the economy; the Federal Reserve said so itself when, on the basis of this sort of reasoning, it *raised* the discount rate from 1½ percent to 2½ percent on 9 October 1931 and then to 3½ percent on 16 October, a week later. (By 1931 the Great Depression was something more than a speck on the horizon; GNP had already fallen 25 percent below its 1929 level, and unemployment had already risen to over 15 percent of the labor force.)

The Gold Standard

The gold standard, which was in effect throughout much of the Western world during the last half of the 1800s and the first few decades of the 1900s, represented the Marciano Principle in action. What was the gold standard and how was it supposed to work?

Under the traditional gold standard, nations fixed the value of their money in terms of gold and stood ready to buy or sell gold freely at the established price. This necessarily resulted in a fixed exchange ratio of one nation's money in terms of another's, called the par (or parity) rate of exchange. Say the United States fixed 20 dollars an ounce as the price of gold and Great Britain decided upon 5 pounds an ounce: then the par rate of exchange would be 4 dollars for 1 pound, for both $4 and £1 could purchase equal amounts of gold.

This fixed rate of exchange was quite stable. It would not vary above or below par by more than the cost of shipping gold across the Atlantic. If an American importer of £100 worth of British goods (woolen underwear) found that he was being charged more than $400 plus gold shipping costs in order to get the 100 British pounds he needed to pay his supplier, he could always buy $400 worth of gold (20 ounces) from the U.S. Treasury and ship it to England at his own expense to discharge his obligation. Thus the price of a unit of foreign money could only rise to an upper limit, known as the gold export point, which was above the par of exchange by the amount of gold shipping costs.

Similarly, the price of foreign money could not fall below par by more than the cost of shipping gold. If an American exporter of $400 worth of snuff boxes to England found that he would be offered less than $400 minus gold shipping costs for the 100 British pounds he had coming, he could always simply request that 20 ounces of gold be shipped here at his expense. Thus the lower limit of the foreign exchange rate was called the gold import point.

Under the rules of the gold standard, the money supply of every nation was tied rigidly to its gold supply. The gold standard was then expected to be a self-equilibrating mechanism in which balance of payments deficits and surpluses were automatically corrected by flows of gold among nations. This gold flow mechanism was expected to work just like the hickory stick treatment. Say the United States had a deficit in its balance of payments because it had been importing more than it had been exporting. It would make up this deficit by shipping gold abroad. This would mean less gold here and more gold in Great Britain, which would decrease the money supply in the United States and increase the money supply in Great Britain. Tight money here and an enlarged money supply abroad would lead to lower prices and wages here and to higher prices and wages abroad. With lower prices and wages here relative to abroad, Americans would be discouraged from buying any more woolen underwear from England and the British would find our snuff boxes even better bargains than before. So our imports fall, our exports expand, and our balance of payments deficit is corrected. This is precisely the same as the Marciano Principle: We drive the domestic economy into recession in order to improve our international balance of payments!

This sacrifice of domestic stability on the altar of international stability led to the downfall of the gold standard in the early 1930s, and there is little likelihood that it will ever return. Nowadays, no nation is about to abdicate control over its domestic financial affairs in favor of gold or anything like it. Before the development of modern monetary and fiscal policies, government intervention to influence the economy was unknown; because they knew no better, nations suffered through depressions and inflations and simply waited for times to improve. But it is not possible to turn back the clock. It is an open question whether modern monetary-fiscal policies actually do more good than harm, but any administration that failed to take strong action to alleviate recessions and inflations—and tried to invoke gold as the reason for its inaction—would hardly remain long in office. Today monetary policy is expected to actively alter monetary and credit conditions to influence domestic economic activity, not to passively adapt to changes in our gold stock merely because it might restore equilibrium in our balance of international payments.

Historically, a main function of the gold standard was to serve as a safeguard against inflation, by tying the money supply to gold and thereby providing an upper limit on the money-issuing power of the state. Insofar as governments of all sorts have a propensity to print excessive amounts of money in order to finance wars and circuses, it was thought that gold would play a useful role by forcing governments to live within their means. No more gold, no more money.

However, in reality gold has usually proved to be extremely unreliable in preventing inflation. Even in the good old days (remember them?), when coins were the sole circulating money, kings and princes found ways to circumvent any gold shortage by clipping the coins and changing the rules. And today, with most of our money in the form of demand deposits at commercial banks and with electronic money on the horizon, any conceivable connection between gold and the money supply is too tenuous to rely on as an effective means of preventing excessive monetary expansion. The need to prevent inflation is undeniable, but gold has never been dependable in that respect and is even less likely to be so today.

Nevertheless, one remnant of the gold standard did manage to hang on until rather recently—until 1973, as a matter of fact. At the end of World War II the nations of the world agreed to maintain fixed and inflexible exchange rates, more or less as under the gold standard. This led to periodic financial crises, as we shall see in the next chapter. Before turning to the performance of fixed exchange rates in the postwar period, however, let's examine another alternative: flexible (or floating) exchange rates.

Floating Exchange Rates

Another possible cure for a balance-of-payments deficit, one that does not clash so violently with the goals of high employment, stable prices, and economic growth, is to permit flexibility in the price of foreign money (or, what amounts to the same thing, in the foreign price of dollars). Say a Mexican peso costs Americans 5 cents and a French franc costs us 25 cents. Until early 1973, such prices of one kind of money in terms of another—or exchange rates—were rigidly fixed by international agreement under the overall supervision of the International Monetary Fund (IMF), an institution established at an international monetary conference held at Bretton Woods, New Hampshire, in 1944.

The IMF's main function was to oversee the stability of exchange rates, although it was really unable to prevent unilateral exchange rate alterations when nations individually decided it was in their self-interest to make such changes. From World War II until 1973 world monetary arrangements were based on a network of more or less fixed (or pegged) exchange rates, supervised by the IMF.

The alternative to a system of fixed exchange rates is to unpeg them, and let them float freely in accordance with supply and demand conditions for each particular country's money. An increase in the *supply* of Mexican pesos would lower their price, say from 5 cents to 4 cents a peso; an increase in the *demand* for French francs would raise their price, say from 25 cents to 30 cents a franc. This was not permitted under IMF monetary arrangements until 1973; actually, it wasn't *officially* permitted until 1976.

Remember that a deficit in our balance of payments means we are paying out more money abroad than we are taking in. American importers are paying out more dollars for Swiss cuckoo clocks and Scotch whisky than foreigners need to buy our exported Frisbees and Fords. Result: An excess supply of dollars (or an excess demand for foreign money, since you can look at it either way) builds up throughout the world.

When exchange rates are free to fluctuate in response to supply and demand, the excess supply of dollars—due to our spending so much abroad—depresses the price of dollars to foreigners. The dollar *depreciates* relative to other monies. (Instead of the French having to pay 4 francs to get a dollar, something *less* than 4 francs would get them that much of our money.)

Or you could look at the same thing from the other side of the transaction, in which case an excess supply of dollars translates into an excess demand for other monies. When we import toenail clippers from Hong Kong or hitchhike along the not-so-sunny coast of Portugal, we have to buy their money to make payments. You can either say we are supplying dollars or buying (demanding) foreign money. From the

latter point of view, this excess demand for foreign money—
due to our spending so much abroad—raises the price of
foreign money to Americans. Other monies *appreciate* relative to the dollar. (Instead of Americans getting a franc for
25 cents, we would have to pay *more* to get 1 franc.)

This depreciation of the dollar (or appreciation of other
monies) has two effects. First, dollars become cheaper for
foreigners, so our goods and services automatically become
less expensive for them even though our domestic price tags
remain unchanged. After all, it makes no difference to them
whether our goods are less expensive for them because our
price tags are lower (the Marciano method) or because each
United States dollar costs them less of their own money while
our price tags stay the same (the flexible exchange rate
method). In either case our goods are cheaper for foreigners
to buy, and our exports are likely to expand.

Second, foreign monies now cost us more, so that foreign
goods and services automatically become more expensive for
us to buy. With foreign products costing us more, because
foreign money costs more, our purchases from abroad—our
imports—are likely to fall.

Thus the end results are the same as the Marciano route:
more exports and less imports. We take in more francs and
pesos as we receive payment for our enlarged exports, and
pay out less dollars abroad because of our lower imports,
thereby putting an end to both the deficit in our balance of
payments and the depreciation of the dollar. However, we
achieve these results by letting exchange rates decline while
keeping our economy stable, instead of by sending the economy into a nosedive while keeping exchange rates stable.

Freely floating exchange rates are a sharp departure from
international monetary arrangements as they existed prior to
1973. Until then, fixed exchange rates—called par values—

ruled the roost. The 1973 crisis in international finance (to be discussed in the next chapter) moved the world toward exchange rate flexibility. In January of 1976 the IMF officially approved the present system of floating exchange rates.

Most academic economists, both Monetarist and Keynesian, lean toward floating exchange rates. Most bankers and government officials, on the other hand, seem to favor a system of fixed exchange rates; they argue that freely floating rates create so much uncertainty regarding the price of foreign money that *international* trade is seriously impaired. Advocates of rate flexibility reply that fixed rates often create so much disruption at home—by forcing countries to adjust their economies instead of their exchange rates—that they seriously inhibit *domestic* trade (that is, GNP).

Since early 1973 flexible exchange rates have gained the upper hand. But the advocates of fixed rates have not given up the fight by any means; they are waiting in the wings, hoping that floating rates sink so that fixed rates can surface once again.

21

INTERNATIONAL FINANCIAL CRISES

AND THE COLLAPSE OF FIXED

EXCHANGE RATES

One thing that fixed exchange rate arrangements provided in abundance was intermittent crises in world financial markets, tremors that nearly everyone agonized over although hardly anyone was really quite sure what was going on. Just to say that exchange rates were fixed didn't necessarily make it so, especially when forces of supply and demand were constantly impinging on them. It is in the story of how they were fixed, and in what had to be done to keep them from fluctuating, that we find the reasons underlying almost every monetary crisis that erupted abroad during the past quarter century—as well as the seeds of the two Big Ones that finally exploded both at home and abroad in 1971 and 1973, and at long last brought the House of Fixed Rates tumbling down.

The Genesis of International Monetary Crises

Remember how floating exchange rates operate? When a country runs a balance of payments deficit, its money *depreciates* relative to other monies; its outflows of funds exceed inflows, pumping too much of its own money abroad, and this burgeoning supply leads to a decline in its relative value. In turn, this relative depreciation of its money should expand the deficit country's exports, contract its imports, and thereby restore its balance of payments to equilibrium.

But with fixed exchange rates, as they existed from the end of World War II until 1973, the process never got off the ground. By international agreement (under the IMF), a deficit country that saw its money start to depreciate had to promptly step in to stop the decline. It did so by buying up its own money in order to mop up the excess supply. However, it couldn't buy up its own money by offering more of the same in exchange—which, as a government, it could simply print—because that's what people were *selling*, not buying. It had to use *other* money to buy up its own, and this other money is called its international reserves.

Traditionally, international reserves have been held in the form of gold, because of its general acceptability. Since the end of World War II, however, most foreign countries have held a substantial portion of their reserves in the form of U.S. dollars, which generally have been just about as acceptable as gold in making international payments. They also hold other kinds of "foreign exchange" among their reserves—pounds, marks, francs, and so on—but mostly they hold U.S. dollars. Other nations acquire dollars when we run our deficits and then hold them as their reserves.

In general, countries use their reserves in the same way

individuals and business use their cash balances—to bridge temporary gaps between the receipt and expenditure of funds, to tide them over periods when inflows of funds are slack, and to meet unexpected or emergency needs. *In particular,* with a system of fixed exchange rates, countries also used reserves to intervene in foreign exchange markets whenever the value of their money threatened to slide away from par (its agreed-upon fixed value). A foreign country generally used U.S. dollars for this purpose, paying out dollars to buy up any excess supply of its own money, thereby preventing its own money from depreciating relative to other monies. Or, if it was a surplus rather than a deficit country, selling its own money to keep it from appreciating relative to others.

This means, by the way, that since dollars are the reserves of foreign countries, the United States was in the unique position of not having to intervene itself to keep *its* money from changing in value relative to other monies. All other countries were intervening to keep their monies from changing in value relative to the dollar, and this prevented the dollar from changing relative to them. Read that again to make sure you are still with us.

Now let us see how things used to work and watch a mini-crisis develop under a system of fixed exchange rates. A deficit foreign country—Great Britain, for example—seeing its money start to depreciate, promptly steps in to maintain the par value of the pound by paying out its reserves to buy up excess pounds. *But what if Great Britain continues to run payments deficits?* Then it must continue to shell out reserves to absorb pounds. However, its reserves are far from infinite. Sooner or later, when it runs out of reserves, its "defense of the pound" must come to a halt. When the authorities sense that propping up the exchange value of the pound is becoming too costly in terms of the drain on reserves, and no end appears in sight, *then,* having stopped defending the pound, they start attacking the IMF—to win a decrease in the exchange rate. Great Britain devalues the pound—that is, it lowers the par value of the pound.

Once the financial community senses that devaluation is a possibility, however remote, it is likely to undertake actions that increase the probability of its occurrence. To illustrate with the same hypothetical example: Anyone who owns pounds (or liquid assets payable in pounds) and suspects that the pound may be devalued would be inclined to get out of pounds and into some other kind of money—say West German marks or Swiss francs—until the devaluation has been completed; then, with the same marks or francs, he could buy back more pounds than he originally had. Such "speculative" sales of pounds by private holders must of course also be purchased by the British monetary authorities, as they try to prevent the pound from depreciating below par. This puts an added strain on their reserves, thereby increasing the likelihood of devaluation, which in turn stimulates renewed "speculative" activity. "Keeping the faith" under such circumstances is all but impossible.

International transfers of short-term funds stemming from fears of devaluation can feed on themselves in this fashion and rapidly build up to the point where they generate massive reserve drains. Such short-term flows of funds include the purchase of Treasury securities as well as shifts of time and demand deposits. Since devaluations are an ever-present fact of life under a fixed exchange rate system, countries with balance of payments deficits have traditionally been viewed with some suspicion by those who manage large pools of mobile funds—treasurers of multinational corporations, bankers, Arab oil sheiks, financial consultants to private investors, and others with similar responsibilities. Indeed,

fund managers often got nervous about holding a country's
money as soon as that country's rate of inflation exceeded
that of other countries, since this was taken as an early
warning signal of future devaluation (a rise in prices that is
more rapid than elsewhere hurts exports, encourages imports, and thereby invites balance of payments deficits).

All of this at least produced a convenient by-product for
the monetary authorities *after* they devalued: they could
always blame the devaluation on "the unprincipled specula-
tors in foreign exchange who mounted a disloyal attack on
the [pound] and finally, despite a staunch defense, succeeded
in bringing it to its knees."

There always has to be a scapegoat!

The Special Case of the United States

The above recital of a typical European monetary crisis and
ultimate devaluation is similar to American experience, except that where the United States was concerned the scenario
was slightly different because of the unique role of our dollar
as a reserve in world finance. As we have seen, the monetary
reserves of other countries consist mainly of U.S. dollars; in
turn, the reserve behind the dollar consisted mainly of gold.
Thus the saga of our dollar has been closely intertwined with
that of gold, which calls for a moment's digression on that
subject.

Gold played a pervasive role in international finance under
the system of fixed exchange rates, since par values were
customarily calculated with reference to it. As an illustration, suppose the dollar is defined as equal to four-tenths of
an ounce of gold, while the mark is defined as equal to

one-tenth of an ounce of gold. From these ratios, fixed par values emerge: in this example, $1 = 4 marks (or each mark = ¼ of a dollar).

Devaluation refers to a country formally lowering the fixed ratio between its money and gold, as if the United States were to redefine the dollar so that it would no longer be equal to four-tenths of an ounce of gold but to only two-tenths of an ounce of gold instead. As a consequence, $1 would be equal to only 2 marks (and each mark would now be worth ½ of a dollar).

In the American devaluation of 1934, to take an historical illustration, a dollar that had been worth about one-twentieth of an ounce of gold became worth only one thirty-fifth of an ounce. If United States devaluation means that $1 becomes worth a smaller fraction of an ounce of gold, then of course it takes more dollars to buy an ounce. When a dollar was equal to about one-twentieth of an ounce of gold, then about $20 = one ounce; with a dollar equal to only one thirty-fifth of an ounce of gold, then $35 = one ounce. Thus it became customary to speak of a devaluation of the dollar simply as a rise in the price of gold.

With this as background, let us turn to the main crises that involved the United States during the 1960s.

Crisis Number 1. The 1960s had hardly begun before rumors erupted that dollar devaluation was imminent—that the United States was about to raise the price of gold above the $35 an ounce that had prevailed since 1934. Underlying these reports was the hard fact that we had been running balance of payments deficits steadily through the 1950s, thereby supplying dollars to the rest of the world in excess of the foreign exchange we were taking in. Some of these foreign-held dollars were returned to the U.S. Treasury with a request to please exchange them for gold, if you don't mind. As a result, our gold stock—*our* reserves—dwindled. At the same time, many U.S. dollars were *not* presented for gold; instead, they were held by foreign countries as *their* reserves. But if they had been sent in for gold, we would have been hard put to honor them, because by 1960 our short-term dollar liabilities to foreigners had grown larger than our gold stock. We couldn't have redeemed all the outstanding claims on our gold even if we wanted to.

There was nothing secret about these facts, and they quite naturally gave a lot of people reason to suspect that we might very well devalue, thereby automatically increasing the value of our gold stock. As a result, in anticipation of gold soon being worth more than $35 an ounce, in late 1960 a heavy private demand for gold drove its price to $40 an ounce in London and Zurich, where the main free gold markets of the world, open to anyone, are located. (In financial circles this was called a "speculative attack on the dollar" and was widely regarded as un-American.)

Free market gold at $40 an ounce posed a threat to our gold reserves. Foreign central banks might be tempted to buy gold from the U.S. Treasury at the official price of $35 an ounce and then sell it in London or Zurich for $40. (Others would be tempted, too, but the Treasury would sell only to a government or a central bank.) The crisis remained on the front pages until it was resolved early in 1961, when the world's leading financial nations formally established a "gold pool" to peg the market price at $35. The central banks of the United States, Britain, Belgium, Holland, West Germany, Italy, France, and Switzerland began to act in concert, as a syndicate, to sell gold to the free market when the price threatened to rise above $35 and to buy it when it started to fall below.

Crisis Number 2. All of this worked tolerably well for several years, until the gold pool's sales (to keep the price down) started draining so much gold out of their coffers that the central bankers became somewhat disenchanted at the prospect of playing the game much longer. The reason the gold pool had to keep selling, and hardly ever buying, was the same reason it had been organized to begin with: persistent U.S. balance of payments deficits, feeding dollars abroad, continued to arouse the same anticipations that had run up the price of gold in the first place.

Under the circumstances, it was only a matter of time before the next crisis. It arrived late in 1967 as the war in Southeast Asia accelerated the flow of U.S. dollars abroad. The private demand for gold was so great during 1967 that by year's end the central banks in the gold pool had almost $2 billion less in their gold reserves than they had at the start of the year. So in March 1968, to front-page headlines, they called it quits.

The gold pool was replaced by a "two-tier" gold price system. This time the world's central bankers decided to build their own version of the Berlin Wall, separating once and for all the official monetary gold market from its private counterpart. In brief, they picked up what chips were still theirs and went off to play strictly among themselves, with all transactions within the fraternity to take place at the official price, then $35 an ounce, agreeing by blood oath not to sell or buy any more gold in the private market. As for the private buyers and sellers, they could do as they wished and trade at whatever price they pleased.

In one tier, the central banks agreed to buy and sell gold only among themselves and at the official price, and they agreed not to buy any newly mined gold nor to sell or buy gold on private markets. The other tier was represented by the private market, where all newly mined gold was to be channeled, and where the price was allowed to vary in response to supply and demand. Thus from March 1968 until November 1973, when the two-tier system fell apart, there were two gold prices: the official price and the free market price. The official price was the price at which all governmental and IMF settlements were recorded; this was $35 an ounce until it was increased to $38 in December 1971, and then to $42.22 in February of 1973. The free market price, however, fluctuating with the tides of private supply and demand, soared to well over $100 an ounce during this five and one-half year period, reaching the then-record high of $125 in mid-1973. So long as the two tiers did not deal with each other, or with intermediaries, there was no necessary relationship between the two prices—like fire trucks and bananas, they went their separate ways.

Although the two-tier system worked from early 1968 to late 1973, it contained within itself the seeds of its own demise: the higher the free market price rose above the decreed official price, the greater became the incentive for those governments with relatively large gold holdings to push for worldwide devaluation up to the market price. Or, alternatively, to sell some of their gold to the private market. Countries have violated blood oaths for much less.

So in November 1973 the two-tier gold price system collapsed under the strain of trying to keep the official and private gold markets in separate watertight compartments. Governments agreed that if any of them wished they were once again free to buy or sell gold in the lucrative private market.

But one tier or two, United States balance of payments deficits continued and even became larger.

Why Did Dollar Devaluation Take So Long?

How could this country continue to run payments deficits for over twenty years, and all that while avoid the consequences (i.e., devaluation) that other countries would face had they tried the same? As we have seen, Great Britain or France or West Germany would have had to step in much earlier and pay out reserves to stop their money from depreciating below par—pay out reserves to buy up excess supplies of their own money. Continued losses of their reserves in this fashion, accelerated by the inevitable "speculative" transfers of liquid funds into other kinds of money, would force devaluation upon them within a relatively short time. Surely it could not continue for over two decades!

But the United States was (and to an extent still is) in a uniquely fortunate position. While other countries could run deficits only so long as their reserves held out, we were able to run deficits for much longer because our dollars *are* the reserves of others. Thus there has been (and still is) a rather special demand for U.S. dollars that nothing else, except gold itself, can satisfy. As a reserve money, the dollar was utilized by *other* countries, under IMF agreement, to intervene in foreign exchange markets to keep the exchange value of *their* money at par relative to the dollar. This automatically kept the dollar from changing relative to other monies, as we have already noted before, without the United States having to intervene itself. If the dollar started to depreciate in relative value, then other countries would find their money *ap*preciating relative to the dollar and *they* would step in and sell their own money (buy dollars) to keep exchange rates at their fixed par values. Thus the reserve role of the dollar put the United States in a uniquely fortunate position, especially in a world of fixed exchange rates.

Nevertheless, even those upon whom fortune smiles risk running out of luck if they push it too far. Until mid-1971 the entire world monetary superstructure was erected on the basic premise that other countries could always come to the U.S. Treasury and exchange their dollars for gold. By the end of 1970, however, that superstructure looked precariously unstable; the U.S. gold stock ($11 billion) had become much smaller than foreign central bank holdings of U.S. short-term Treasury securities plus U.S. bank deposits ($20 billion), with the differential widening. It was evident the United States was at long last in danger of running out of *its* reserves.

In light of our diminishing gold reserves, both absolutely and relative to our commitments, other countries became increasingly reluctant to hold the additional dollars spewed forth by our payments deficits. But instead of getting smaller, U.S. balance of payments deficits grew larger; as a consequence, worldwide expectations of impending American devaluation grew even greater, despite (because of?) repeated official denials that the United States would ever think of such a thing.

By 1970 the view had become commonplace that the dollar was "overvalued" relative to other monies—that is, at prevailing (fixed) exchange rates a dollar was able to buy too many Dutch guilders, too many West German marks, too many Japanese yen. To put it the other way, others could get too *few* dollars for their money. This contributed to our payments deficits by encouraging us to import too much (foreign goods were relatively cheap for us, partly because foreign money was so cheap) and export too little (foreigners found our goods relatively expensive, partly because our money was so expensive).

The particular sequence of events that set off the inevitable explosion was sparked by vast international transfers of short-term funds in 1970 and the first half of 1971, actually at first more in response to intercountry interest rate differentials than to nervousness over imminent U.S. devaluation. International capital movements, whether in response to interest rate differentials or because of expectations with respect to exchange rate alterations, of course contribute to balance of payments deficits (or surpluses) just like imports (and exports) of goods and services. That is, the purchase by Americans of foreign securities or foreign bank deposits, for whatever reason, involves our making payments abroad (like U.S. imports), and the purchase by foreigners of U.S. Treasury bills or deposits in American banks involves our receiving payments from abroad (like U.S. exports). During 1969, short-term money had moved *to* the United States, attracted by the high interest rates here during that tight money period. In 1970 and 1971, however, with recession in the United States and interest rates lower here than abroad, funds moved back to Europe, contributing to our payment deficits.

Eurodollars

It is useful to mention at this point that international capital movements have been given added impetus in recent years by the rapid growth of Eurodollars. These unusual creatures are deposits in foreign banks, mostly in Europe, that are on the foreign banks' books as payable in U.S. dollars, rather than in the money of the country where the bank is located. For

example, Eurodollars are born when an American transfers
a dollar deposit from an American bank to a foreign bank
and keeps it there *in dollars* (rather than switching to
pounds, say, if the bank to which the money is transferred
is in England). They are similarly created when a foreign
holder of a deposit in an American bank does the same thing,
as when a French exporter gets paid with a check on an
American bank and deposits it in a local bank outside Paris
with instructions to retain it as a dollar deposit (instead of
exchanging it into the equivalent amount of francs). For that
matter, anyone in another country can create Eurodollars by
exchanging local money for dollars and then depositing them
in a local bank, with instructions to keep the deposit in dollar
form. The original Eurodollar deposit can then serve as the
basis for dollar loans by the foreign bank, and if redeposited
the process can be repeated, thereby creating additional
Eurodollars.

Close to E$400 billion are now on the books of commercial
banks abroad, including the overseas branches of American
banks, and they represent a particularly mobile pool of interest-sensitive funds. Indeed good old Regulation Q had a
great deal to do with the growth of Eurodollars: the interest
rate ceilings on deposits in the United States induced many
corporate and institutional depositors in American banks to
shift their deposits to foreign banks, to get higher yields, but
to keep them payable in dollars for the sake of convenience.

In the tight money years 1966 and 1969, when the Federal
Reserve was putting severe pressure on bank reserve positions, its policies were partially offset by Eurodollar transactions. Unable to compete effectively for domestic funds because of Regulation Q, American banks borrowed large
amounts of Eurodollars from their overseas branches in
order to restore the lending power the Federal Reserve was

just as diligently trying to deplete. These Eurodollar borrowings so blunted the bite of monetary policy that in mid-1969 the Federal Reserve imposed reserve requirements on them in an effort to restrain their growth.

The Real Storm: 1971

But to return to our unfolding story. We left the particular sequence of events that set off the inevitable explosion (that brought down the house that IMF built) just as we were mentioning that it was sparked by vast international transfers of short-term funds in 1970 and the first half of 1971, at first more in response to the attraction of higher interest rates abroad than to nervousness over imminent U.S. devaluation. These interest-sensitive short-term capital outflows worsened our already weak balance of payments position, so apprehension rapidly mounted with respect to possible dollar devaluation. A flight from the dollar ensued during the first half of 1971, including large-scale conversions of Eurodollars into other monies, especially the "strong" ones most likely to appreciate (such as West German marks, Swiss francs, and Japanese yen).

To maintain the fixed par values of their own money, as required by the IMF, the central banks of these "strong money" countries had no choice but to buy up the flood of dollars being offered in the market, for that purpose paying out their own money. To give you an idea of the enormous magnitudes involved: at the end of January 1971 foreign central bank dollar holdings amounted to $20 billion, *already an historic high;* by the end of May, only four months later,

STEVENSON

"OK. The forward rate for marks rose in March and April, combined with a sharp increase in German reserves and heavy borrowing in the Eurodollar market, while United States liquid reserves had dropped to fourteen billion dollars, causing speculation that the mark might rise and encouraging conversion on a large scale. Now *do you understand?"*

Drawing by Stevenson; © 1972 The New Yorker Magazine, Inc.

they had swollen to $32 billion. In only four months, foreign central banks had bought up twelve billion dollars, almost none of which they really wanted!

Such an avalanche of dollar purchases by these central banks, like any other open market buying by a central bank, laid the basis for an enormous expansion of their domestic money supplies—in most cases contrary to the prevailing monetary policies of the countries involved. Forced to buy up vast amounts of dollars, and shoveling out their own money to pay for them, other countries were rapidly expanding the reserves of their own banks and losing control over their domestic money supplies. In the process of maintaining the *external* value of their money, they were losing their grip on its *internal* value.

West Germany wanted out first. In early May of 1971, after buying up several billion dollars in the first few days of the month, West Germany ceased its dollar purchases, abandoned fixed exchange rates, and let the mark float to find its own level. Holland did the same. For a short while the crisis seemed to have been weathered successfully. During June and July there was actually a fair demand for dollars, and foreign central banks were able to get rid of about five billion of them.

But that turned out to be only the calm before the *real* storm. In the first half of August there was again a feverish rush to convert dollars into other monies—by midmonth, foreign central bank dollar holdings soared to close to $35 billion, well above the May peak. And then it was, on 15 August 1971, that President Nixon ended the convertibility of the dollar into gold.

Faced with jittery and panic-prone international financial markets, with $35 billion in the hands of foreign central banks, obligated to pay out gold to any central bank that wanted to exchange its U.S. dollars for it—but with only about $10 billion worth of gold left in the Treasury—Nixon announced that the game was over. There weren't enough chips left.

Actually, the termination of the dollar's convertibility into gold caused little disarray in international finance. Everyone had known for the better part of a decade that the commitment of the United States to pay out gold in exchange for dollars was more symbolic than real. If it had ever been put to a real test, it would have ended years before. Fixed exchange rates also went out the window for four months following 15 August. Most major countries joined West Germany and Holland and permitted exchange rates to float, with each country's money finding its own value relative to the others on the basis of supply and demand conditions. And do you know what? International trade did not come to a halt!

But good things rarely last. In mid-December 1971, the leading nations resurrected fixed exchange rates as part of a "new look" in international financial arrangements. The December 1971 Smithsonian Agreement provided that exchange rates could fluctuate a little (but not much) more than before. Previously, exchange rates had been permitted under IMF rules to fluctuate by 1 percent above or below par before a central bank was required to intervene to stabilize them. The Smithsonian Agreement widened those limits to 2¼ percent on either side of par. The world's Financial Authorities felt this was such a drastic change it deserved a new name to memorialize the event; they decided that from then on the fixed rate would no longer be called the par value, but rather the "central" value. (A rose by any other name is still. . . .)

Par—pardon, central—values were simultaneously realigned, to produce an average depreciation of the dollar of about 12 percent against the major trading nations, with the expectation that this would inhibit U.S. imports, stimulate U.S. exports, and thereby help remedy our payments deficit. Also as part of the Smithsonian Agreement, the dollar was *finally* devalued, for the first time since 1934—from the equivalent of one thirty-fifth of an ounce of gold to one thirty-eighth of an ounce. This raised the official price of gold from $35 to $38 an ounce.

But for a number of reasons, things didn't work out as planned. Within fourteen months—in February 1973—the United States devalued again, this time raising the official price of gold an additional 11 percent, to $42.22 an ounce.

Repeat Performance: 1973

The Smithsonian Agreement of December 1971 was hailed by President Nixon as "the most significant monetary agreement in the history of the world." However, again words didn't necessarily make it so; by February 1973, only fourteen months later, the Smithsonian Agreement had almost completely disappeared, leaving hardly a trace.

The basic premise of the Smithsonian Agreement was that fixed exchange rates are a viable foundation for an international financial system, that the trouble lay not in fixed rates per se but in the particular levels at which the rates had been fixed. Conclusion: Realign the rates, fix them at new, more "realistic" levels and then everything will be just fine. But it didn't work out that way. With exchange rates pegged once more, and thereby prevented from reflecting shifting supply and demand pressures, the lid blew off again in early 1973.

A minor event sparked the explosion. In late January, Italy established new exchange rules for the lira. Fearing that the value of their money would decline, many Italians sold lire for dollars and then exchanged the dollars for Swiss francs. The inflow of dollars panicked the nervous Swiss monetary authorities, who stopped buying dollars and let the Swiss franc float. This brought the treasurers of multinational corporations and the Arab oil sheiks into action. Sensing that another flight from the dollar might be imminent, they promptly proved it, dumping dollars for German marks and Japanese yen. (It was no longer profitable to move into the Swiss franc, since it had floated upward to the point where it was not a bargain any more.) Within a week the West German Bundesbank had to (reluctantly) buy $6 billion, and the Bank of Japan had to swallow over $1 billion, to keep the dollar from falling below (or the mark and yen from rising above) agreed-upon levels.

On 12 February 1973, not unwillingly, the United States announced that it was again devaluing the dollar, raising the official price of gold from $38 to $42.22 an ounce. The news was fresh that in 1972 we had run a $6 billion trade deficit —devaluation against the mark and yen could help correct that imbalance. Even so, large-scale selling of dollars—in anticipation of *further* devaluation—broke out again within weeks. Finally, in the so-called Brussels Agreement of 12 March 1973, Germany and the major Western European nations decided they had no choice but to let their monies float vis-à-vis the dollar, and so they abandoned fixed exchange rates.

Since March 1973 the international monetary system has been characterized mainly by floating exchange rates. Several Western European nations fix the value of their monies relative to each other, permitting only limited fluctuations above or below par. And almost all small less-developed countries peg the value of their money to that of a larger country, typically a major trading partner. But by and large floating rates are the order of the day, with demand and supply continuously moving exchange rates up and down.

Strictly speaking, floating rates existed "illegally" for almost three years, since the IMF's regulations still required fixed par values until early in 1976. However, no one seemed to worry about such technicalities. Finally the rules of the game were officially changed at the IMF's meetings in Kingston, Jamaica, in January 1976. At those meetings the entire structure of mandatory fixed exchange rates, erected at Bretton Woods near the close of World War II, was formally dismantled and a new international monetary system was constructed in its place, one that permits flexible exchange rates (although it does not require them). None of the participants at the Jamaica meetings, by the way, appeared to think it strange that the new exchange rate regulations were being drawn up almost three years *after* they had been put into practice.

The Jamaica Agreement also altered the nature of the International Monetary Fund, from an exchange rate supervisor and regulator to a forum for debate and an agency to assist the underdeveloped nations. In addition to legalizing floating exchange rates, it was agreed to "demonitize" the international monetary role of gold by terminating the concept of an "official" gold price. The IMF also agreed to sell 25 million ounces of its own gold on the open market and use the proceeds to aid the poorer nations.

Floating Rates: Success or Failure?

Have floating exchange rates been a success? In some respects they undoubtedly have been an improvement over fixed rates. Had fixed rates still been in existence late in 1973, for example, it is not hard to imagine the financial crises of vast proportions that would have exploded when the Organization of Petroleum Exporting Countries (OPEC) announced a fourfold increase in oil prices. All things considered, floating rates have absorbed the shocks of that and similar episodes remarkably well.

But floating rates have nevertheless fallen far short of expectations. In the last section of Chapter 21 we noted that floating rates would hopefully end a persistent balance of payments deficit without destabilizing the economy in the process. Unfortunately, things have not worked out quite that way. The dollar has depreciated rather steadily on international financial markets since floating began early in 1973, but our economy has been far from stable. What *has* resulted is a worsening of inflation here at home. We have to pay more for imports (since foreign money costs us more) and the amount of our exports demanded by foreigners has increased (since our goods are cheaper for them because our money is cheaper). For both reasons—cost-push and demand-pull—inflation in the United States has been exacerbated by the depreciation of the dollar.

At the same time, the decline of the dollar relative to foreign monies has *not* wiped out our chronic balance of payments deficit. If there was anything floating rates were expected to do, it was to rectify that situation by making our imports more expensive and our exports more competitive. But in fact our payments deficit has grown *larger* rather than smaller. We seem to have gotten ourselves into the worst of all possible worlds: a falling international dollar, a rising domestic price level, and a balance of payments deficit larger than ever.

There are several explanations for this unhappy state of

affairs, none of them entirely satisfactory. One is that the balance of payments corrective process takes time—that although the payments deficit may get worse for a while in response to depreciation, eventually it will get better. Economists often refer to this as a J-curve phenomenon: at first things deteriorate, but at some point they turn around and improve dramatically. Things get worse initially because imports are resistent to the price increases caused by the depreciation of the dollar, implying that imports actually rise in dollar volume in the short run; similarly, it takes time before exports are stimulated. In the short run, therefore, the depreciation of the dollar is likely to enlarge the balance of payments deficit rather than contract it. *Eventually,* however, there will be a meaningful turnaround.

An alternate explanation is that we have never really given floating rates a sufficient chance to float freely so they could produce their results. Instead, nations have continuously intervened in foreign exchange markets, nudging exchange rates higher or lower, refusing to let the free market operate. Instead of "clean" floats, we have had managed or "dirty" floats.

For example, in November 1978, President Carter and the Federal Reserve announced a barrage of measures intended to stop further foreign exchange depreciation of the dollar. These measures included the authority to borrow $15 billion worth of marks, yen, and francs from foreign central banks in order to buy dollars, higher commercial bank reserve requirements, and a 1 percent increase in the discount rate (to attract foreign funds by raising short-term interest rates here). This massive support of the dollar was aimed at combating inflation at home—since, as noted above, a continuously depreciating dollar accentuates both cost-push and demand-pull inflationary pressures. Nevertheless, we can't have it both ways: if we want floating rates, we have to let them float.

So far, then, the verdict is mixed. Floating foreign exchange rates are neither a clear success nor an unmitigated disaster. Everything considered, they have probably been an improvement over fixed rates since they came into being in 1973. Many bankers and business executives would still prefer to return to fixed rates, but the likelihood appears slim that it will happen in the near future.

22

WHAT ABOUT GOLD?

Once upon a time, long ago and far away, the natives of a small island in a remote part of the world had a monetary system of which they were extremely proud. Although they lacked commercial banks and had no Federal Reserve, they had something many people consider much more important —a monetary standard. It was not a gold standard, but it was somewhat similar. It was a rock standard. Near the southeastern edge of the island, on a high cliff, sat a handsome and enormous rock, awesome to behold and thrilling to touch, and it was this that they decided should serve as "backing" for their money.

Naturally, the rock was too heavy, and indeed too valuable, to use as an actual means of payment. Instead, for circulating media itself, corresponding to our coins and dollar bills, they used special clamshells. People had confidence in these because boldly inscribed on them were the words:

Will Pay to the Bearer on Demand One Dollar in Rock

The very fact that this statement was made meant that no one ever demanded any rock. The assurance that it was there was sufficient.

For many years all went well. The economy was simple but prosperous, and those from the Great Civilizations across the sea who occasionally visited the island marveled at its stability and its thriving commerce. The natives were not reluctant to explain the reasons for their prosperity: hard work, thrift, clean living, and, above all, sound money. Sound as a rock.

Unfortunately, one night a severe storm struck the island. The inhabitants awoke the next morning to find the rock gone, evidently hurled into the sea by the furies of nature. Consternation! Panic! Luckily, however, they were saved from the potential consequences—worthless money and economic collapse—by an accident of fate that took place within the week. One of the younger natives, a child of no more than eight, perched on the very cliff where the rock had once been, was looking at a rainbow arching far out over the horizon. Following it down, he suddenly saw—or thought he saw—the rock, fathoms deep, under the water.

After much excitement, it was finally ascertained that on very clear days, when the sea was calm and the sun at a certain angle, some who had especially strong eyes could see it. Those who could not, which included almost everyone, were assured by those who could that the outlines of the boulder were indeed discernible. And so, the backing still there, confidence in the money was restored, and in a short while the island became more prosperous than ever.

Of course, all the outstanding clamshells had to be called in, so that the elders of the community could strike out the words:

Will Pay to the Bearer on Demand One Dollar in Rock

In their place was painstakingly inscribed:

Will Pay to the Bearer on Demand One Dollar
in Lawful Money

"Then it's agreed. Until the dollar firms up, we let the clamshell float."

Drawing by Ed Fisher; © 1971 *The New Yorker Magazine, Inc.*

Now if anyone brought in a clamshell to be redeemed, it would simply be exchanged for another clamshell. As it turned out, however, no one bothered. After all, with the backing assuredly there, the money obviously was as good as rock.

Gold at Home

Our own monetary system, of course, has always been much more rational. Until the early 1930s all of our money was redeemable in gold at the United States Treasury. Every dollar bill, and for that matter every demand deposit as well, actually or implicitly bore the following inscription:

The United States of America
Will Pay to the Bearer on Demand One Dollar in Gold

Then overnight, in 1933, it was declared illegal for anyone in this country to own or possess gold, except for industrial or numismatic purposes. Gold ownership by Americans was made illegal by an Executive Order issued by President Franklin D. Roosevelt on 5 April 1933. The prohibition was formalized by the Gold Reserve Act of 1934. Accordingly, the inscription on the currency was solemnly, officially, and duly altered to:

The United States of America
Will Pay to the Bearer on Demand One Dollar
in Lawful Money

In 1947 a literal-minded citizen of Cleveland, A. F. Davis, sent the Treasury a $10 bill and respectfully requested, in exchange, the promised $10 in "lawful money." He received back, by return mail, two $5 bills.

Seventeen years later, in 1964, the venerable inscription was finally removed from our currency. All that remains is an unpretentious observation: "This note is legal tender for all debts, public and private." Also (in considerably larger print): "In God We Trust."

Pursuing the same theme somewhat further, until 1965 the

Federal Reserve was required to hold reserves in the form of warehouse receipts for gold, called gold certificates. The amounts required were 25 percent behind member bank deposits at the Federal Reserve banks (member bank reserves) and also 25 percent behind all outstanding Federal Reserve Notes (most of our currency). These gold certificate reserves were considered the ultimate backing behind our money, both demand deposits and currency. Indeed, economics textbooks were fond of portraying our monetary system as an inverted pyramid, with a base of gold that supported an equal volume of gold certificates, above that a fourfold expansion of member bank reserves and currency, and atop that a further multiple expansion of demand deposits. It was clear to any conscientious reader that without its Atlas-like foundation of gold the entire U.S. monetary system would collapse.

But then, as the U.S. gold stock dwindled from over $20 billion in 1958 to less than $16 billion at the end of 1964, the gold backing behind member bank deposits at the Fed was quietly eliminated by Congress and the President on 3 March 1965. Three years later, on 19 March 1968, the corresponding gold reserve against currency was also abolished, just as casually. No one seemed to care. The newspapers hardly mentioned it. Was somebody covering up?

All of which raises an intriguing question. There is, we are told, billions of dollars worth of gold buried deep beneath the surface of the earth in heavily guarded Fort Knox, Kentucky. Have you ever seen it? Do you know anyone who has?

Why don't you write a letter to the Federal Reserve or the Treasury, tell them you're going to be in Kentucky anyway, and ask them to let you stop by and take a look at the gold in Fort Knox? On second thought, don't bother. We did and got back a rather chilly reply: "With reference to your inquiry relating to Fort Knox, all the gold is stored in sealed compartments and no visitors are allowed."

Sealed compartments? No visitors allowed? It sounds more like King Tut's tomb or Count Dracula's crypt than a twentieth-century monetary system. A curse on all who shall enter here! Do you *really* believe there is any gold there? Does it really matter?

Gold Abroad

We seem to have broken free from our superstitious attachment to gold here at home. We appear to be perfectly capable of transacting business without using little gold coins of the kind we had before 1933. And although U.S. citizens are once again allowed to have gold in their possession—since the beginning of 1975—the change in the law created less excitement than the rumor that the Rolling Stones were planning to replace Mick Jagger with Frank Sinatra.

Private citizens still hoard gold in many countries where there is no law against it, and in some countries where there is. And nations do the same, since they continue to settle up their net debts among themselves by playing house with small gold bars of a specified purity and weight. (Each bar, about the size of an ordinary brick, contains 400 ounces of 99.5 percent fine gold, which at $42.22 an ounce—the last "official" price—makes a typical bar worth almost $17,000.) In fact, you can even see some of this gold. Foreign governments store much of their gold in the basement of the Federal Reserve Bank of New York. A guided tour takes you down to the crypts. You can even hold one of the bars. Curious, isn't it?—we can touch theirs but not ours.

The "official" price of gold is worth a brief historical recapitulation. When gold was truly the legal basis of our monetary system, the official price was the price that the U.S. Treasury would pay for gold and at which dollars were redeemable back into gold. That is, with full convertibility at $20.67 an ounce, for example, you could turn in $20.67 and receive in exchange one ounce of gold. The official price was set at $20.67 an ounce by the Gold Standard Act of 14 March 1900, and it remained there until it was raised to $35 an ounce by President Roosevelt on 31 January 1934, even though starting in 1933 U.S. citizens were no longer permitted to have gold. In August of 1971 President Nixon stopped selling gold to foreigners as well, but the official price stayed at $35 until December of that year when it was raised to $38 as part of the Smithsonian Agreement. It was hiked once again by President Nixon in February 1973 to its final figure of $42.22 an ounce.

But dollars have not been redeemable into gold domestically since 1933 or internationally since 1971. The two-tier gold price system fell apart late in 1973, and ever since 1968 the free market price has been well above the official price, making the latter sort of academic. The free market price has ranged between $100 and almost $900 an ounce since late 1973, so no one would sell at the official price of $42.22. It became a little silly to talk about an official price of $42.22 when there was no longer any buying or selling taking place at that "price." So in January 1976 the concept of an "official" price was formally abolished at the IMF meetings in Kingston, Jamaica. The price of gold is now simply whatever it brings on the open market. We keep referring to $42.22 here only because it is convenient to use that figure as a reference point. A more realistic present-day figure would be about fifteen times that, or around $600 an ounce.

There is probably about $1,500 billion worth of gold in existence in the world today (calculated on the basis of the free market price)—roughly 2½ billion ounces, at $600 an ounce. Actually, estimates range from 2 to 3 billion ounces, which at $600 an ounce implies a dollar value between about $1,200 and $1,800 billion. So much of the estimating approaches sheer guesswork, however, that one might as well slice it down the middle and settle for $1,500 billion as a reasonable figure. For instance, none of the Communist-bloc nations will reveal their gold holdings; private hoarders, regardless of their politics, are even more discreet.

The United States has stashed away about $160 billion (at $600 an ounce), we are told, and other governments and central banks outside the communist sphere have close to $600 billion. The Soviet Union is estimated to have official gold holdings somewhere between $70 and $200 billion (most likely in the neighborhood of $140 billion), and other Communist countries, including China, perhaps $60 billion. Finally, there are substantial private hoards secretly squirreled away, some from the dawn of time, by peasants and potentates from France and Switzerland to India, Kuwait, and Tibet. Lord only knows what these amount to, but brave men calculate between $480 and $600 billion, with around $540 billion a likely figure (which includes a few billion in private hoards in the Communist countries).

With 2½ billion ounces in existence, and each brick-size bar containing 400 ounces, that amounts to about 6¼ million bars. That much could fit into one ocean liner and still leave enough room for 100,000 copies of *Mad* magazine.

The annual production of newly mined gold adds relatively little to this stock—about 50 million ounces emerges annually from the bowels of the earth. About 70 percent of this, sometimes more, comes from South Africa, a little over 10 percent from the Soviet Union, and 5 percent from Canada, the three largest gold producers. In many years this is not enough to satisfy all the *nonmonetary* demands for gold, not to mention the monetary ones. Jewelers, dentists, and manufacturers use a considerable amount every year, and hoarders frequently acquire and then promptly rebury at least as much. So even though newly mined gold adds about 2 percent to the total supply every year, some years end with *less* gold on hand for worldwide monetary uses than was available when the year began.

Paper Gold?

The ending of the external convertibility of the dollar into gold in 1971 and the formal abandonment of fixed exchange rates (and an official gold price) in January of 1976—both discussed in the previous chapter—have severely ruptured the umbilical cord connecting international finance and chemical element 79. But the attachment has by no means been severed. Many governments are still convinced that, of all possible stores of value, gold is the safest, the least susceptible to manipulation by other governments, and the most likely to appreciate in value over the long pull. The spectacular rise in the price of gold on the free markets of London and Zurich in recent years, to well above the old official fixed price, only reinforces many foreign governments' desire to hold on to what gold they have and to get as much more as they can. General de Gaulle was no doubt articulating the views of more central bankers than would care to admit it when, in 1965, he rhapsodized over the beauty and desirability of gold, which "does not change its nature, has no nationality, and is eternally and universally accepted as the unalterable fiduciary value par excellence."

In fact, gold does indeed frequently change its nature; it can be refined, melted, molded, minted, sweated, and has often been debased. In terms of its nationality, it is no different from hula hoops, turnips, or aardvarks. It is universally acceptable only because of the belief that it will continue to be so. And its value is certainly not unalterable, as recent history dramatically attests. Gold is not a help but more a nuisance, and frequently a considerable handicap, in international monetary affairs, as nations discovered long ago with respect to their domestic finances.

In 1970 the potentially most hopeful step of all, away from gold, was hesitantly taken with the introduction into the world's monetary system of International Monetary Fund Special Drawing Rights (SDRs)—more commonly known as "paper gold." Actually, SDRs were agreed upon in principle several years earlier, at the 1967 annual meeting of the IMF in Rio de Janeiro, but it took two years before international consensus could be reached regarding their details, and still another year before they could be implemented. (Only three years of study, debate, discussion, and hassling around the conference table is tantamount, in international monetary circles, to acting on impulse.)

SDRs are a new form of money, an international reserve asset, usable (only by central banks and governments) to settle international debts in much the same way as gold. But instead of having to be panned, dredged, or mined from the earth, they are created out of thin air—just like demand deposits—by a purely man-made entry on the books of the

IMF. About $20 billion of SDRs have thus far been made available for member nations of the IMF to draw upon when needed.

SDRs were originally valued in terms of gold, but since mid-1974 they have been valued in terms of a weighted average of exchange rates for the monies of the major trading nations. As a result, some international trading contracts have been drawn up calling for payment in the dollar or pound equivalent of SDRs rather than simply in dollars or pounds, because the value of an SDR is likely to be more stable in terms of worldwide purchasing power than the value of any single kind of money. If the dollar depreciates, for instance, it will take more dollars to equal one SDR, and a foreign seller who has priced his goods in terms of the dollar equivalent of SDRs will therefore get more dollars for his goods. In other words, the pricing of internationally traded products in terms of the dollar equivalent of SDRs, rather than in terms of just dollars, gives the seller some protection against any depreciation of the dollar vis-à-vis other monies. This commercial use of SDRs has enhanced their prestige in recent years.

One purpose of SDRs is to assist those countries with balance of payments or reserve difficulties: a nation with a shortage of reserves, currently running a balance of payments deficit (e.g., Brazil), can draw on its SDR allotment to meet its payments needs. When it receives its SDRs, Brazil can then transfer them to a strong reserve position country, say West Germany, that is "designated" by the IMF to "purchase" them. In exchange, Brazil will receive West German marks, which it can either convert into U.S. dollars or other foreign exchange, or use directly in making necessary payments. Countries "designated" by the IMF to buy SDRs do not have to accept them above a specified limit.

The term "paper gold" is, strictly speaking, a misnomer. SDRs are still far from the true equal of gold in terms of general acceptability. Countries "designated" by the IMF to surrender some of their money for SDRs are not nearly so enthusiastic about the transaction as they would be had they been "designated" to receive gold itself.

It is obvious that if SDRs are to be a success, they will require continued cooperation among nations. Nevertheless, they represent an inching away from mysticism in international monetary affairs—one small step for mankind. Provided they receive tender loving care, they may hopefully grow and prosper; but by any realistic assessment, it does not appear likely that they will soon topple gold from its pinnacle.

Is Gold a Good Investment?

Since it is legal for Americans to own gold once again (ever since the beginning of 1975), and since it is highly unlikely that gold will soon disappear from the world monetary stage, the question naturally arises: Is gold an attractive investment? Is buying gold a wise way to get rich or a dumb way to go broke?

Because gold earns no interest or dividends, it immediately suffers in comparison with such alternatives as savings accounts, bonds, stocks, and rental property—although in this respect it is similar to diamonds, stamps, rare coins, art objects, and nonincome-producing real estate. Because it yields no current income, the wisdom of buying gold thus depends entirely on the prospect for future price appreciation.

If gold can be expected to rise in price by more than about 5 to 10 percent annually, which is roughly what one can earn in a savings account or in bonds or stocks, then it is worth considering seriously as an investment. But if it is not likely to match that rate of price appreciation, one can do better —and with greater safety—in one of the more customary forms of investment. In terms of this criterion, the historical record indicates that there have been only three periods in the past hundred years when an investment in gold would have paid off. One was the period just prior to 1934, the second was the period from the end of 1967 to the end of 1974, and the third was from mid-1976 through *early* 1980.

In January of 1934 President Roosevelt increased the price of gold by 69 percent, from $20.67 to $35 an ounce. Thus anyone who had the foresight to buy gold at $20.67 from February of 1929 through February of 1933, and who sold it at $35 in February of 1934, would have been rewarded with a compound rate of return of anywhere between 11 and 70 percent per annum, the exact figure depending on when it was bought. In recent years gold buyers have done even better: the free market price of gold rose from $35 an ounce in 1967 (unchanged since 1934) to a peak of almost $200 in December of 1974, a compound annual rate of price increase close to 30 percent for the entire seven-year period. Indeed, between late 1972 and late 1974 the price of gold more than *tripled!* And from mid-1976 to *early* 1980 it rose from $105 to almost $900 an ounce!

But be careful, because these figures greatly exaggerate the likely profits obtainable from gold in recent years. The free market price did not rise without interruption from 1967

I was born in 1929, when gold was selling for $20.67 an ounce...I married in 1968, in an outwardly happy marriage. That was the year gold began to go up again...For the past few years my wife has been having an affair with another man...

...Six months ago she went off to live with him...If I had bought gold in 1929 I could sell it today at 9 times the price at $180 an ounce, up from $20.67 then...Last week she came back 'To give our marriage another chance,' she says...'To give our marriage another chance?' I tell her, 'Until next time you leave, you mean'...

Some say gold stocks yes, gold bars no. I say gold bars yes, gold stocks no... Yesterday she left 'forever'...This morning she's back again...'I want to say something,' she says...

Drawing by Lou Myers; © 1975 *The New Yorker Magazine, Inc.*

through 1974. During much of 1971, for example, the price was below 1969 levels, and similarly from June through November of 1973 the price of gold fell by 30 percent. Or how do you think people felt who bought gold at $195 an ounce in January of 1975, as soon as ownership by Americans again became legal, and then watched it fall to $105 by July of 1976? That's a 45 percent drop in value in just a year and a half. Not to mention the decline from $875 per ounce in January of 1980 to $490 in March of 1980—only two months later.

Supply and demand factors make the price of gold highly volatile. With respect to supply, new production adds to the existing stockpile at the rate of only about 2 percent a year. This means that the overwhelming element on the supply side is not the amount of current ore production but uncertainty as to how much holders of the existing stockpile might try to unload. For instance, the U.S. Treasury deliberately (and successfully) cracked the price spiral in January of 1975 by selling 750,000 ounces from its gold hoard, and then auctioned off another 500,000 ounces in June 1975. Similarly, at the January 1976 IMF meetings in Kingston, Jamaica, the IMF agreed to sell 25 million ounces of its gold on the open market and use the proceeds to aid developing countries. Since then there have been periodic sales of gold by both the U.S. Treasury and the International Monetary Fund. In other words, sales by large holders, including the Soviet Union, are always a threat to break the price.

On the demand side, again, a significant portion of the demand for gold is not for current industrial or artistic use but rather is motivated by psychological considerations—in particular, by fear regarding an uncertain social and economic future. Gold has traditionally been thought of as a hedge against inflation; when consumer prices threaten to rise rapidly the private demand for gold expands, but when inflation subsides that demand often vanishes overnight. This sort of demand typically fluctuates erratically on short notice, and rather small changes in supply or demand can produce wide price swings.

Thus gold is a highly speculative investment in which the warning *caveat emptor* is particularly appropriate. Large gains can occasionally be made, but large losses are just as likely on the basis of the historical record over the past hundred years.

It is appropriate to end this chapter as we began, with a story. A man on a sinking ship ran to fetch his gold hoard before jumping overboard. When he landed in the water, the weight of the gold made floating impossible, so down he went. The crucial question is: Did he have the gold, or did the gold have him?

Epilogue

23

IS MONEY BECOMING OBSOLETE?

What might the financial system look like in the year 2000?

Buck Rogers and Flash Gordon are passé, Jules Verne is old hat (around the world in *eighty* days), and *1984* draws too close for comfort. The science fiction of yesterday has become the reality of today. An excursion into financial science fiction for the "Brave New World" ahead should provide a fitting ending for this book.

The Decline of Demand Deposits

"He spends money," they say, "as though it's going out of fashion." And perhaps money is indeed going out of fashion.

When checkbook money first began to gain popularity in this country, in the nineteenth century, it took decades before people finally realized what was happening. For a long time checking accounts were not even considered part of the money supply. They were viewed as proxies or substitutes for "real" money, namely hard cash. Somewhere in the vaults of the banks, it was thought, nestled the coin and currency, dollar for dollar, behind every checking account.

As a matter of fact, even coin and currency were suspect.

Dimes and dollar bills were considered mere stand-ins for the *really* genuine article—gold coin or bullion. That, and only that, was truly money. Anything less was, like Daylight Saving Time, a violation of the Lord's will.

Today, demand deposits are gradually losing their monetary importance, just as currency did a century ago. Checking accounts still constitute the bulk of our money supply, but the money supply itself has been diminishing in importance in our evolving financial system. Thirty years ago the money supply—currency plus checking accounts—amounted to half of our gross national product. Twenty years ago it was equal to around a third of GNP. Today it has shrunk to less than one-sixth of GNP. We are carrying on more and more business, both financial and nonfinancial, with a relatively smaller and smaller supply of money.

Just as a hundred years ago coin and currency gradually gave way to the convenience and efficiency of demand deposits, so today demand deposits, as we have known them, are gradually giving way to even more convenient and efficient payment mechanisms. The growth of credit cards, for example, has made it unnecessary to write twenty-five checks when making twenty-five purchases. One check, at the end of the month, will do for all. And often that one check is not even needed. Your friendly neighborhood bank can make an automatic debit to your account at regular intervals, relieving you of the need to write even that one check.

If you have your paycheck sent directly to your bank by your employer and make most of your purchases with that bank's credit card, with payment then settled up at stated intervals by the bank automatically reducing your account by the amount of the charges incurred, you will soon find your check book obsolete.

If we combine the essence of this already realistic payments system with the potentialities of the high-speed computer, magnetic tape storage, remote feed-ins, and satellite transmission, it does not take too much imagination to make a stab at the shape of things to come.

Debits and Credits in the Year 2000

A few decades from now, coins will probably still be with us for inserting into vending machines that we can then shake and bang to release our aggressions. But checks may well have vanished as quickly as they came. Check payment is really nothing more than a bookkeeping operation to begin with. As a method of information dispersal as to how the books should be kept, checks are—in light of present and foreseeable technology—notoriously cumbersome, slow, unreliable, and inefficient.

More in keeping with the twenty-first century will be a vast nationwide balance sheet and clearing system in which debits and credits can be rung up virtually instantaneously by electronic impulse. Every individual and every transacting organization of whatever sort will be tagged at birth with a number and a slot on the "books" of a computerized nationwide accounting and payments system, a National Ledger as it were.

Credits and debits to each individual account will be made by the insertion of a twenty-first century version of a credit card into a twenty-first century version of a telephone or teletype. Instead of a written piece of paper instructing a bank to credit this account and debit that one—that is, a check, with its necessary physical routing from place to place

—the insertion of a plastic card into the appropriate recept-
acle will automatically credit and debit both accounts instantaneously. It should not be too difficult to devise a system
whereby the proper code will serve as a means of verifying
the validity of the electronic instructions to the Great Master
Bookkeeper in the Sky.

Eliminating checks would be only one of the many advantages that would emerge from such a system. All financial
assets are nothing more than a representation of someone
else's liability or evidence of equity. Current practice, which
consists of inscribing same on embossed parchment, has been
absurd for at least two generations. There is no need for
stocks and bonds to look like Pronouncements of State by
King Henry VIII. As everyone is fully aware, a simple computer print-out would do just as well. However, by the year
2000 even that will not be necessary, since it will all be
recorded automatically on the magnetic tape of the National
Ledger as soon as a stock or bond is issued or a transaction
made.

An even more important advantage will be the saving in
time and effort currently devoted to keeping the books in a
society slowly but surely being inundated by paperwork. We
are only kidding ourselves if we think we have made much
progress in this area since quill pens replaced whatever it was
they replaced.

In any event, peoplepower will have to be saved somewhere to provide personnel for the army of computer repairpeople who will in all certainty be busy around the clock
answering customer complaints and fixing breakdowns in the
equipment. One supply source for repairpeople, of course,
will be the cadres presently known as the Monetarists and
the Keynesians. Their hard-learned skills will be obsolete in
the twenty-first century. After spending a lifetime ac-

cumulating regressions and correlation coefficients designed to test the role of money in economic activity, what else will they be able to do when money itself becomes no more than a historical *curiosa?*

A National Ledger payments system will be possible in a surprisingly few years. Already its introduction depends more on costs and financial evaluations regarding its profitability than on purely technological considerations. It remains to be seen whether the necessary services will be provided by one firm, by an association of private financial and nonfinancial firms, or by the government, alone or in partnership with private enterprise.

There are obvious advantages inherent in its being a governmental function. For example, for many years employees of the Communist Party USA were not permitted to receive social security benefits. If they and other malcontents could similarly be denied access to the National Ledger, and thus barred from making or receiving payments of any sort, the American Way of Life could be made even more Secure.

Implications for Financial Markets

With methods of communication and the dissemination of information perfected to the ultimate degree by the year 2000, in all likelihood financial markets will finally take on the characteristics of the purely competitive markets that economists have been talking about in classrooms since the days of Adam Smith. Instead of simple buy and sell orders, or bid and offered quotations, potential buyers and sellers of financial assets will be able electronically to transmit complete demand and supply schedules to a central clearing computer, specifying the amounts of various securities they wish to buy or sell at a range of alternative prices.

Of course, this in itself would not be quite sufficient to meet classroom standards for a purely competitive market, since one of the prerequisities for such a market is that the participants possess perfect foresight regarding the future as well as perfect knowledge of the present. But even that might be incorporated by feeding probability forecasts into the Giant Maw of the computer. Is it too farfetched to suggest that such forecasts might even involve some of the parapsychological techniques—like clairvoyance and precognition—currently under intensive study at some of our most prestigious universities and on several all-night radio programs?

Implications for the Economy

Economic policy making, Monetarist or Keynesian, will also mean something quite different in the twenty-first century from what it means today. Monetary and fiscal policy are far too uncertain in their impact for use in the Century of Efficiency that will follow the present Century of Progress.

By that time, all assets and liabilities as recorded on the National Ledger will be subject to increase or decrease by any given percentage by Executive Order, thereby instantaneously altering the wealth of every individual and every business firm in the country. If aggregate spending does not respond promptly in the direction and amount desired, further asset-valuation adjustments can be fine-tuned until the reaction on the part of the private sector conforms to what is deemed necessary to assure the Good Life for all.

Given human nature, this may possibly give rise to the problem of "valuation evasion"—that is, an illegal market in which assets are valued and transactions effected at prices other than those recorded on the National Ledger. The result would be the accumulation of unrecorded wealth for those involved in such dealings. If this gains currency, so to speak, an entire underground financial system—complete with (unreported) deposits, handwritten checks, and a subterranean check-routing network—is likely to spring up in opposition to the more efficient computerized and satellite-supervised official payments system.

The most effective remedy to prevent such undermining of the common welfare would be to bar all participants in Financial Subversion from access to the National Ledger. Practitioners of too-private enterprise would thus be consigned, along with employees of the Communist Party USA, to deserved financial ostracism as Subverters of the National Happiness.

Such a solution would have the self-evident virtue of safeguarding the Sinews of our Efficiency, while at the same time being consistent with the preservation of our Cherished Freedoms.

SELECTED READINGS

Data and Current Comment

A comprehensive source of information on current monetary data, credit conditions, general economic trends, and the policies of the central bank is the *Federal Reserve Bulletin,* published monthly by the Board of Governors of the Federal Reserve System. However, more sparkling comment and analyses are generally found in the monthly reviews of the various Federal Reserve banks. Each of these banks will put you on its mailing list without charge if you drop a postcard to its Public Relations Department.

Also well worth reading are the annual *Economic Report of the President* and the publications of several private financial institutions, most notably Morgan Guaranty Trust Company's monthly *Survey,* Citibank's *Monthly Economic Letter,* and the Bankers Trust Company's annual *Credit and Capital Markets.* The main offices of all three of these banks are in New York City.

Books on Money and Policy

If you can still stand us after what you've been through, a basic money and banking textbook that goes into all this in more detail is Ritter and Silber, *Principles of Money, Banking, and Financial Markets,* 3rd edition (Basic Books, 1980).

A highly recommended advanced work is Milton Friedman and Anna J. Schwartz, *A Monetary History of the United States, 1867–1960* (Princeton: National Bureau of Economic Research and Princeton University Press, 1963).

A convenient summary of Milton Friedman's views on monetary issues can be found in his *A Program for Monetary Stability* (New York: Fordham University Press, 1960). Keynesian ideas all stem, of course, from John Maynard Keynes, *The General Theory of Employment, Interest, and Money* (New York: Harcourt, Brace and World, 1936).

INDEX